CAPTIVE MEMORIES

CAPTIVE MEMORIES

MEG PARKES
& GEOFF GILL

Meg Parkes MPhil
Honorary Research Fellow,
Liverpool School of Tropical Medicine

Geoff Gill MA, MSc, MD, PhD, FRCP, DTM&H
Emeritus Professor of International Medicine,
Liverpool School of Tropical Medicine

First published in 2015
by Palatine Books,
Carnegie House,
Chatsworth Road
Lancaster LA1 4SL
www.palatinebooks.com

British Library Cataloguing-in-Publication data
A catalogue record for this book is available from the British Library

Paperback ISBN 13: 978-1-910837-00-9

Designed and typeset by Carnegie Book Production
www.carnegiebookproduction.com

Printed and bound by Jellyfish Solutions

DEDICATION

Captive Memories is dedicated to:
the former Far East prisoners of war, their wives and widows,
who made a permanent record of their memories for the benefit of future
generations; the former and current staff at the Liverpool School of Tropical
Medicine who have been a part of a unique collaboration with veterans
of Far East captivity during the past 70 years; Roderick Suddaby, the late
Keeper of the Department of Documents, Imperial War Museum, London.
Over the years his department became the trusted guardian of the written
memories of countless veterans of conflict during the twentieth century,
including many former Far East prisoners of war. Rod Suddaby was both
friend and mentor to many researchers of this still little-known aspect of
Second World War history; and finally, in gratitude to all Far East POW
who during captivity and since, put pen to paper so that others might try to
understand their monumental struggle to survive.

All things to nothingness descend,
Grow old and die and meet their end.
Man dies, iron rusts, wood goes decayed,
Flowers fall, walls crumble, roses fade.
Nor long shall any name resound
Beyond the grave, unless't be found
In some clerk's book: it is the pen
Gives immortality to men.

(Master Wace, twelfth century – from his Chronicles of the Norman Dukes)

CONTENTS

FOREWORD

IN THE LATE 1970S as a member of the Royal Army Medical Corps I was posted to the Queen Elizabeth Military Hospital at Woolwich and, as was their right, former Far East Prisoners of War (FEPOW) could be admitted to the hospital for treatment. This was my real first encounter with these fascinating gentlemen. After Woolwich I was posted to the Far East and during my two years in Hong Kong I spent much of my spare time researching and studying the military history of the colony including the invasion and occupation by the Japanese during the Second World War. I was introduced to a former FEPOW, Jack Edwards, and we became quite friendly during those two years in the colony.

Jack wrote and lectured on his experiences as a prisoner of war, spent mainly in the copper mines of Kinkaseki on the island of Taiwan. He told me of his health problems whilst a prisoner and how the Canadian doctor, Major Ben Wheeler, had saved his life. He showed me the documentary film made by Wheeler's daughter, a truly moving story. Some of the men of the Hong Kong Volunteers who had been captured in Hong Kong were on occasion admitted to the British Military Hospital whilst I was there and the ward staff, knowing of my interest would let me know and I was able to meet and talk to them. It was ironic that during that time, Shamshuipo, notorious as a prisoner of war camp during the war was once again in use to house Vietnamese boat people, some of whom I met during clinics; they had themselves been prisoners of the North Vietnamese for many years and now suffered from deprivations of a similar nature experienced by the men in this book.

Some ten years later I was appointed firstly as Curator of the Royal Army Medical Corps Museum and then the Director of the Army Medical Services Museum and it was then that I was fortunate to meet some of the Far East POW who had served in the medical services (both male and female). I was spellbound hearing their fascinating story, especially one of them, the marvellous David Arkush, who features in this book. David went on to make a short film for the museum relating his experiences as a dentist whilst a prisoner.

During my time at the museum I was fortunate to make the acquaintance of both Meg Parkes and Geoff Gill. I had first heard Geoff speak about the work of the Liverpool School of Tropical Medicine at the Royal Society of Medicine in 2006. Later, in 2010, I was fortunate to be invited to one of their conferences at Liverpool where several former prisoners of war related their experiences. Both Meg and Geoff spoke about the Tropical School's FEPOW research projects and in particular the wide range of oral histories featured here in this book. It was moving, not only the work they had done but also listening to the men themselves; after all they had experienced in those dark days, they were so spritely and full of life in their advancing years.

This book is mainly the culmination of over twelve months spent by Meg interviewing former prisoners and then turning it into her Master of Philosophy degree. But this did not just result in an achievement for her; it has produced a ground breaking study of the experiences of these men during captivity in the Far East and their consequent health issues post-war. It is a great privilege to be asked by Meg to write the Foreword to this important work. It is a book that should be read by all military historians and those involved in medicine, especially tropical medicine, and both Meg and Geoff should be commended.

Pete Starling MA, DHMSA, FRHistS
Former Director, Army Medical Services Museum

INTRODUCTION

CAPTIVE MEMORIES REPRESENTS A distillation of the Far East POW historical research undertaken at the Liverpool School of Tropical Medicine (LSTM, or the Tropical School) since 2001. Beginning in 1947 right up to the present day, LSTM's involvement with the health (and latterly the history) of these veterans, represents the longest collaborative partnership ever undertaken by the Tropical School. Out of this unique and enduring relationship came knowledge which has improved the diagnosis and treatment of some tropical infections, together with a greater understanding of the long-term psychological effects of Far East captivity. Using eye-witness accounts and the personal perspective of this group of elderly veterans of Far East captivity as the backdrop, *Captive Memories* charts this fascinating history.

Geoff Gill, now Emeritus Professor of International Medicine at LSTM, has been closely involved for four decades. In this first part of the Introduction Geoff outlines the background history to a six-decade long collaboration between the School and this unique group of veterans.

PART I: LIVERPOOL SCHOOL OF TROPICAL MEDICINE'S FAR EAST POW COLLABORATION Geoff Gill

My work with these fascinating and inspirational patients has, for me, proved to be a life-changing experience which started with a chance meeting in the spring of 1975. I was a junior doctor at the Royal Victoria Infirmary in Newcastle-upon-Tyne, where I had trained and graduated in medicine. I was working on a general medical ward and had just passed the main professional examination in medicine for membership of the Royal College of Physicians (MRCP). My job was due to end in late July when I was getting married to Helen, a paediatric nursing sister at the same hospital. Before we met, both of us had visited different parts of Africa and we had decided to take a year or two out of the UK system to live and work in Africa. Finding jobs and obtaining work permits would take some time, so we planned to leave the UK in early 1976. What we would do in the four or five intervening months after getting married was undecided.

One afternoon, I was in the Sister's office of Ward 15 when one of my colleagues came in for tea, bringing with him a visiting lecturer, Dr Alistair Reid from the Liverpool School of Tropical Medicine, who was due to give a talk on tropical illnesses that evening. He and I got chatting and I mentioned my plans to work in Africa. Alistair Reid was forthright and decisive. 'You must come down to Liverpool and do the DTM&H' he said, 'and I'm pretty sure that we have an SHO job vacant for you also.' The DTM&H is the Diploma in Tropical Medicine and Hygiene, a three month full-time course internationally acknowledged as the basic qualification in tropical medicine. The SHO job was as Senior House Officer responsible for LSTM's four tropical beds at Sefton General Hospital in Liverpool (formerly known as Smithdown Road Hospital). With such a small number of patients clinical duties were fairly light, so there was ample time to attend the DTM&H course (and also not have to pay tuition fees!).

This was the shortest interview I have ever had and within two or three weeks the job was confirmed. So, in September 1975 Helen and I relocated to Liverpool and moved into the Doctor's Residence at Sefton General. Helen was lucky in obtaining a short-term theatre sister post at Alder Hey Children's Hospital. We had a happy four months there and after Christmas flew out to work in Zambia for two years.

Whilst at Sefton General my tropical clinical work involved almost entirely looking after ex-Far East POW, who were there for several days at a time undergoing Tropical Disease Investigations (or 'TDIs'). This was a series of screening tests which POW themselves had long campaigned for and which had finally been agreed by the government in the late 1960s. The background was the growing evidence and realisation that veterans of Far East captivity, even 30 years after release, were suffering significant tropical and other diseases as an aftermath of their experiences in captivity. The Tropical School's Far East POW clinical unit had become the national centre for these investigations in 1968. However, before describing this work in more detail, it is worth tracing the history of the Tropical School's involvement with the Far East POW story in more detail.

Brief history of the Liverpool School of Tropical Medicine

The Liverpool School of Tropical Medicine is the oldest academic establishment in the world dedicated to the study of tropical medicine. It opened officially on 22nd April 1899, some six months before its London counterpart.[1] Liverpool's need for a tropical centre was due to its status as the 'second port of the Empire'. Boosted by the slave trade initially, during the nineteenth century Liverpool increasingly traded with America, the Caribbean and Africa. Along with imported tobacco and cotton came an increasing number of sick crew and passengers with obscure tropical infections. The report of Liverpool's Medical Officer for Health in 1889 recorded 294 cases of malaria, 42 of dysentery, 10 with beriberi, and two with yellow fever. Unsurprisingly, the medical establishment locally had difficulty with both diagnosis and management of these conditions.

The British Colonial Office supported the establishment of centres for tropical disease treatment in Liverpool and London, but (as could be expected!) offered no financial support. In Liverpool it was a group of local medical men, led by Dr William Carter, who led the initiative. They petitioned for support Mr Alfred Lewis-Jones, head of the Elder Dempster shipping line. Carter and his colleagues knew that it was in the clear interest of the shipping industry to support a tropical diseases unit in Liverpool. After a meeting with Lewis-Jones in November 1898, he pledged his support, eventually donating a total of £32,000 during the first 10 years.

When it opened in April 1899, the school was geographically scattered. There was a tropical ward at the Royal Southern Hospital and laboratories (the 'Johnson Laboratories') in the University College Liverpool. In 1903, a new field centre at Crofton Lodge, Runcorn, was opened. Despite this lack of focus, there was enormous energy and activity in these early years. A major 'catch' was the appointment of Ronald Ross initially as Lecturer, and later Professor, in Tropical Medicine. Ross brought extensive malarial experience from India, and it was in the Johnson Laboratories that he confirmed the mosquito-borne transmission of malaria. For this he was awarded the Nobel Prize in 1902. Another early star was John Dutton, a parasitologist who identified the protozoa *Trypanosoma* as the cause of sleeping sickness, and the bacteria *Borrelia* as the cause of relapsing fever. On an expedition to the Belgian Congo in 1905, Dutton sadly died of relapsing fever. In his honour, the organism is to this day known as *Borrelia duttoni*.

Back in Liverpool, the tropical ward treated over 1800 patients in its first twelve years of existence, 78 per cent of whom were associated with the shipping trade. Educationally, a taught diploma course in tropical medicine (DTM) was initiated in 1904. This runs to the present day as the DTM&H, with over

Figure 1 The 'Old School' (courtesy LSTM)

150 doctors coming to Liverpool annually from various parts of the world for this recognised and prestigious qualification.

The Tropical Ward moved to the Liverpool Royal Infirmary in 1914 and the next year a dedicated building for Tropical Medicine research and teaching was opened adjacent to the hospital on Pembroke Place. As this coincided with the outbreak of the First World War the new building was initially used for military personnel with tropical diseases. By the mid-1920s the School had consolidated activities in the new building which is still in use today (see Figure 1). This building stood alone until 1954 when a new teaching block was built. Further extensions have subsequently been added, most recently the Centre for Tropical and Infectious Diseases (CTID) in 2007 and the Wolfson Building in 2015 (see Figure 2).

After a prolonged sojourn at Sefton General during the Second World War and for 40 years afterwards, in 1985 the Tropical Unit returned to central Liverpool, to the new Royal Liverpool University Hospital (RLUH, opposite the 'Old Royal' and close to the Tropical School). Today the Tropical School is a centre for research, teaching and clinical tropical disease diagnosis and treatment. It comprises offices, laboratories, lecture theatres, library, seminar rooms, clinics and wards (at RLUH). Hundreds of postgraduate students

Figure 2 LSTM's newest buildings (top) Centre for Tropical Diseases (CTID) and (bottom) Wolfson Building *(courtesy LSTM)*

attend LSTM each year, studying for diplomas, masters degrees and doctorates. Millions of pounds in research-funding is won by the School, which leads international research in major tropical diseases, including malaria, tuberculosis and HIV/AIDS. Though traditionally part of the University of Liverpool, the School has recently been awarded its own degree and diploma-awarding status. Over 110 years since its opening the Tropical School has grown beyond recognition, though its mission to research into tropical diseases and improve diagnosis and treatment in some of the poorest communities in the world, remains unaltered.

The Tropical School and Far East POW collaboration

The original link between the Tropical School and Far East POW was forged by Brigadier (later Sir) Phillip Toosey, a survivor of captivity on the Thailand–Burma Railway. Before the war, Toosey had worked for Baring's Bank in Liverpool. He lived in Wirral and was an officer in the Territorial Army (TA).

Captured in Singapore and sent to work camps in Thailand, Toosey spent his captivity in various camps, most notably Tamarkan where he was the senior British officer. This was where the prisoners built the famous bridge (subject of the otherwise fictional film *Bridge over the River Kwai*). Toosey's leadership at Tamarkan was legendary, his organisational skills and care for 'his' men undoubtedly saved many lives.[2] On his return to Merseyside he resumed his banking career, but was very soon approached by local men who had served with or under him in captivity. These men had varying problems (health-related, psychological, financial etc.) and they needed his help. Within months of his return Toosey managed to facilitate the referral of a sick former Far East veteran to the Tropical School. The man had a relapse of amoebic dysentery and was successfully treated.

This 'index case' was the beginning of a collaboration between Far East POW and the Tropical School which was to last over six decades. After this initial case, Toosey met with Professor Brian Maegraith, Professor of Tropical Medicine and the School's newly appointed (and third) Dean, to ask for his help. The two men became friends and Toosey had a distinguished association with the Tropical School, later becoming its President. More importantly from the Far East POW viewpoint, Toosey had found help for his men, as Maegraith gladly accepted other sick Far East veterans from the area for tropical investigation and treatment. This was an essentially informal arrangement but it became more secure with the creation in 1950 of the National Federation of Far Eastern Prisoners of War (FEPOW) Clubs and Associations of Great Britain and Northern Ireland, representing the growing number of local FEPOW clubs around the country.

The Merseyside club was one of the earliest and was particularly active, meeting regularly at the Boot Inn in Wallasey, Wirral.[3] Its existence strengthened the links with the Tropical School bringing forward more veterans with ongoing health problems, particularly intermittent fevers and diarrhoea. Many were seen by the School's tropical physicians and frequently diagnosed with relapses of malaria or dysentery. The clinical records prior to 1968 no longer exist, so it is not known how many north-west Far East POW were seen under the 'Toosey/Maegraith' arrangement, but it was undoubtedly several hundred.

The Liverpool Far East POW Project

This account now returns to my own move to Liverpool in September 1975 to work on the Tropical Unit at Sefton General Hospital, and study for the DTM&H qualification at the Tropical School. Though recruited by Dr Alistair Reid I worked mostly under Dr Dion Bell, Senior Lecturer in Tropical Medicine and

Honorary Consultant Physician. Dion was a gritty Yorkshireman with a dry sense of humour, and a kind and empathetic demeanour. He was widely regarded as a leading tropical clinician and also a gifted teacher. He had taken over major responsibility for the tropical beds, so it was under his supervision that I worked. Dion became one of my major career mentors and later a close friend.

Up to the late 1960s many Far East POW particularly from the south of England were investigated at Queen Mary's Hospital in Roehampton, south London. This was a military hospital until 1968, when it became part of the National Health Service (NHS). At this point it could no longer see Far East veterans and Liverpool's Tropical School became the main national centre for the TDI programme. From 1968 to 1999 a total of 2,152 Far East veterans were seen in Liverpool; in the 1970s four or five men each week were investigated at the Tropical Unit.

The range of health problems suffered by these men is detailed in Chapter 5 but suffice to say that a number had persisting tropical conditions as well as long-term psychiatric consequences. The tropically related problems included chronic infections with the worm *Strongyloides stercoralis,* and long-term nerve damage due to beriberi and other nutritional deficiencies during captivity. The men were usually admitted from Monday to Friday for full investigation, assessment and, where possible, treatment. They were frequently seen by other specialists, in particular for associated mental health problems. The TDI week would begin with Dr Bell seeing each man for at least a full hour's interview and examination, time he set aside and something most had never experienced before. Traumatic and previously unrecounted memories were often revealed at these consultations and, unsurprisingly, Dr Bell became a hugely respected and almost iconic figure amongst British Far East prisoners of war.

At Liverpool I also met Steve Cairns, a former POW who was the National Welfare Adviser to the National Federation of FEPOW Clubs and Associations. Steve lived in Manchester and frequently visited both the Tropical School and the men admitted for TDIs, having encouraged many of them to volunteer for the screening as this would facilitate his work on their pension claims. Through him I realised that a major problem was the lack of published medical evidence concerning Far East POW health issues (see Appendix II for more about Steve's welfare work). I reviewed the literature myself and could only find two brief reports on *Strongyloides* infections in Far East veterans from the late 1940s. It seemed to me that the effect of Far East imprisonment on future health was of huge medical importance and needed recording in respected medical journals. I was also aware that this would be of enormous use to Steve, and the push for individual pension claims, as well as more general acceptance of Far East POW health problems.

Dion and I published our first paper in 1977 in the *British Medical Journal.*

This recorded the high prevalence of persisting strongyloidiasis more than 30 years after return from the Far East. Over the next fifteen years we published a further series of papers including more detailed research on *Strongyloides* infections, persisting nutritional nerve damage, liver disease, psychiatric problems and many other aspects of Far East POW health.[4] Much of this research demonstrated for the first time the potential long-term effects of tropical exposure, particularly in a military setting. This experience and information has benefitted modern military medicine in relationship to recent conflicts in tropical regions.

From clinical research to medical history

On my return from Zambia in 1978 I undertook specialist training as a physician while continuing my Far East POW research, gaining my MD on the subject in 1980. By 1985 I was a registered specialist in both general and tropical medicine and was appointed consultant physician at Arrowe Park Hospital in Wirral, with an honorary Senior Lecturer appointment at the Tropical School. In 1990 I moved my clinical work to Walton Hospital in Liverpool and in 1996 transferred from the NHS to the University of Liverpool, with a substantive academic appointment at the Tropical School.

The Far East POW research continued during this time, but after the year 2000 it changed direction. Attendance had been declining for some time due to the advancing age and reducing POW numbers, and the last one referred for a TDI at the School was seen in 1999. For some time I had felt that these men had a remarkable story to tell and that the historical record of the Far East POW experience was poorly recorded. As well as the general history of their captivity, I was particularly interested in their medical story, the patterns of disease during imprisonment and how the POW doctors coped with this challenge.

In 2001 I obtained funding from the Wellcome Trust for a three -month sabbatical leave period to make a preliminary exploration of medicine on the Thailand–Burma Railway, using interviews with surviving Far East POW doctors as well as archive material at the Imperial War Museum. This project continued and extended over the next eight years, culminating in a PhD thesis in 2009.[5]

In 2007 I was joined by Meg Parkes as Research Assistant, initially to record oral history interviews with Far East prisoners of war. *Captive Memories* sets their testimonies and unique long-term perspective into the broader context of this long and rich collaboration between doctors, researchers and a remarkable group of patients. In the next section, Meg explains more about this work.

PART II: FAR EAST POW MEDICAL HISTORY
RESEARCH Meg Parkes

This section gives the background to the Tropical School's Far East POW oral history study which underpins *Captive Memories* and which formed the basis for my MPhil dissertation. Research for the MPhil required further interviewing and to date 66 veterans have been recorded. Seven years on from the start of the study, over two thirds of those interviewed have died.

Historically, very few veterans of Far East captivity chose to speak openly about their experiences and over six decades since their return from captivity time was running out. In 2007, commissioned by the Tropical School in association with the Imperial War Museum (IWM) Sound Archive, I was asked to find and interview, during a twelve-month period, up to 50 former British servicemen who had been Far East POW. By that time these veterans were all in their late 80s or 90s. All had endured and survived captivity by the Japanese between 1942 and 1945. In addition, four widows of Far East POW were also interviewed as well as several wives who sat in on their husband's interviews. Finally, two other people, both connected to this history, were also interviewed. The oral history study was broad, seeking men from all services, former officers and Other Ranks (ORs) and significantly, covering as many different areas of captivity across the Far East as possible.

Interviewees and interviews

The main reason that 66 front doors opened so readily was the respect felt for the Liverpool School of Tropical Medicine, an institution revered and highly regarded by Far East POW and their families. All those interviewed expressed gratitude towards the School, despite few of them actually having had personal contact with it.

These men were some of the last survivors of the 37,500 servicemen who returned to Britain from the Far East during the autumn of 1945. Their testimonies create for both listener and reader a vivid personal impression of three and half years of captivity, as well as an insight into the effects wrought on the post-war lives of these men and their families. Surprisingly perhaps, not all their memories were bad. The events they recalled happened a long time ago and memory can dull as well as excite the recall of events. It can also alter them, which should be borne in mind when reading oral history testimonies. That is not to imply they are not valid. Some memories fade into insignificance, others remain vivid; each interview is simply what the individual recalls.

Over half of those interviewed (39) had been captured at the Fall of Singapore in February 1942 and shared captivity there; one was captured in Malaya before

Singapore fell. Most were transported up country to Thailand to camps along the Thailand–Burma Railway. While they had all endured similar conditions, each man had his own unique experience. The building of the Thailand–Burma Railway has dominated British public awareness of Far East captivity since 1945 largely because the majority of British Far East prisoners of war (over 30,000 of 50,000 captured) were held in those areas for at least part of their captivity. Naturally therefore, among survivors into old age, the railway camp experience continues to dominate collective memory as well as public perception.

The aim of the oral history study was, however, to seek a broader picture of Far East captivity; to better understand what men remembered and to learn about the conditions and experiences prevailing in other parts of the region, in Sumatra, Java, the Moluccas, Borneo, Taiwan (Formosa), Korea, Indo-China, Hong Kong, Japan and New Guinea, about which still comparatively little is known when compared to the Singapore/Thailand experience.

Of the remainder, 22 were captured in the Dutch East Indies, mainly in Sumatra and Java, most moving to other locations, including Borneo and the Moluccas. Three ended up working on the Sumatra railway. Four were captured in Hong Kong with two of them moved elsewhere. Four men survived the sinking of the ships they were transported on, one twice.

Many of the men interviewed were speaking out publicly for the first time in their lives; two told me that I was the first person they had felt able to share their story with. I found it profoundly moving to be invited into their homes and to sit, often for several hours, and listen to their reminiscences.

These men were eye-witnesses to history. As well as their memories, they also wanted to share long-ago hidden diaries and notebooks, photographs, drawings, ID badges and documents of all kinds, including letters from loved ones received while in captivity. These precious artefacts seemed to symbolise endurance and survival.

The men represented all walks of life. At the outbreak of war they had been young doctors, students, teachers, solicitors, clerks, engineers, plumbers, artists, lorry drivers or career soldiers. All were determined to record their memories and feelings for posterity and they were grateful to the Tropical School for inviting them to do so. They knew time was fast running out; if they did not take part then very soon it would be too late. Some said they were doing it in the name of friends who did not return. A list of semi-structured questions was drawn up to guide the interviews and these were revised as the interviewing progressed. Given the nature of the experiences and the memories they were recalling, at the outset of each interview they were told they could stop the recording whenever they wished. Few chose to do so. All wanted to bear witness so that future generations would know more about what had been endured. That it was real. It did happen.

Their testimonies are far from self-pitying. They did not regard themselves as 'heroes', merely survivors. Far East captivity affected all who experienced it, shaping men's lives and their deaths. It encouraged the best, and the worst, in human behaviour. While for some, experiences remembered were dreadful, others felt it was important to say it had not all been bad. Many felt it had made them better men. They remembered the way they had shared, been entertained, been cared for and learned how to care for others, and they acknowledged that not all men had behaved well all of the time. Above all else, they got through it. It was a time when friendship was worth more than anything else. For some there was peace, a sense of reconciliation with the past, if not actually with their captors. For others that was not possible, nor could they imagine ever changing their viewpoint.

A few had kept secret diaries during captivity despite knowing that it was forbidden to do so. Some of those interviewed had written memoirs in later life for their family, a few had been published.[6] Interestingly, many of those interviewed said that while never having wanted to speak about it to their family, including their children (many of whom grew up feeling that they could not ask questions), they did find it easier to talk to grandchildren. A full list of all interviewees is in Appendix III.

Collectively these men have created a personal view of captivity in the Far East during the Second World War and the effect that it had on their post-war lives. Some were speaking publicly for the first time. All speak of the will and the struggle to survive, to endure, and for many, to know that ultimately life can be good. There is much to learn from these men and we do well to listen. We owe them all a debt of gratitude for sharing their experiences with us.

Post-war medical treatment

Approximately 37,500 British Far East prisoners of war returned home, the majority by means of a long sea voyage. This had benefits, allowing these men time to come to terms with their new-found freedom and to slowly adjust to the demands of peacetime and family life. But, many men felt it was also convenient for the government of the day, as it meant they were out of sight for longer, allowing time for them to put on weight and lose their sickly appearance, reducing the possibility of the public outcry that may have ensued if relatives had seen them in the first few weeks of freedom. Many exhibited the effects of chronic malnutrition combined with tropical infections which required highly specialised medical care for many years, though few were to receive it.

There was a network of military hospitals around the country, the largest being Queen Mary's Hospital, Roehampton in Surrey and Queen Elizabeth's

Hospital at Woolwich for Army personnel. There were the RAF hospitals at Cosford near Wolverhampton and Ely in Cambridgeshire and the Royal Naval Hospital at Haslar in Hampshire. Queen Mary's Hospital Roehampton had been established as a military hospital in 1915, initially specialising in rehabilitating amputees but later on it developed expertise in tropical medicine. It became the referral point for thousands of Far East veterans from late 1945 onwards. In the north of England, specialist doctors at the Tropical School in Liverpool saw POW patients in the early post-war years, some of whom had self-referred.

Historiography

The speed of the war in the Far East resulted in the surrender of over 50,000 British servicemen alone, up to a third of all nationalities of Allied Far East military captives. Despite growing public interest in the Second World War over recent years and a plethora of films and books released and published since 1945, the experiences of those who endured Far East captivity remains a comparatively little-known aspect of that history.

Only a few oral history studies relating to Far East captivity have been conducted in Britain over the years and involved very few of the veterans. One of the major difficulties for those studying Far East POW history is the dearth of primary source material available, particularly when compared to that which is available to researchers of European POW captivity during the Second World War. A search of war-related literature published in the immediate post-war decade reveals how little Far Eastern captivity was represented at that time. While numerous books, films and articles about the battles, victories and prisoner of war escapades in Europe appeared both during and after the war, by comparison only a handful of accounts relating to the Far East campaign and captivity were published in addition to the few authorised official and regimental histories.

Due to the threat of reprisals by the Japanese, few men chose to risk their lives keeping diaries, notes or drawings documenting life in captivity. Of those men who did many were officers as generally they had more time to do so. Contemporaneous accounts by ORs are rarer as most had neither the time nor the energy or the materials with which to keep diaries. One exception was RAMC medical orderly Doug Skippen, who noted in his secret journal in early 1944 in camp in Burma, that he would have to curtail his writing as he was running out of pages in his notebook and 'of course, we have no idea yet as to how long we have to go yet before freedom … I must mention, that I would have been in serious trouble had the Japs found my notes.'[7]

Great ingenuity went into hiding such records. The manuscript of *Banpong*

Express was written by Major H. H. Coombes while he was in Non Pladuk camp in Thailand in 1943. This survived, hidden in the lining of a one gallon thermos container in the cookhouse, being retrieved after liberation while awaiting repatriation. He published his book in 1948, one of the very first British Far East POW to do so.[8] But even when documents returned home with the author, it did not necessarily follow that he wanted to share the contents, even with those closest to him.

According to the late Roderick Suddaby, Keeper of the Department of Documents at the IWM from the early 1980s until 2011, the museum saw a gradual increase in the number of acquisitions of private memoirs, diaries, reports, artefacts and memorabilia belonging to veterans of Far East captivity. In 1983 the museum published the diaries of the late Captain Robert Hardie, a Malayan Volunteer medical officer captured in Singapore and sent to Thailand. Later, following the 50th anniversary of VJ Day in 1995, more memoirs were published, written by veterans, relatives or with the help of researchers or journalists. Such accounts can provide useful information though when written in old age and without contemporaneous notes to underpin them, there is a greater risk of altered or false memory and the mythologizing of events.

In recent years more contemporaneous diaries, reports and artwork have come into the public domain, usually following the death of a veteran. They provide invaluable insight for the historian (both academic and family), describing the personal details of daily life in captivity, naming places, camps, the characters and incidents. By their nature such accounts may be biased to the views of the author, but as they were written at the time the events took place, they are not subject to the altered memory of later life.

During the course of this study items have come to light, for example, a detailed neurological study undertaken by RAF Flight Lieutenant and Medical Officer Nowell Peach during late 1942 at Tandjong Priok transit camp in Java. It comprises 54 original patient records clipped together with a rusty pin (see Chapters 2 and 3).

The fact that many prisoner of war diaries remained 'hidden' from public view for four decades or longer, reflects the reticence felt by so many men; they did not, or could not, share details of their experiences. Shame and guilt may have had a part to play in this. Many POW described at interview a collective sense of shame following the capitulation, in swift succession, of Hong Kong, Singapore and the Netherlands East Indies, feelings which many harboured for much longer than their captivity. They had surrendered, given up. Some recalled how, once back home they felt as if they were a visible reminder of the humiliation of unconditional surrender that had led to Britain's catastrophic defeat in the Far East. Former Gunner Fergus Anckorn, from Kent, made this point succinctly when he stated that, 'we were a disgrace really.'

This is in stark contrast to the veterans of captivity in Europe, whose home-coming came about as a result of the nation's victory over the enemy and was the cause of sustained celebrating and approbation. Nowadays, survivor guilt is widely recognised as an understandable reaction by those who have suffered severe trauma and survived incidents which caused the deaths of others. It is prevalent among those who witness the arbitrary and often needless deaths of comrades on active service. But this was not the case back in the late 1940s. In 2007 former merchant seaman Harry Hesp exemplified the long-term effects of such feelings when he said, 'It's very difficult to live with yourself and you wouldn't think after 60 years … I'm the only bloke from Warrington left. I'm the only *Empress of Asia* bloke left. So, I have a feeling of guilt.'

Another factor which was cited several times during the study was a fear of being accused of exaggerating, or worse being branded a liar. Many POW became adept at grossly understating the reality of captivity as a means of deflecting interest, dismissing questions with remarks such as, 'Oh it wasn't much fun.' But post-war, the British public's perceived indifference to these men was, I believe, neither conscious nor callous. The war in Europe had finished nearly five months before the first Far East POW returned home in the autumn of 1945. Significantly, as the number of British forces held in captivity in the Far East was barely a third of those captured in Europe, only a minority of the population was related to a Far East POW. There were also many who had menfolk returning home from the fighting in Burma, the so-called 'Forgotten Army', but to the rest of the population the Far East was a very long way away, in every sense.

Academic studies into this history fall into two categories: primary and secondary sources. Primary sources include research papers, like Nowell Peach's neurological study, written by the clinicians, doctors, dentists and nutritionists in captivity. Some published papers in the immediate post-war period, like Dr (later Professor) Hugh Edward de Wardener MBE, a captain and medical officer in the Royal Army Medical Corps (RAMC) in camps in Singapore and Thailand. In 1946, while still unwell and being treated for TB, Hugh had his research studies undertaken while in captivity, on cholera and Wernicke's Encephalopathy, published in *The Lancet*. In the same year, former Flight Lieutenant Leslie John Audus RAF (who post-war became Professor of Botany at Bedford College, University of London), published his work on manufacturing yeast supplements in POW camps in Java and the Moluccas (on the island of Haruku), in the scientific magazine *Discovery, Magazine of Scientific Progress from the Year 1946*. Their work is explored in Chapter 3.

Those, like Nowell, Hugh and Leslie, who kept records of any kind during their captivity took huge personal risks in secretly undertaking and recording research, diaries or artwork and then safely concealing it. Retrieving it all at liberation was another problem for many. Perhaps the need to do this work was part of some unwritten survival strategy? Defiance and determination are powerful weapons, especially when combined with courage and guile.

Publishing academic papers so soon after their return must also have required Herculean strength and determination, especially as Hugh, Leslie and others who did so, were unwell for some time post-war. They must have felt compelled to publish their work and in so doing they ensured it was not only shared within their professions, but it also served to inform the readership about the conditions under which they were held. At the time these and other papers added greatly to medical knowledge. Today they provide us with a fascinating insight into the skills, expertise, resourcefulness and tenacity of the medical staff and those who worked closely with them.

Secondary sources include more recent scholarly works that make a valuable contribution to a wider understanding of the history, such as Dr Bernice Archer's *The Internment of Western Civilians under the Japanese 1941–1945, A Patchwork of Internment*; Rob Havers' *Reassessing the Japanese prisoner of war experience: the Changi P.O.W. Camp, Singapore, 1942–1945*; and Clifford Kinvig's *River Kwai Railway*.

Previous oral history studies relating to Far East POW history in this country have tended to be concerned with sequential facts related to captivity: the battles, defeats, camp life, working parties, brutality and disease. But this fragmented approach does not address how men coped, how they survived, their personal outlook and memories and, significantly, their feelings about what they went through so long afterwards.

In contrast *Captive Memories* documents and highlights the unique long-term perspective of the 66 Far East POW interviewed. It charts the experiences of these men during captivity and the impact that they had on post-war lives, as remembered over six decades later. The study further explores what these men remembered about their homecoming and post-war lives. Why did there appear to have been a conspiracy of silence shrouding their experiences?

These men, facing the end of their lives, chose to speak out and share their memories. It has not been possible to put into *Captive Memories* all that each man said, but extracts from every interview have been used throughout the book ensuring that each man has a voice. Extracts vary in length, with some men quoted several times, in order to piece together the wide range of topics and aspects of the history from the interviews. After introducing each man in turn, giving his wartime service and rank, they are subsequently referred to by name.

The book contains many contemporaneous illustrations, a few of which were provided by interviewees, others from archives and other sources. This artwork is significant. Very few cameras and little film survived captivity in the Far East and photographs by POW were taken hurriedly and in secret, poorly exposed, grainy and in shadow. Art provides the only other visual reference to life, death and survival in Far East captivity. It is vital and compelling work. As record-keeping was forbidden, artists, whether gifted or amateur, worked clandestinely and at great risk. Their work reveals so much about the battle to survive. This subject is explored further in the Postscript.

Captive Memories has been written with a general readership in mind while being underpinned by rigorous academic research. To aid readers with an interest in further study there are endnotes, a bibliography and a full index. There is also a website – www.captivememories.org.uk – where there are audio extracts from the oral history study as well as background to the earlier clinical and scientific work of the Tropical School and the Heritage Lottery Fund's Far East POW history education project (see Postscript for more details of the latter).

A personal perspective

My father had been a Far East prisoner of war. Captain (later Dr) Andrew Atholl Duncan served with the 2nd Battalion Argyll and Sutherland Highlanders, was captured in Java and later shipped to Japan. He was lucky, he always said so. He had survived. He returned from captivity in late 1945, bringing with him handwritten diaries of his experiences.[9] He married his fiancée straightaway, returned to university swapping degrees from engineering to medicine and graduated in 1950, settling down to life as a GP with his growing family in Wirral (I am the second of four daughters born during the early post-war years).

We knew from the earliest time, in all sorts of subtle (and not so subtle) ways, that Dad had been a prisoner of war of the Japanese. In my late teens I read his diary for the first time and went on to transcribe all nine original notebooks to provide copies for us all. In so doing I became more familiar with, and fascinated by, his experiences. How does someone go through what he did and be able to make the life he had for himself, and us? After he died I inherited the diary and its archive and as custodian felt an overwhelming obligation to share with others the information he had kept so assiduously. He had named so many of his fellow captives and had drawn camp plans to scale and with compass bearings. I felt sure there would be other families with an interest in the four camps he had been in. In 2002 I self-published the first of two volumes, sharing the story the diaries and family's wartime correspond-ence told; the sequel was published in 2003.[10] Subsequently, I was contacted not only by relatives of other Far East veterans, but also by a former prisoner who had known Dad, Ed Knight (Flight Lieutenant Frank Edgar Knight RAF), who I met and later interviewed for this study. His granddaughter had bought the first book for him having been told by Mr Suddaby at the IWM that her grandfather was mentioned on the first page! My research interest continued to grow.

In 2005, the 60th anniversary of the ending of the Second World War and the repatriation of Far East captives was marked by the opening of a dedicated museum to Far East POW history at the National Memorial Arboretum (NMA) in Staffordshire (organised by COFEPOW, a charity representing the children and families of Far East POW). Soon afterwards, together with three other researchers, we set up the Researching FEPOW History (RFH) group. Our aim was to organise conferences, at the NMA initially, bringing internationally acclaimed historians to share their research with audiences comprised of family as well as academic historians from around the world.[11]

Then in 2006, Geoff Gill invited me to undertake a one-year oral history project for the Tropical School, finding and interviewing British former Far East prisoners of war. After two brief courses in the rudiments of oral history taking (at the British Library and the North West Sound Archive) I set off in April 2007 armed with a Marantz PMD660 digital recorder to start interviewing. In just over twelve months I had travelled over 28,000 miles around Britain. Soon after starting, the study became the basis for my MPhil dissertation (awarded in 2012).[12]

Gathering the oral histories has represented a final window of opportunity for the Tropical School. Bringing Far East prisoner of war history to a wider audience, and in particular the younger generation, has long been part of my motivation; the testimonies of these men (and women) deserve to be shared widely.

Structure of the book

The chapters which follow focus on specific areas of study drawn from the interviews.

Chapter 1 gives a brief outline of the history, an overview of general conditions in captivity including eye witness accounts of the 'hellship' voyages many experienced. Chapter 2 examines survival and how the prisoners of war coped with the deliberate and wanton neglect and deprivation imposed by their captors. Chapter 3 explores the scope of the medical ingenuity and inventiveness of a 'citizen's army' of skilled men who enabled doctors to save thousands of lives in camps across the Far East. This is drawn specifically from the Thackray study into medical ingenuity and inventive medicine which is outlined in the Postscript along with other studies undertaken. More interviews were conducted with former medical officers and orderlies and the chapter contains a rich seam of medical eye-witness accounts.

Chapter 4 explores the background to the repatriation process, their memories of coming home and what life was like in early years. In Chapter 5 Geoff Gill explains in greater detail the medical aftermath and the clinical and scientific work undertaken at the Tropical School from the late 1960s onwards. He had joined the team of doctors and scientists in the latter part of the 1970s and has remained closely involved with all aspects of this work ever since. Chapter 6 sets out the men's long-term perspective, reflecting on if, and how, the experiences they endured and survived affected later life.

The Postscript provides a summary of the Tropical School's social history research: the Thackray inventive medicine study (2008–09), the Tropical School's Far East POW round table meeting (2010) at which eight veterans were present, the Far East POW History Education project (2009–11, see www.captivememories.org.uk), funded by the Heritage Lottery Fund and the Medical Art Behind Bamboo study, awarded a Wellcome Travel grant (2012–14).

Finally, there are three appendices. The first is a summary of Dr Kamaluddin Khan's PhD thesis, published here for the first time since completion in 1987. Dr Khan was a consultant psychiatrist based at Arrowe Park Hospital in Wirral.[13] He was invited to join the Tropical School's Far East POW research team in 1974 by Dr Dion Bell (clinical lead in Far East POW medicine at the Tropical School). Dr Khan worked with scores of veterans until the early 1990s and his thesis is based on research undertaken with these men. His compassionate care and understanding was to be a lifeline to many men, and their families and we are indebted to him for giving permission to publish his key findings.

The second appendix outlines the extraordinary welfare work undertaken by Far East POW since their return to Britain. It includes a brief account of the setting up of the clubs and then the National Federation of FEPOW Clubs and Associations (NFFCA), and the establishing of two, separately administered, Welfare Trust Funds, the history of latter having been provided by former Trustee former Far East POW Robert Hucklesby. Finally, we pay tribute to the work of NFFCA's incomparable National Welfare Adviser, former POW Steve Cairns MBE OBE, who for over six decades maintained links between generations of doctors at the Liverpool School of Tropical Medicine and their Far East POW patients.

The third appendix provides a list of all the interviewees.

CHAPTER 1

A BRIEF HISTORY AND OVERVIEW OF CAPTIVITY

THIS CHAPTER IS NOT intended as an in-depth history of the origins of the conflict in the Far East during the Second World War but rather an outline, giving context to the experiences that the interviewees lived through in captivity. The origins of the war in the Far East are rooted in Japanese expansionist policies which sought to destroy western colonial power in the region. This had swift and devastating consequences for the large number of Allied Forces sent out, or diverted from their previous course to the Middle East, to protect the colonies upon which so much of western prosperity had depended.

These servicemen were mainly volunteers and not regular soldiers, sailors or airmen. They had signed up expecting to fight a war in Europe or North Africa but not in the tropics of the Far East. Japan's military success not only took the Allies but also the Japanese by surprise. The consequences for 132,000 Allied prisoners of war captured across the region were equally swift and devastating: theirs was to be a war of survival which would be fought against disease, starvation and despair. Estimates of the total number of Allied Forces captured by the Japanese vary widely but approximately 50,000 were British forces.

The colonising of the Far East by the great seafaring nations of Europe, namely Portugal, Spain, Holland, Britain and France, stretched back over four centuries. Each nation laid its claim to large parts of the Far East in pursuit of commerce and particularly the valuable spice trade. These colonial powers exploited the abundant natural resources and by the second half of the nineteenth century had interests in tin, rubber and oil, which provided vital fuel for the fast growing industrial economies of Europe and America.

By the beginning of the twentieth century Britain was the largest colonial power in the Far East controlling India, Burma, Malaya, Borneo, New Guinea and small but strategic parts of China namely, Hong Kong and Shanghai. Portugal, the earliest European colonist in South East Asia, still controlled Macau in China and Goa in India. The Dutch were the oldest colonial power having ruled over the Netherlands East Indies (NEI), extending from Sumatra across two and a half thousand miles of islands, since the seventeenth century; the French had colonised Indo-China including Laos, Tongking (Northern Vietnam) Cochin-China (South Vietnam) and Cambodia; the United States occupied the Philippines which had been taken from Spain in 1893, as well as many Pacific islands.

Throughout this period of European expansionism Japan remained isolated, cut off from international affairs. By the mid-nineteenth century it sought the support of the industrialised West in order to modernise and so gradually sought links with Britain, Russia and America. Its nearest neighbour was China, a vast but poorly led country which during the late nineteenth century had engaged in a series of disastrous wars with Japan, Great Britain and France. After the final Sino-Japanese war in 1894–5, China lost Manchuria to the Japanese who immediately established a military garrison at Mukden. Japan went on to take control of both Taiwan (also known as Formosa) and Korea.

Britain signed a Treaty of Alliance with Japan in 1902 to safeguard her Far East interests from growing Russian interference, an agreement which bolstered Japan's esteem as an emerging modern nation and gave her renewed confidence to challenge Russia. The Alliance held and enabled Britain to keep her navy in the west while relying on the Japanese to come to her defence in the Far East if necessary. At the outbreak of the First World War Japan allied itself with Britain and for a while the Alliance was mutually beneficial though Japan's increasingly acquisitive attitude to China caused disquiet in both Britain and the USA. However, at the peace conference at Versailles in 1919 Japan emerged as one of the world's leading nations and was granted a permanent seat on the League of Nations. As Japan's manufacturing capacity and prosperity had grown so too had support for the fledgling 'Taisho democracy', Japan's two-party, anti-militaristic political system which had been developing since the turn of the century. However, it wasn't easy for the ruling parties to keep the balance between the gradual westernization of ideas and soaring inflation, and the views of the traditionalists. In the early 1920s there was a proliferation of new political parties influenced by democracy, socialism and communism. Japan was becoming polarized and there was growing support for both extremes. The sudden financial crash in the West at the end of the 1920s saw catastrophic economic depression rippling around the globe, causing rising unemployment and hardship. Japan, unlike the United States, Britain and the Netherlands, had no empire to rely on to ease the burden and so therefore looked to China's vast natural resources and markets as the solution.

In 1931 a dissident group of Japanese Army officers stationed at the Mukden garrison in China engineered a fracas with the local Chinese, known as the Manchurian Incident, which quickly escalated into all-out conflict. In 1936 Japan signed the Anti-Comintern Pact with Germany, thereby securing against attack from Russia. The Chinese, though vastly outnumbering the Japanese, had neither cohesive leadership nor a united Army and it was the nationalist leader Chiang Kai-Shek who retaliated against repeated Japanese aggression. In December 1937 Japan's response culminated in the massacre of over 200,000 civilians in Nanking. It was a portent of what was to come. Despite Japan's military supremacy it couldn't control the whole of China but by 1938 had captured most of the coastline and taken control of the north of China. Japan's Prime Minister, Prince Konoye, declared that Japan was at war with China, stating that Asia was to be known as the Greater East Asia Co-Prosperity Sphere, bringing an end to Western colonial rule.

Britain, though concerned by the deteriorating situation, was determined not to seek outright confrontation with Japan and relied on the hope that the Japanese would be ensnared in the conflict in China. In 1939 the United States, after years of isolationism and a long history of uneasy relations with Japan, decided to act. President Roosevelt proposed to Congress that the United States assist Chiang Kai-Shek's resistance forces by supplying them with military aid and at the same time threaten Japan with oil sanctions, in the belief that the threat alone would make Japan back down. It did not. The Japanese depended on oil imports from the USA and had barely eighteen months' supply left but there were other sources of the vital raw materials it needed to wage war; controlling the oil fields of the Dutch East Indies and the tin mines and rubber plantations of Malaya and the DEI became a necessity.

Within months Europe was at war. By the summer of 1940, France and the Netherlands were defeated and Britain was facing the real possibility of invasion; their Far East colonies had never been more vulnerable. Japan seized the moment and signed the Tri-Partite Pact with Germany and Italy which agreed to mutual support if any one power was attacked by a power not a party to the Sino-Japanese dispute or the hostilities in Europe. The threat to the United States was clear. Roosevelt, in his Arsenal of Democracy speech on 29 December 1940, told the American people that he was determined to fight Japanese expansionism in South East Asia because, 'if Great Britain goes down, the Axis powers will control the continents of Europe, Asia, Africa and Australasia and the high seas – and they will be in a position to bring enormous military and naval resources against the hemisphere.'

Japan knew that in order to take control of European and US colonies in the Far East the US Fleet must be stopped from intervening. Their unprovoked attack on the Pacific Fleet at anchor at the US Naval Base in Pearl Harbour, Hawaii, early on the morning of 7 December 1941 took the USA and the rest of the world completely by surprise. Within hours the Japanese had launched simultaneous invasions of Malaya, Thailand, Hong Kong and the Philippines.

Since 1938, Hong Kong had become increasingly isolated after Japanese forces landed 35 miles away at Canton. Britain had long realised that defending the colony from a determined attack would be impossible but, rather than abandon it, decided to strengthen the garrison by sending two Canadian battalions to join the 1st Battalion of the Middlesex Regiment and the 2nd Battalion of the Royal Scots plus two Indian regiments.

In 1941 the population of Hong Kong stood at approximately 1,750,000, of whom the vast majority were Chinese. By December that year the garrison numbered over 8,900 British, Canadian and Hong Kong voluntary reservists, plus 4,400 Indians and over 600 Chinese. Most of the defence forces, especially those newly arrived from Canada, were poorly trained and ill-equipped to meet such a determined and organised force as the Imperial Japanese Army. From 8 December it took the Japanese just eighteen days to take the garrison at Hong Kong, the Allied forces surrendering on Christmas Day 1941.

Malaya was the most advanced country in South East Asia following industrialisation, with over half the world's tin ore and at least one third of the world's rubber produced there. It had an excellent road system running the length of the west side of the peninsula from Thailand to Singapore. However, Britain's strategy for the defence of Malaya and Singapore was muddled and inadequate. The country was divided into distinct areas each with its own local government system: the Crown Colony of Straits Settlements (SS) which included Singapore; the Federated Malay States (FMS) and the Un-Federated Malay States (UMS). Since the end of the First World War the colony had suffered from lack of investment, with disagreements between Singapore and London about whether funding was for 'local' or 'Empire' defence, and decisions constantly being deferred. In 1921 the British government reluctantly agreed to a permanent naval base in Singapore but it took 15 years to complete and was never properly used.

The situation was further compounded by the lack of co-operation between the civilian Straits Settlements government, the military authorities and the garrison forces based there. In the whole of Malaya before 1936 there were only two airfields, both on the northwest coast at Port Swettenham and Alor Star. With the rising threat from the East they were of little use as an early warning of any seaborne threat from the South China Sea because of the short-range capabilities of the 'planes. There was also the prevailing belief that with the Malayan jungle impenetrable, particularly during the monsoon season from October to March, landings could not succeed on the east coast. In mid-1936, the decision by the RAF to build three more airfields in dense jungle on the east side of Malaya, at Kota Bahru and Kuantan, was carried out without reference to the Army or Navy who were expected to defend them. According to Lieutenant General Sir Lewis Heath, commander of 3rd Indian Corps during the Malayan campaign, 'These new airfields proved impossible to defend and were considered detrimental to the interests of the Army.'

By September 1939 there were nine battalions stationed in Singapore. The RAF had eight squadrons, though with insufficient and inadequate aeroplanes. In addition to the regular forces there were also the volunteer forces drawn from the colonial and native populations of Malaya and Singapore. However, for years pre-war the Japanese had established an extensive espionage system throughout Malaya and Singapore. Despite warnings, it was decided this did not pose a significant threat to security and in the event of trouble the fleet could be despatched. Both complacency and the 'impenetrable jungle' of politics and military one-upmanship contributed to the fall of Malaya and Singapore.

Allied Forces captured by the Japanese were mainly from Britain, Australia, New Zealand, Canada, Holland, India and America. They surrendered between December 1941 and April 1942 and became Far East prisoners of war (or FEPOW as they are known) in three specific areas: Hong Kong (over 8,000 British, Indians and Canadians), Malaya and Singapore (over 50,000 British and Australians), Java, Sumatra, Borneo and the Celebes (over 42,000 Dutch and 10,000 British) and the Philippine Islands (over 11,000 Americans).

The sheer numbers of captives overwhelmed the Japanese, as did the speed of their capture. In Singapore large numbers of Allied Forces were herded together on the Padang next to the Singapore Cricket Club down by the water-front. RAMC Sergeant John Brown, who had trained in the catering section, recalled what happened to his group at the time. 'We were captured in the cricket club in Singapore ... They didn't interfere with us ... they rounded us all up and took us all to Roberts Barracks. That was Changi. I suppose I was fairly lucky being in the catering, they never interfered with us, not for a long time.'

Tens of thousands made that seventeen mile march from the Padang out to the Changi peninsular, Captain Bill Drower among them. A British Intelligence Officer attached to the Hertfordshire Yeomanry, he described in his 1993 memoir their arrival at Changi POW camp in February 1942.[1] 'Over 50,000 British and Australian troops then sorted themselves into unit groups, without help from their captors who were jubilant and to a degree bewildered by the vastness of their prize.'

He was right. The Japanese had made little, if any, provision for the taking of captives. The idea of surrendering to the enemy was anathema to their military code of Bushido which expected every man to fight to the death rather than be taken prisoner. They would prove to be harsh and unforgiving captors, unlike in 1904–05 during the Russo-Japanese war when they had behaved in an exemplary way towards captured Russian forces. During the inter-war years the Japanese military developed a rigid, aggressive regime of physical hardship and punishments within their Armed Forces, a brutal system of authority that was endured by all Japanese soldiers during military training and service.

This fundamental difference between western and Japanese military culture and conduct was to have a profound effect upon the lives, and deaths, of Allied prisoners of war. From the outset FEPOW were left in no doubt that their lives meant nothing to their captors. They also discovered that they were not protected by the 1929 Geneva Conventions as Japan had not ratified their agreement and therefore had no obligation to respect international law in respect of enemy combatants.

All prisoners of war, no matter where they were captured, endured similar basic conditions throughout captivity: they were routinely humiliated and abused, lived in overcrowded and insanitary conditions, deprived of both food and the most basic medical care and were cut off from news of the home front and isolated from their families. Prisoners lived in daily fear of disease, industrial injury, random beatings and torture meted out by sadistic and unpredictable captors. Allied prisoners of war were regarded as a dispensable slave labour force to be worked to death if necessary.

Living conditions varied initially according to the climate and location of capture. Those held captive in the tropics had to battle not only disease and malnutrition, the latter attributable in part to being at the furthest reaches of the supply chain, but also the merciless heat and monsoons (and resulting mud), in addition to the extremes of life in the jungle or on bare coral islands. Meanwhile FEPOW who ended up in northern locations like Taiwan, China, Korea and Japan, had to contend with the bitter cold.

Overview of captivity

The type of accommodation varied widely. In colonial outposts such as Hong Kong, Singapore and Batavia (the capital of Java, now Jakarta), former administrative buildings and institutions such as schools, hospitals, army barracks, native gaols and native labour camps, were hurriedly converted into prison compounds. Of the men interviewed 38 were captured in Singapore, mostly British Army personnel, with 30 of them sent to Thailand to work on the railway. On Singapore Island the largest POW camp was Changi which initially held up to 50,000 British and Australian servicemen. This whole area on the South Eastern corner of the island was barbed-wired off. It had within its confines both jungle and woodland in an undulating landscape, a long sandy coastline and good roads linking villages to new pre-war purpose-built military barracks for British garrison forces and the town. Across the island there were many other smaller camps housing men on different working parties building shrines, clearing bomb damage and loading and unloading goods at the docks.

The Japanese left the day-to-day running of Changi camp to the senior Allied officers who quickly organised the administration on strict military lines. This was imperative early on, to combat the health risks in the over-crowded and chaotic conditions which gave rise to frequent outbreaks of dysentery and malaria. Prisoners were required for daily working parties which for some provided a welcome opportunity to escape the oppressive overcrowding. This work could bring tangible benefits especially if it was on the docks where there were plenty of opportunities for stealing food and other essentials.

The second largest groups of interviewees were the 22 men captured across the Dutch East Indies, thirteen of whom were RAF personnel. Six men were held in Sumatra, several more were transported to other countries and the rest remained in Java. In Java former Dutch air bases became forced labour camps with prisoners repairing airfields. When the Netherlands East Indies capitulated in March 1942, a derelict former native labour camp on the dock-side at Tandjong Priok outside Batavia was hurriedly converted into a large transit camp for marshalling large numbers of prisoners of war awaiting over-seas working parties. One of the first groups into the camp was an advance party Royal Engineers (RE) who were sent to wire-off the compound in preparation for the influx of several thousand POW from up country.

A few months later, a large draft of prisoners left Tandjong Priok camp and joined others, notably Lieutenant Colonel Dunlop's medical party from Bandoeng, on board a ship bound for Burma. There they joined thousands of men transferred from Singapore to work on the construction of the Thailand–Burma Railway. This was built to provide a supply line to Japan's frontline for its assault on India and it eventually stretched for 415 kilometres from Bangkok in Thailand to Thanbyuzayat in Burma, through jungle, swamps, across plains and around mountains. There was little or no habitation waiting for the thousands of men who arrived early on and so, after clearing the jungle, they set to work building bamboo and attap huts, a process which was to be repeated time and again as the railway progressed through thick jungle.

Though in general the basic rice ration was hopelessly inadequate, particularly in view of the heavy workload, food was more abundant in Thailand than in many other places. The prisoners of war were quick to exploit this by establishing clandestine trade with local Thai villagers to augment their diet. This railway was the largest construction project undertaken by the Japanese involving over a quarter of a million people, mostly enslaved, of which around 61,000 were Allied POW. As seen in the table below, 22 per cent of the 30,131 British POW died in Burma and Thailand.

Table 1 Death rates of the different nationalities of enslaved labour on the Thailand–Burma Railway[2]

NATIONALITY	EMPLOYED	DEATHS	%
Malay (1)	75,000	42,000	56%
Burmese	90,000 (2)	40,000 (3)	44%
British	30,131	6,648	22%
Javanese	7,500	2,900	39%
Australian	13,004	2,710	21%
Dutch	17,990	2,737	15%
Chinese (Singapore)	5,200	500	10%
American	686	132	19%
Aminese	200	25	13%
Total	**239,711**	**97,652**	**41%**
Japanese/Koreans	15,000	1,000	7%

Notes: (1) The people transported from Malaya included native Malays, Tamils and Chinese.
(2) Approximately 175,000 Burmese were drafted to work on the railway but large numbers deserted before arriving at Thanbyuzayat.
(3) This figure does not include the many believed to have died after deserting.

There was another railway built through jungle in the Far East, this one on the island of Sumatra and three of the men interviewed had worked on the construction. Though shorter in length than the Thailand–Burma Railway, the track in Sumatra was forged through thick jungle at a terrible cost in lives. By far the greatest number of deaths, upwards of 80,000, were among the 100,000 Sumatran and Javanese labourers (or romusha, the Japanese word for labourer) sent in 1943 to begin construction. From mid-1944 onwards approximately 3,800 Allied POW worked on the railway, the British numbering just over 1,000. In all, 673 or just under a third of all Allied POW, died. In addition, around 1,450 Allied POW and 4,200 Javanese labourers were sent from Java to join them in September 1944. They were on board the unmarked Japanese ship, *Junyo Maru*, when it was torpedoed and sunk by the British submarine, *Tradewind*, on 18 September. Only 720 survived. Interviewee Leading Aircraftsman Rouse Voisey 151MU (maintenance unit) RAF, was one of only 520 survivors picked up, as he describes on page 34.

Running from east to west roughly across the centre of the island, when completed the Sumatra railway was to provide a supply line to the west coast in preparation for Japan's plan to seize India. Despite his experiences there, Sumatra Railway veteran Aircraftsman 2nd Class Derek Fogarty RAF, described in his interview the beauty of Sumatra.

> They drove these wagons all the way across Sumatra to Pakenbaroe. And one thing I do remember was we were up in the hills and we went through like a hole in the top of a mountain and ... came out the other side and there was just a panoramic view of a hundred miles probably of Sumatran jungle ... It was wonderful. I mean you could not but admire the beauty of Sumatra ... all the time I was there I always admired the beauty of everything.

Conditions in the camps across Sumatra were, if anything, at times worse than in Thailand, as the island was at the western limit of Japan's newly acquired territories. Disease raged largely unchecked despite the heroic efforts of the few Allied medical staff and there were no large base hospital camps like those in Thailand. Derek vividly recalled how they had to build their camps.

> We got into the camp and ... you had to build [it]. So, people who knew, they lay out the templates for the uprights of the buildings ... then somebody dug the holes every so many feet ... the wood was from the jungle ... somebody got the bamboo, there was plenty of bamboo everywhere ... and you split that and you make the pieces across to hold the attap, and the pieces that come down and so on and the pieces to go across. And you put the attap on, somebody had been making the attap within the party, I mean there were hundreds of people about a thousand people there, and we made the camp ... trees were still left and they came out the top of the huts and you slept on the floor the first night and gradually you made what they called bali-bali ... it means 'sides' ... eventually they put planking in it. But all the other camps we'd been in, in Java it was just split bamboo ... you split it and you just open it out and you've got a, not a plank but you've got a board, like a strip and you just sort of tie them down ... normally it would be rattan ... in Sumatra it was all boarding, all the flooring was boarding, and that would be about that high [two feet] off the ground.

It was a similar story in the Celebes Islands, north of Java, and on the coral islands of Ambon and Haruku, known as the Spice Islands. Six of those interviewed were among the hundreds of British POW (mainly RAF personnel) who together with thousands of Dutch POW left the port of Surabaya in the east of the island in March 1943 on ships or coastal steamers bound for the Spice Islands. The scene on arrival at Haruku was vividly described by former RAF medical assistant Arthur Turbutt.

> Having arrived at Haruku at night it was the monsoon season, torrential rain came down in sheets, and we were taken off the boat, up a very small beach to a cleared area not very big, just a few trees had been hacked down. And of course it was about three inches deep in mud from the monsoon, and we were told to lie down and go to sleep ... the following morning we were herded down to the beach again and we had to wade out to the boat which was lying off, and they were throwing the drums of oil overboard and we had to push them back to the shore. Well some of our lads couldn't swim, I think some drowned actually, but eventually all these drums were pushed back and we had to roll them up the beach ... When the boat was unloaded it set off and we settled down into our new camp, which was still being built by the natives, bamboo huts, and putting attap roofs on and when they were completed we were allowed to go inside.

Armed with nothing more sophisticated than hammers, spoons and trowels, prisoners were soon given the task of reducing two nearby adjacent hills. The spoil was removed in baskets and tipped into the gap between the hills. Months later, once levelled and compacted, a serviceable airstrip was created. As the soil was poor there was little hope of growing much-needed vegetables to supplement their diet and consequently vitamin deficiency diseases were rife and the death toll high. Only the expertise and improvisational skills of former botanist, Flight Lieutenant Leslie John Audus and Dutchman and fellow academic, Dr J. G. ten Houten, a plant biologist from Kuala Lumpur, saved the death toll from rising further. This and other extraordinary medical ingenuity is explored in Chapter 3.[3]

The 8,000 Allied prisoners captured at the fall of Hong Kong in December 1941 were among the first to be taken into captivity, herded together in former British and Canadian army barracks, schools and other buildings. Of those interviewed only four had been captured in Hong Kong and two of them were later sent to Japan. In the early months there was constant movement of POW between the camps at Shamshuipo, Stanley, Argyle Street and North Point with overcrowding, starvation, illness and unrelenting working parties the norm. However, from the autumn of 1942 numbers in Hong Kong fell drastically as drafts of prisoners left, destined for Japan, Taiwan and Manchuria. In both Taiwan and Japan prisoners of war were enslaved to Japan's heavy industries, coal and copper mining, steel and aluminium works and shipbuilding, taking the place of the rapidly growing numbers of Japanese needed to serve overseas. Here prisoners were housed in what had been Japanese workers' camps, primitive wooden huts affording little protection against the long cold winters. Again the supply and quality of food was a major problem, and as the war dragged on this only worsened as not only were the prisoners of war starving but so too were the local population. Opportunities for supplementing their diet were nonexistent. In Taiwan the incidence of malaria was high but so too were outbreaks of diphtheria, tuberculosis (TB) and skin lesions caused by chronic malnutrition.

Disease among prisoners of war in all regions was exacerbated by the deliberate neglect of their captors. There was never enough food to satisfy even basic human needs, unpolished and filthy rice being the staple for all, seldom accompanied by anything other than thin watery soups. When Red Cross supplies of food and medicines arrived in camp they were stored under lock and key. The guards helped themselves and only a fraction filtered through to the prisoners. Typically, accounts in diaries speak of one box of supplies having to be shared by up to 10 or more men when they should have received a box each. There can be no doubt that if these supplies had been distributed as intended then not only would productivity have increased but many more prisoners of war would have survived.

From the beginning of captivity both malaria and dysentery were the twin scourges of life in camps. These serious and debilitating conditions were very soon complicated by a combination of tropical disease and malnutrition, vitamin deficiency diseases such as pellagra (causing dermatitis and diarrhoea), beriberi and dengue fever. Symptoms such as loss of vision and peripheral neuritis (damage to nerve endings in limbs, resulting in unrelenting pain in the legs and feet) were the result of gross malnutrition. Such painful symptoms caused abject misery while chronic vitamin deficiency could lead to life threatening conditions such as cardiomyopathy (enlargement of the heart muscle), weakness and breathlessness which if left untreated could be fatal. Added to this were periodic outbreaks of cholera, diphtheria and typhus, major threats for those incarcerated in the equatorial and tropical regions.

Another excruciatingly painful problem was tropical ulcers. These were the result of untreated wounds either caused by trauma, for example beatings or minor scratches and cuts from thorns, stones or coral. Injury was commonly to the legs or feet (another consequence of lack of clothing and protective footwear) but could affect any part of the body. These wounds quickly became infected and, combined with malnutrition and poor circulation, the loss to life or limb was catastrophic.

Being sick was no barrier to work and desperately ill men were shown little mercy. Allied doctors and medical staff did what they could to alleviate suffering, and medical officers repeatedly bore the brunt of Japanese fury when working party numbers fell below demand. In the absence of medicines and equipment doctors relied on skill, judgment and ingenuity. Despite these difficulties they worked miracles, assisted by the medical orderlies whose self-less care for their fellow man has rightly become legend among these veterans. A First Aid certificate in pre-war life was sufficient qualification for an Other Rank to become camp doctor where none existed, just as being a Sunday School teacher could elevate others to the rank of padre. Few sought such promotion, they just did what they could do, but it often meant the difference between life and death to their comrades.

In the jungle camps of the Thailand, Burma and Sumatra, Allied doctors devised makeshift operating theatres and successfully operated on thousands of patients, treating everything from the removal of in-growing toenails to mid-thigh amputations. The subject of disease, and how it was combatted, is covered in more detail in Chapters 2 and 3.

With tens of thousands of prisoners being used as a slave labour force in different countries, some were transported overland, like those captured in Singapore who travelled by train, locked in steel wagons up to 30 at a time, north through the Malayan peninsular to Thailand. Many thousands more were shipped around South East Asia and the Far East in what became known to all Far East POW by the lasting sobriquet, 'hellships'; lying deep below the decks, battened down in the filthy, cramped, airless holds of small coastal steamers, often for weeks at a time.[4]

In late October 1942, the *Singapore Maru* sailed from Java via Singapore to Japan, a voyage lasting over five weeks. It carried approximately 1,100 British FEPOW, my father Captain Duncan among them. He kept a detailed diary of the voyage which later, in camp in Japan, he wrote up as a narrative. Luckily for him and the rest of the human cargo, there was no torpedo that time. But still, approximately 240 prisoners died during or shortly after the voyage and were buried at sea or left on quaysides en route north. The following eyewitness account, lodged at the National Archives at Kew, was given to the US War Crimes Investigation team in late 1945, by American POW medical officer, Lieutenant Commander T. I. Moe.[5] He had been sent with his medical team from their nearby camp to evacuate the sick left on board the *Singapore Maru* for two days after it had docked at the port of Moji in late November 1942. 'Conditions on the *Singapore Maru*, which was an old freighter, the filth and stench of bloody mucous, pus, and faeces which covered living spaces, effects, mess gear and the persons themselves, surpass description.'

Deaths at sea mounted due to neglect, disease and malnutrition. These ships, with their Japanese flag flying for all to see, had no markings to distinguish their cargo from that of the ordinary coastal traders which sailed to and from Japan supplying its new found empire. This made them legitimate targets for Allied submarines; over 22,000 Allied prisoners of war were lost at sea in

"PRISONERS WERE TRANSPORTED THUS

Figure 1 Prisoners were transported thus
… drawn by American Far East POW, Lt
Johnson, given to Captain Duncan at
Zentsuji POW camp, Japan
(A. A. Duncan collection)

this way. The first reported case of a POW transport ship being torpedoed was the *Lisbon Maru* on 2 October 1942. It was sailing from Hong Kong to Japan carrying 1,800 British prisoners of war, one of whom was 23-year-old Royal Scots' bandsman Denis Morley. At interview he recalled what happened.

All I can remember is the blackness of the hold and the stink and the stench … you had to stay calm and collected, it was no good panicking … we were battened down, hence the darkness and the stench. Later on somebody who had smuggled a knife in managed to get up … and cut the canvas so you could lift one of the boards up. The first few that got out unfortunately got shot, but there were so many eventually did get out, they got the Japs and finished them off and we were then able to get out … somebody opened the front hold, the third hold unfortunately was getting to be under water. Anyway, I took my time … then you could hear shots, and the Japs were shooting the chaps in the water and they weren't picking them up either. Any rate, I went in and I just lay on my back and floated and let it take care of itself. Eventually, Chinese fishermen came out and started picking up. The Japs saw this and then they … started picking us up … I got taken near one of these … anyway I did swim towards it and I climbed up the ladder and got on board … whether he was a rating or an officer … come out of the laundry sort of thing and he pointed me to sit there, which I did. And lo and behold he came up with a little bowl of tea and a cigarette, lit it for me … eventually there were more being picked up and I'm a tough little blighter and I went and I just helped people to get on, until it got dark and that was it …

The *Lisbon Maru* was sunk by the USS *Grouper* with the loss of 843 POW. News of this disaster quickly reached the camps across the region, many of whom had men awaiting embarkation. Several of those interviewed vividly described these voyages. The following three interviewees shared memories of conditions on board the ships. First, former Lance Corporal John Leonard Pratt, Royal Corps of Signals, shipped from Singapore to Indo-China, who was only too aware of the threat from Allied submarines:

We got a feeling that they cut the voyage short for some reason, maybe because of American sub-marine activity, I don't know … the torpedoing, I mean that was awful being down below and you were locked in like that, in tiers [shelving] … we didn't [get hit], as I said we were the only boat that survived with one destroyer, the other two transports and other two destroyers were sunk … as far as we know, 'cos we heard the explosions during the night. And we think that the Japanese then curtailed the voyage, y'know, said Ok for some reason, dump them in Saigon for some reason because there was work to be done there for the Japanese…

Next, former Private John Tidey, 1st Battalion of the Cambridgeshire Regiment, recalled his voyage to Japan after working in Thailand,

… back down to Singapore, there the terror started, loaded on to these hellships … the bowels of the boats … we were crammed in man for man and we weren't allowed to go up on deck until things got worse when they had to allow people to go to latrines … boxes strapped to the side of the ship that you climbed over the side to do whatever you had to do. When the sea was rough enough it hit the box and put you back on deck, this was quite funny in some cases.

Then Gunner Peter Barton, 'B Troop' 242 Battery 48 Light Anti-Aircraft, Royal Artillery, in his broad South Shields brogue, described his two voyages, the first from Java to Singapore, when they were

> literally packed in, we'd had now't to eat for about a day and a half and I mean the rice was full of weevils and rubbish ... we got on board and had to go down this thirty foot vertical ladder. When we were all on, the Japanese brought stacks of tiny little loaves and instead of giving us one each as we went down, they waited till we were all down and they tipped them on top of us, w'aye you bugger – eeh I'm sorry! And we just fought amongst each other, y'know some blokes would have three, that was it, like, you just had to dive in ... And then we had this boiled rice for the next few days till Singapore.

There they were subjected to an undignified and uncomfortable process on Singapore docks before boarding the next ship.

> We all got off and stood bollock naked on the quayside and we had a water hose turned on us. That was our bath, no soap, towel or 'owt. And then we were marched naked, it were brilliant sunshine, right the way down to where another ten Japanese doctors were sitting on chairs with white coats on. And we had to stand in front of them in numbers of twenty, bend down and they pushed a glass rod up your rectum. That was your medical for dysentery. And then they put all the ten tubes in a glass jar, how could they tell which was which, y'know?

The Japanese were looking for signs of blood or mucous on the glass rod. The procedure was done in camps as well, and routinely with little finesse as many accounts reveal. Despite this, dysentery raged on regardless. Peter continued describing the next, much longer voyage.

> [Then] we went on the *Dai Nichi Maru* from there ... we were at the stern part of the ship [on] wooden shelves and we just lay both sides [of] a narrow passageway ... we were a few days out at sea and, of course the Japanese troops were above us going on leave see, and we were way down. And there were no toilets, there were buckets, but they'd be filled in seconds and you'd be splashed and you actually waded in urine and dysentery and phew, it stank! ... and this particular night was a bit rough and it was only a tramp ship and there must have been at least two thousand of us right the way through. And, it was funny, the lamp went out, a forty watt lamp on a long flex, and in the darkness a Geordie voice shouted out,

'Oi, mate, is that shit or water?' [when] some moisture fell on him. And a titter went round the hold and a bloke said, 'Listen t' that daft bugger,' and somebody shouted, 'Taste it and see!' … [then] a cultured voice rang out from the darkness, 'Now boys, don't let these Nip bastards see we're enjoying the cruise.'

As noted earlier Rouse Voisey survived the sinking of the *Junyo Maru* off the coast on Sumatra. This was his second journey by sea. The first, on board the *Amagi Maru*, had taken him from Java to Haruku in April 1943. That voyage, while unpleasant and fraught with anxiety due to submarine activity, was uneventful, as was the return journey to Java in May 1944. Four months later, on 18 September 1944, Rouse was not so lucky.

We [were off the] west coast of Sumatra when, we were very tightly packed on that boat … conditions were really stifling in the hold … on the Monday afternoon I believe, we heard the two, I call them thuds … we'd been hit by two torpedoes. There wasn't pandemonium … but all of a sudden Lieutenant Commander Upton, his voice came quite clearly, 'Abandon Ship!' And he … could see what was happening, the Japs were getting off, so he knew it was pretty bad obviously, and we then began to get out of the hold as best we could … The only escape from the hold was an iron ladder in one corner which went vertical from top to bottom and a knotted rope, which I took I don't know but I got out. I jumped overboard … into the sea some twenty, thirty feet down, presumably because by then it began to tilt up. And the sea was very calm and I swam over to where people were gathering. I didn't go to the escort boat … I could see what was happening people were being beaten off … by the Japs, obviously they were protecting themselves at this stage because if we'd all got on it would've gone under because there were so many of us … there were some 6,000 souls on that boat, 2,000-odd prisoners and 4,000 native labourers. And no attempt was made to pick anybody up at that stage, some people were trying to get on the escort vehicles and some did … I eventually got to some debris in the water with a couple of Dutch chaps and we, there were bales of cotton … and we got hold … and roped this stuff together and made a little raft and the three of us sat on it …
I think I was picked up on the Wednesday morning and from Monday after-noon it was something like 40 hours and … I wasn't terribly sunburnt … I made a sling on this thing and they were like a couple of pieces of wood, arrow shaped, and I made a sling and I sat in the sling with my arms over the things and I wore little holes in there [his side] which the salt water treated. And gradually I found myself on my own. I tried to drink at one stage but I realized I couldn't drink the salt water so all I did was wash my mouth out with salt water to keep it moist, I didn't drink it. I think it was sometime on the Wednesday … that I saw this boat

slowly coming in amongst us, it was in reverse going very, very slowly and I saw one or two chaps go towards it so I made up my mind to have a go at getting on it. It was a Jap, Japanese boat which had been one of the escort vehicles, it was a submarine chaser which had the depth charges on the back and it was going very, very slowly in reverse. Incidentally I only learned to swim in Singapore … I swam towards it and there was a sailor standing at the top of it, it was only about, a small boat as I say about five or six feet out of the water, with a rope ladder down and I managed to grab hold of this ladder and pull myself up. I thanked him and he brought me over to where twenty or so lads were sitting over in the stern of the boat. Told me to go and sit down. Went over, being an obedient type of chap I was, and another Jap came with a little sip of water and a little dry biscuit which I thought was pretty good because I was pretty parched by that time … On the way there [Padang] one of the Dutch chappies went a bit delirious and he crawled up the deck towards the Japanese quarters and two sailors came out, picked him up and just threw him overboard again. And that was a, a moment when you thought well I'm going to sit still, I'm not going to do anything stupid. We arrived at Padang and we were put into the local jail there.

Such vivid eye witness accounts, given over 60 years after the event, help us to visualise something of the reality that faced thousands of Allied servicemen. Distress, disease and death were all around them; there was absolutely nothing they could do to protect themselves from danger. They had to learn to live with a constant fear of the unknown.

The Far Eastern prisoner of war experience is unique in the annals of British military history. Never before or since have such large numbers of our Armed Forces been subjected to the extremes of geography, disease and man's inhumanity to man, as exemplified by Far East captivity. Almost 25 per cent of British Forces died during captivity as opposed to just under five per cent in Germany and Italy.

The differences between Allied captivity in the East and West are stark. Prisoners of war in Europe remained in the northern hemisphere and therefore had few problems with the climate and diet (albeit food rations were meagre). Many servicemen arrived in Singapore just days before the surrender allowing little time to acclimatise. Some were already sick with malaria and dysentery before they were forced to capitulate. Then, once in captivity in such a debilitated state, they had to manage without medicines and exist on an almost exclusively rice diet. Many could not and quickly succumbed.

In Europe, Allied prisoners of war were protected to some degree by the Geneva Conventions, while those in the Far East were not. Lines of communication throughout Europe, both official and clandestine, were more easily established and maintained and so prisoners did not feel the same depth of isolation and despair as that experienced by Far East POW over 6,000 miles away. Most Allied prisoners in Europe had one vital advantage over their Far East comrades: they were Europeans, as were their captors. If they escaped they had a chance of survival especially if they had an aptitude for language, acting skills and a fair measure of luck. Not so in the Far East. No amount of luck could make Europeans look like native Malays, Javanese, Thais or the Japanese. If Allied prisoners escaped, and very few succeeded and survived, they did not have a chance of passing themselves off as 'locals' and they were utterly dependent on resistance forces taking huge risks to smuggle them to safety.

In the Far East Allied prisoners of war battled for survival of body, mind and spirit. Most were completely isolated from reliable news or contact with family for the first two years or more, some for the duration. However, former Royal Navy Petty Officer Writer, William 'Bill' Bolitho, who was held in Sumatra throughout his captivity, described at interview how he briefly landed a job during 1944 which made a huge impact on camp morale. This was entirely due to him being blessed with a phenomenal memory which had come to the attention of his captors. They needed someone who knew every man in the camp and Bill was their man.

> On one occasion ... the Japanese interpreter, a wizened old man, came along and said there was some mail for us had arrived from Singapore ... and because I knew everyone's name and whatnot I was to go to Japanese HQ and to sort it out ... And when he'd seen what I'd put aside, if he approved, it would be brought back to camp and distributed ... I went to this room and it was stacked with mail and they said sort it out. I did this for eight days and got through it, and the mail ... was going the rounds of all the camps ... and every night I got back it was just about dark and there was a queue, 'Was there a letter for me?' ... I felt it was so wonderful to be able to do this for the others and it gave me enormous pleasure.

While not only being kept in isolation from the world outside, they also found themselves at the mercy of a seemingly indomitable enemy, especially in the early days of captivity when, as noted by a British surgeon and ex-prisoner of war of the Germans, P. H. Newman, this was a time when prisoners were likely to be at their lowest psychologically. But captivity for Far East POW was not just a confined, regulated, sparse and alien experience. From the outset it was also accompanied by feelings of humiliation and degradation, in part a result of having surrendered. This was combined with constant fear for their lives, their existence dominated by hunger, disease, gratuitous violence and slave labour.

In some areas, like Changi for instance, the numbers of captives were so great that the Japanese left the prisoners to organise themselves which undoubtedly helped many to adjust and cope better initially. However, quite quickly the Japanese organised the mass movement of prisoners across thousands of miles of sea and land with dreadful consequences for many. The experiences of those who survived up to four years' captivity in the Far East did not disappear once they were repatriated. Many returned home harbouring myriad tropical infections as well as the ravages of malnutrition. Some were also scarred mentally and emotionally. These men, who had had to keep such a tight hold on their emotions, suppressing rage and frustration for so long, then had to try and adapt to normal life.

CHAPTER 2

SURVIVING FAR EAST CAPTIVITY

THIS CHAPTER OUTLINES THE general conditions facing Far East prisoners of war throughout captivity. Using the oral history interviews and other eye-witness accounts, it explores how life changed and the struggle to survive illness, neglect and isolation.

Camps varied greatly in size and local conditions, spread as they were across a vast geographical area, from Burma and Sumatra in the west to Japan and as far south as New Guinea in the east.

General conditions

Camps sprung up initially wherever the Japanese took prisoners. Gradually as men were moved around some camps closed, new ones opened and others grew rapidly. There were some very large camps, for example Changi in Singapore, which initially held over 50,000 Allied POW (over 30,000 of which were British), North Point in Hong Kong (at least 6,000 British, plus other nationalities) and Tandjong Priok transit camp in Java (with over 4,500 multinational prisoners of war at its peak, before it closed in mid-1943).

Accommodation varied widely and in most areas was overcrowded, inadequate with primitive or nonexistent sanitation in the early weeks and months. Depending on the location, men occupied former colonial barrack blocks, aircraft hangars, municipal buildings, bamboo huts and tents. Common to all camps were inadequate food, water supplies and widespread disease, with

Map of south east Asia and the Far East,
most of which was occupied by the
Japanese 1941–1945
(A. A. Duncan collection)

Figure 1 Duncan's sketch of interior of
Room 8 Zentsuji, showing the view from
his bed space (*A. A. Duncan collection*)

little or no provision for the welfare of the sick, including the many battle
casualties at the outset of captivity.

Men, shipped from Hong Kong, Singapore or Java to work in Japan's heavy
industries, often found that home was to be overcrowded, draughty, wooden
shacks which had been workers' dormitories. They were airless and stiflingly
hot during the summer and had little or no heating in the freezing winters.

Captain Duncan's 1943 sketch (Figure 1) looking from his bed space, shows
the interior of Hut 18 at Zentsuji propaganda camp on Shikoku Island, Japan,
and gives the impression of an orderly and clean environment. This camp had
been a Japanese Army barracks pre-war.

Compare this to the stark reality of the view from the artist Jack Chalker's
bed space in Chungkai Hospital camp's dysentery hut in Thailand in the same
year (Figure 2). Jack depicts a hellish scene of pain and misery literally laid
bare before him in this, one of his iconic pen and ink sketches. It is shocking
to realise that the men we are looking at were, like Jack, mostly in their mid
twenties.

This was the state many were reduced to within the first year of their
captivity. We should be grateful we cannot smell it. Nor the scene on page 42

created by Lieutenant Stanley Gimson, a Glaswegian who served with the 2nd Indian Heavy Anti-Aircraft (AA) Regiment, which shows the interior of the dysentery hut at Kanyu River Camp, up country from Chungkai Hospital camp (Figure 3). It is a similar scene to Jack's, the degradation and suffering of more young men, stooped, squatting and restless, struggling in the oppressive, unrelenting tropical heat. Gimson gives us a better understanding of the hut's bamboo and attap construction, with its low palm leaf roof, so typical of the camp buildings in tropical regions. The artist, a capable amateur, trained as an accountant pre-war and worked for the cotton thread manufacturer, J. and P. Coates. In the early days of captivity took advantage of Changi University's classes in Law. He and the lecturer, Captain Charles Elston, a fellow officer in the Indian Army (1st Indian AA Regiment), were friends and Gimson's interest in the Law grew from then. Charles, who had read Law in Liverpool and was a practicing solicitor at the outbreak of war, said at interview that Gimson had an aptitude for the Law, 'After the war he asked me for a reference, he wanted to apply to Glasgow University, which I was happy to provide. I told them he was a diligent student.' He was. Gimson had a distinguished legal career, rising rapidly through the Scottish legal profession as an

Figure 2 Dysentery hut, Chungkai
(courtesy of Jack Chalker)

Advocate and ultimately as Sheriff Principal. They parted company in Changi when Charles was drafted to Thailand in early summer 1942, but met up again two years later at Chungkai. Charles worked with a small advance bridge-building party to speed the progress of the main construction teams on the railway. They were left to get on with the work, unhindered by their captors for most of the time.

Post-war both men kept in touch and were life-long friends. Charles took an active role in the FEPOW Club movement, initially alongside Brigadier Sir Philip Toosey in Liverpool and later became a trustee on the Central Welfare Fund (see pages 52, 229 and Appendix II), while Stanley joined and eventually led the Scottish FEPOW Clubs Association. In 2010 Charles took part in both the Tropical School's Far East POW Round Table discussion and two months' later gave an interview to pupils at Pensby High School for Girls in Wirral as part of the Heritage Lottery Fund's Far East POW History education project (see Postscript for more details).

Wherever they were held initially, within a very short time many POW were dispersed in large drafts to wherever the Imperial Japanese Army (IJA) needed a workforce. In Singapore and Java many of the newly arrived troops

Figure 3 Kanyu River camp, Thailand, 1943 drawn by Lieutenant Stanley Gimson
© *Imperial War Museums (Art.IWM ART 16893)*

G.H.Q. ORDERS
by
MAJOR WHITING.

No. 1.   24.4.42.

1.   MORNING ROLL CALL will take place 5 mins. after REVEILLE.

2.   With effect from to-day all officers and men will arise at Reveille,
     only men who have been detailed by the M.O. will remain in bed.

3.   MORNING INSPECTION. All ranks below that of Sergeant will parade
     at 8.30 a.m. for inspection, washed, shaved and suitably attired.

4.   N.C.O's i/c rooms and men occupying small rooms will ensure that
     their room has been scrubbed and all kit is packed as per barrack
     room before the inspection by Major Whiting, Officer Commanding,
     G.H.Q. at 10.30 hrs. daily. Also that that portion of verandah
     and drain in the immediate vicinity of room is washed and cleaned.

5.   PHYSICAL TRAINING. All officers and men under 35 years of age
     excepting those excused by M.O. or engaged on essential duties will
     parade at 10.30 a.m. for physical training. Failure to comply with
     this order will result in disciplinary action being taken against
     offender.

6.   BATMEN. As from to-day no man will fulfill duties as batman for
     more than one officer. L/Cpl. Boyden will be N.C.O. i/c Batmen
     and all requests, complaints etc. will be made to him for necessary
     action. Where batmen are desirous of volunteering for fatigue
     parties arrangements for their duties to be performed by another
     batman must be made with the officers concerned the night previous.

7.   OBSCENE LANGUAGE. The use of obscene language in barrack rooms
     will cease forthwith.

8.   URINATING. The practice of urinating into drains or through the
     barbed wire surrounding No. 1 Camp is to cease forthwith. Action
     will be taken against any offender committing these offences.

9.   PARADES. It has been noticed that members of G.H.Q. do not exhibit
     the usual promptness or smartness when answering roll calls or parading
     for duty, from to-day onwards disciplinary action will be taken
     against all persons who fail to act in a prompt and soldier like manner.

10. COMPLAINTS. Complaints will be made in writing and signed and handed
     to W.O. II. Roberts, and will be given every consideration. Those of
     a frivolous or trivial nature will NOT be accepted.

11. RETREAT. "Retreat" will be sounded at 19.45 hrs. daily and will serve
     as a signal for those outside camp to return by 20.00 hrs. On hearing
     this call all men will stand at "attention" irrespective of place or
     nature of work.

quickly succumbed to tropical diseases for which they had no time to build up any resistance. Fortunately for the captives the Japanese were initially over-whelmed and largely left them to organise themselves, demanding only that sufficient numbers reported for working parties each day. After a while as the camps became more organised interference from camp guards became the norm.

From the outset the British established Army regulations as the basis of organisation of camp life. A senior British officer (SBO) was appointed, often from the Army. In larger camps the SBO worked alongside senior officers of other nationalities. Camp rules, separate from Japanese regulations, were issued and adhered to. These daily orders provided a useful framework for organisation, discipline and healthcare.

One example is the list of daily orders issued three weeks into captivity, on 24 April 1942, by Major Whiting the SBO at Tandjong Priok in Java. It ran to 16 points (see Figure 4) and makes interesting reading. Point No. 8 highlights the lack of self-discipline and hygiene exhibited by some of the men. Such behaviour was a great cause for concern to medical officers desperately trying to minimise the spread of disease. While such rules and regulations may not have been universally welcomed, to the vast majority of the 50,000 British Far East POW, army life was at least familiar.

In Hong Kong early on, thousands of prisoners were gathered at Shamshuipo camp, including Lieutenant James 'Jim' Wakefield of the Royal Engineers. At interview Jim recalled an unexpected communal reaction to war. They discovered that the latrines did not work as the copper piping had been looted by the Chinese. The order went out dig pit latrines 'which were never used for the first fifteen to twenty days, every man had virtually reacted to the war ... they just couldn't go to the loo and pass a stool ... it was an anomaly that I'd never sort of met up with before.'

Allied prisoners of war had to learn to adapt to their new surroundings quickly. The many nationalities included British, Dutch, Eurasian (mixed Dutch and Javanese parentage), Australian, American and romusha e.g. Thai, Malay and Javanese, initially sorted themselves into groups by nationality, services, regiments and rank within the larger camps. Some of these groups stayed together, many did not. At various times the Japanese separated the ranks, moving officers from men, or senior officers away from the rest. On 16 August 1942 in Changi, New Zealander Captain David Nelson, administrator of the clandestine Changi Bureau of Records, recorded that all officers above the rank of lieutenant colonel held at Changi camp were to be moved off the island. These senior Allied officers joined their counterparts from other camps and were sent to Taiwan first then moved to China. Not long after captivity had started the prisoners were informed that Japan was called Nippon and that the Japanese were known as Nipponese. According to Lieutenant Owen Eva of the 9th Royal Northumberland Fusiliers, 'from then onwards Japanese soldiers, guards etc. were known amongst us as "Nips".'

Understandably, there was friction between different groups of prisoners of war. Language difficulties, low morale, overcrowding, lack of privacy and boredom, were all causes for dissent. Senior Allied officers were responsible for providing set numbers of men for daily working parties which added to tensions.

From the outset the Japanese had demanded that all prisoners of war paid obeisance. All signs of rank were removed from prisoners' uniforms. Badges bearing only their number, in Arabic and Japanese characters, were to be worn at all times and at roll call all men had to number off in Japanese. Irrespective of rank, all prisoners of war had to stop and bow low at the sight of any approaching Japanese or Korean guard no matter how junior, at any time of the day or night. It was the ultimate humiliation and required supreme self-control to minimise confrontations and stand-offs.

Another humiliating ritual was the periodic checks for amoebic dysentery, known as 'glass rodding'. In Chapter 1 Peter Barton vividly described the process before boarding a ship in Singapore. RAF medical officer Aidan MacCarthy was another who described in his book, *A Doctor's War*, undergoing the humiliating and inadequate mass testing, when at River Valley Road camp in Singapore in 1944 being 'told to parade, bend over and drop our shorts. Then a glass rod was inserted into each anus.'

However, RAF surgeon Flight Lieutenant Maurice Kinmonth, who worked with Nowell Peach at No. 1 Allied General Hospital (1AGH) in Bandoeng during the first weeks in captivity, recalled seeing how Japanese officers regarded the battle casualties in the wards. On official visits they would walk round the wards and at, 'each bed bowed to each wounded soldier. They thought they were absolute heroes. But we were absolute dross ... we were all cowards.'

Allied POW medical provision

The Japanese quickly closed down most Allied hospitals like 1AGH, forbidding the transfer of equipment or supplies into camps. Only small portable items could be hurriedly distributed among the medical staff and smuggled out. Both Peach and Kinmonth had worked there briefly with the legendary Australian surgeon, Lieutenant Colonel Edward E. 'Weary' Dunlop ('Weary' from an advertisement for Dunlop tyres, tired, weary!) who had established 1AGH a few weeks before the invasion. Nowell remembered what equipment he was able to take with him.

> We were each given a certain number of them to take with us. I had a little roll made in which I had half a dozen artery forceps and a sharp spoon I think and a tracheotomy tube and some other, the scalpel which I subsequently had made, I also carried in that. So I had my own little roll of equipment I think all the medical officers probably took some of the instruments from the hospital when it was closed down ... 'Weary' probably took a lot of them to Thailand with him.

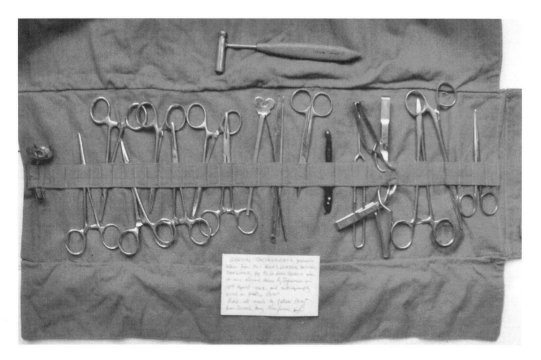

Figure 5 Surgical instruments given to
Fl/Lt Peach at No. 1 Allied General
Hospital, Bandoeng, Java, April 1942
(courtesy Nowell Peach)

The photograph (Figure 5) shows the canvas roll he made from a Dutch kit bag with some of his original surgical instruments. Nowell produced at interview the patella hammer (at the top of the photograph) which was specially made for him by Royal Engineers (RE) at Tandjong Priok camp in late 1942, one of whom was Craftsman John Baxter RE. The steel head was from a dynamo (Wimshurst machine) soldered to a syringe plunger then fixed into a carved wooden handle Nowell had crafted. In the centre there is a homemade metal curette, which has a small scoop at each end, lying vertically, flat, to the left of the scissors also made by RE craftsmen.

Established Allied medical teams fragmented as medical officers accompanied working parties dispatched to different areas. Across the occupied territories, clearing bomb damage and dock work were the main occupations in the early days, the latter affording the greatest opportunity for smuggling food. In different regions there were a few quick-thinking men who risked their lives making contact with local merchants and tradesmen in order to secure clandestine supplies, an initiative that saved many lives. Lieutenant Colonel Cyril Wallace Maisey RAMC (1909–1979) was one such. In his diary, held at the National Archives (TNA), there is a report written at the time detailing his hurried and risky visit to Batavia (now Jakarta) in April 1942.[1] He decided that as the health situation in camps was already so grave he had go, despite Japanese orders forbidding the movement of POW personnel. On 6 April, he met with a Mr Straub of Rathkamps, the largest pharmaceutical company in the Dutch East Indies, to negotiate the supply of medical stores, at the lowest possible price, for use in camps. In his report he described the tense situation in the capital and attributed the success of his mission to his interpreter, the wife of Colonel Larsen of the Dutch Medical Services, who had arranged the meeting, stating that

> the entire success of this week was due to the immense courage of Mrs Larsen. At that time Batavia was a terrified city. The Japanese were killing people for the most trivial offences (for example, laughing at the guards), and apparently there was an order in existence at the time forbidding any white Dutch to appear in the streets unless they had a special Japanese armband ... Undoubtedly our Red Cross armlets saved us from being molested during this week.

He also noted,

> as ADMS (Assistant Director Medical Services) of the South-West Pacific Command, I had undertaken to stay behind in Java and care for our sick and wounded. No one thought we would achieve anything, and I was considered quite mad in refuting the Japanese orders regarding movement. With the exception of Lieutenant Colonel Russell, East Surrey Regiment, no officer could understand that the greatest battle to be fought in the South-West Pacific was disease. Until disease was controlled, it would be impossible to accomplish anything else, and with the long years of being a POW which lay ahead, it was of the utmost importance to establish outside contacts for supplies of medicine at the first opportunity. I never had any doubt that if the medical profession was to save lives, it would be done entirely by our efforts alone: Japanese assistance would be obstructive only.

Not long after he made these arrangements, large scale construction projects elsewhere saw huge numbers of prisoners of war being shipped from Java. His actions undoubtedly benefitted many of those who remained in Java.

Japanese commandants ran the camps, providing daily working parties to construction, industrial or agricultural sites. They were moved on every three to six months and had under their command junior officers, NCOs, privates and Korean guards. Most POW quickly learned not to draw attention to themselves. From the outset, Allied medical officers worked closely with senior officers to establish order, good hygiene, sanitation and the fair distribution of rations. In some larger camps doctors had medical orderlies, clerks and even laboratory technicians working with them, while in smaller or more remote camps there was often no doctor present. Far East POW quickly learnt to utilise whatever was available to help them. The scope for medical ingenuity is explored more fully in the next chapter but in terms of the organisation of camp life and survival, medical teams played a crucial role.

No Work, No Eat

In Japan's heavy industry, dock work or major construction projects like the jungle railways in Thailand, Burma and Sumatra, the Japanese military had to work with their own civilian managers and engineers who, together with the overseers, wielded absolute authority over the prisoner of war labour force during working hours. This arrangement could sometimes work to the advantage of prisoners of war as the overseers were only interested in getting the job completed on time. Former RAF Leading Aircraftsman Tom Jackson recalled working in a dockyard in Japan where

> the military guards who'd marched us there ... handed [us] over to different foreman in different units, the wood yard, the pipe shop, the engineers, all sorts ... walking about in the dockyard doing work there were no guards to stab you with a rifle butt for not working. Some of the gangs had really nasty foremen who used to slap and hit people for no reason but fortunately I, this little gang, we didn't get any of that ...

Royal Navy Petty Officer and wireless telegrapher Reg Davis had been captured in Hong Kong on Christmas Day 1941. Over a year later, in January 1943 he was drafted to Japan to work in the Osaka steelworks. One day he had an accident. Losing his balance, he fell heavily on his right side against a wall, breaking his arm just above the elbow. It was to have horrific consequences which he related at interview in a somewhat matter of fact way.

> The Japanese in their speed to get a quick recovery, get me back to working, they took it off rather than set it in splints. When it happened, instead of taking me to our medics in the camp the Japanese panicked and took me straight down to their hospital which was about a mile, couple of miles, away. They took me down on a handcart with all this [arm] dropping around. Well when I got to the hospital I stayed on this bloody handcart. They just put a strap round me and the surgeon came out and just cut it off. A tourniquet around, and that was it.

And four hours later a couple of the POWs came down and took me back in the camp ... the bloke that looked after me was an RAMC corporal, Flanagan. He slept beside me that night on the tatami, that's a bed, and he got me out of bed about 4 o'clock in the morning and put a fresh dressing on because I was, there was blood everywhere. I was okay then but about a week later I had a terrific temperature, I don't know what it was due to, we had an RAF doctor in the camp by that time. There was no treatment, not even aspirin, but Flanagan he, the medical orderly, he used to wash me down with cold water every so often. And I survived that and after that I started taking an interest in life ... I'd done a medical course in the navy ... Because I had lost my arm I was no further use to the Japanese and I did all the, well I used what Red Cross supplies we had and treated the lads as they became injured and that. We had one doctor who was an RAF doctor and I used to make notes for him. He was very good 'cos after I'd lost my arm I was in his sick bay for some time recovering, about a week actually, and he encouraged me to start writing and make notes of his interviews with the troops.

Post-war Reg learned to manage with a prosthetic arm. He said he just got on with his life, what else was there to do? When asked how he felt about what the Japanese had done to him, Reg replied,

They did what they could do for me ... they were extremely limited to what they could do. I'm not making excuses for them but I mean I never needed to have lost this, but what would've been the consequences if they'd tried to save it? That I'll never know will I? So I accept it's what it is. I'm not happy about it, but devil can't be chooser, can he ... I've tried hard not to let it interfere with me.

Many men were to have lower limb amputations to save their lives. Unlike Reg who had just a stump for his right arm, those who survived the trauma of this surgery were fitted with prosthetic legs manufactured in camps. There is more about this work in the next chapter.

At the start of captivity food supplies within camps had varied enormously. Some men took looted provisions in with them while others were ravenously hungry after days of battle. It took time for the Japanese to organise supplies of rice into camp kitchens and even then the quantity and quality was grossly inadequate. In some areas prisoners traded with the locals but this was soon prohibited and punishment was brutal if discovered. The Japanese philosophy of: 'No work. No eat', meant the sick were not supposed to get rations. Allied POW officers and medical staff tried to ensure that the sick were fed something, while leaving those doing heavy manual work with sufficient to eat.

In Hong Kong Jim Wakefield was sharing a room in Rotingee's Building with several other officers. The sanitation was functioning but they lacked cooking facilities.

> We were able to heat water by having cigarette tins, two different size cigarette tins, circular cigarette tins separated by little bits of asbestos, positive to one tin, negative to the other, pop it in the bucket of water and it heated it up very quickly, but blew the fuses somewhere else in the building ... there was a lot of wire netting ... we got into the habit of untwisting all this, wrapping it round a pencil, using the asbestos ... like an electric coil you have in an electric fire, round in biscuit tins, Jacobs Crackers biscuit tins and you then had a little stove on which you could cook things ... These wires kept burning out and you had to join them up ...

When large drafts of men were transported by train from Singapore to Thailand from mid-1942, food and water were sparse. There were stalls at some stations or halts where they could purchase food and when interviewed Royal Army Dental Corps officer, Captain David Arkush, recalled, 'native women were running little stalls selling fried bananas, banana fritters, and if you had money you went from stall to stall sampling, it was like a holiday atmosphere.'

The reference to money is significant; some men came into camp with money acquired either by luck or during the chaos of battle while others had none. Natives often appeared with food to sell while the men were marching from camp to camp in Thailand. Very quickly men were bartering pens, watches, cigarette cases, clothing and shoes with camp guards or locals, in exchange for food such as eggs, fruit or tinned goods. In time, though not in all areas, the Japanese paid prisoners a small amount for work and in some camps prisoners were allowed to run canteens. Out of their pay, officers were expected to contribute to camp funds which were used to buy clandestine supplies of food and medicines for the sick.

All those interviewed recalled instances when both Japanese and Korean guards meted out random and harsh punishments to the prisoners of war. Unprovoked attacks were a daily part of camp life, as was the fear that they gave rise to. Many men noted the violent behaviour of the Korean guards in particular. In the late 1930s, following Japan's occupation of their country, large numbers of Koreans were impressed into the Imperial Japanese Army. As conscripts they were not only treated with contempt by the Japanese but were also at the end of a long and painful line of punishments, meted out as 'discipline' by each rank to the one below. Once in charge of prisoners of war the Koreans finally found a stratum beneath them on which to exercise authority.

Sergeant Harry Hall was a pharmacist in 197 Field Ambulance RAMC. He stayed on Singapore throughout his captivity, working first at Roberts Hospital and later Kranji Hospital camp. He observed in his diary that, 'quite a few of the guards were Korean, who the Japs thought were almost as low-life as we were. The role of the guards wasn't really to patrol the perimeter you understand, as there was nowhere to go even if you did get out. They were there to make you work, and make you scared.'[2]

Officers and men

The majority of British forces were either volunteers or conscripts, often drawn from distinct regions of Britain, for example the majority of the 9th Battalion Royal Northumberland Fusiliers were from towns and villages between Newcastle and Berwick-on-Tweed; the 18th Infantry Division (known as 18th Div.) were drawn from Norfolk, Suffolk, Cambridgeshire, Hertfordshire and Bedfordshire. Such allegiances, forged before captivity, would later prove to be a great strength as men faced prolonged and unrelenting hardship. However, for some junior officers regional affiliations could be problematic, as Lieutenant Stephen Alexander described.

> My regiment was the 135 Field Regiment RA, also known as the North Hertfordshire Yeomanry … these were TA, Territorial people, and the two batteries came from Peterborough … and round Hitchin in Hertfordshire the other, and they were very strongly regional and I joined them as an outsider from Bristol, together with several other just-promoted officers and we felt very much out of things because we were not from either Peterborough or Hertfordshire. But the regional affinities are very strong and remarkably class conscious … We did stay together and of course this is where the regionalism paid off because people retained the feeling of brotherhood if you like, and of course they could talk of things … they could share memories and this helped to keep them going, undoubtedly. And also it helped with discipline.

In well-organised camps effective leadership and medical care, coupled with firm and fair discipline and a well-developed social structure, kept morale high and a sense of purpose alive. Captured in Java and shipped to Japan, interviewee and former Flight Lieutenant Ed Knight, a munitions expert in the RAF, said he 'never had any experience of mutiny or criticism from the men. They realised we were all in the same position.'

Nevertheless, senior Allied camp leaders had an onerous and precarious job to do. Those individuals imbued with an instinct for leadership combined with diplomacy, guile and courage, commanded the respect not only of their men but also their captors. Men like Territorial officer, Lieutenant Colonel Philip Toosey (1904–1975) Commanding Officer of the 135 Field Regiment, who was also SBO at Tamarkan camp in Thailand, combined high expectations of all his fellow officers irrespective of rank, an unshakable defence of 'the men', with a willingness to show respect when due to their captors.

Toosey was intelligent and strong-willed, an inherently kind man who became a legend among the POW of the Thailand–Burma Railway camps. His sense of fairness and justice brought out the very best in those who served under his command. Even some of the Japanese were in awe of him, appointing him to be the Allied camp leader above other more senior British officers at Tamarkan at the time. His skill was in knowing how to show respect for the enemy without losing the respect of his men. He was determined to get as many men as possible through the ordeal of captivity and return them home. Gunner Maurice Naylor, 135 Field Regiment, had worked as a clerk in Toosey's office at Tamarkan.

> When the bridges were completed … all the healthy, well, able prisoners were sent up country to other camps further up the river. I was left behind because at that time I'd been in a little hut set aside for people suffering from acute dysentery … and I wasn't fit to go … and I thought to myself well I ought to be doing something. If it's going to be a hospital, they're going to need some help. I approached Colonel Toosey on the parade ground on one occasion, I said, 'I've got a degree in administration, I can do clerical work without any problems, if you want any assistance in the camp office, let me know.' And he said, 'Alright, okay, yeah, off you go.' And, a few weeks' later he and Boyle, David Boyle, came charging into the hut I was in and Toosey said, 'There he is, that's the one! Come with me.' So I went to the camp office and Sergeant Neave … Gordon Highlanders, was doing the camp duties or whatever they call them, and he was ill and they wanted me to take over from him.

In the post-war years, up until the time of his death in 1975, Toosey continued to play a pivotal role in the welfare of those he regarded as his men (see Chapters 4 and 5 and Appendix II). Australian surgeon 'Weary' Dunlop was another inspiring officer. He played a big part in raising morale among men, whether they were patients, assistants or fellow officers. Many were inspired by his leadership and determined to follow his example: men like artist Jack Chalker whose help Dunlop sought in recording the range of medical need, ingenuity and achievements. When asked over six decades after his return from captivity what it had meant to work alongside the medical staff, Jack said that the fact also that I could work with these marvellous people, with Marko [Captain Jacob Markowitz, Royal Army Medical Corps] and subsequently with Weary and others, but particularly those two, especially Weary, because you felt you had to support them, you couldn't let them down. I mean these are a godsend, these were magic people to us and so there was, there was a very happy obligation as well. But it was one's own pride that you daren't let them down somehow, and I think that played a huge part in survival.

Weary had been captured while in charge of the Australian field hospital he had set up, 1AGH, in the Crystelyk Lyceum (High School) in Bandoeng in the central highlands of Java.

Nineteen-year-old Dutch nurse, Nini Hannaford (nee Rambonnet), had been a volunteer at 1AGH and at interview remembered working with Weary, Peach and Maurice Kinmonth, one of the young surgeons and someone she much admired.

> I went to the hospital in Bandung ... First of all we went into rented accommo-
> dation and then of course the Japanese had arrived ... Weary Dunlop said, 'It is
> no good you being out there you must come here into the hospital' ... looking
> after people after they had been washed by the Australian nurses ... we used
> to see that they got fed and see if they were comfortable and if they had to be
> operated on ... be there to hold the patient's hand ... and you looked after them
> afterwards.

(Nini met Bill Hannaford, an RAF officer with the liberating forces sent in to relieve her internment camp in Java in September 1945. They married and settled in England).

Weary and the medical staff were allowed to carry on working for six weeks after the occupation before suddenly the hospital was closed and staff and patients dispersed. On more than one occasion during that time Weary physically put himself between his patients and Japanese guards wielding bayonets. He also did whatever he could to encourage and support his junior medical officers. During the early weeks of occupation the hospital still functioned and Dunlop was given permission to go looking for supplies in Bandoeng. In a second hand bookshop he bought an American edition of *Gray's Anatomy* to give to Nowell Peach, as he knew he intended to prepare for his Fellowship (of the Royal College of Surgeons of England). In 1946, just six months after his return from captivity, Peach passed Part I of the Fellowship examination, a feat he owed to having memorised a page a day of *Gray's Anatomy* (Figure 6).

Not all officers were respected. There were the self-serving and selfish in all ranks, just as there were in society at large. But in captivity, when officers

Figure 6 Nowell Peach with the copy of *Gray's Anatomy* given to him by Weary Dunlop in April 1942 *(Copyright The Royal College of Surgeons of England. Reproduced with permission. Source: Peach family)*

failed to show understanding for their men the repercussions were magnified. An incident took place at the Jaarmarkt camp in Soerabaya in eastern Java in late 1942. Senior RAF officers suddenly decided to re-organise the men, re-forming them arbitrarily into official squadrons and splitting up existing friendship groups. This was vividly remembered by former Leading Aircraftman 2nd Class Derek Fogarty.

> [These new] squadrons would be as they were listed on their rolls. Well, the rolls had no bearing on our make-up. We were in groups ... how we were captured, with pals, our squadrons, our stations and all that sort of thing, our own personal welfare, we'd sort of moulded together, we'd been through capture together. And we were made ... to move into a squadron and into a part of this camp, this prison camp, in the group they'd detailed us. And so we were completely alienated [*sic*] from our friends, which was not on ... so, we mutineed against it shall we say, we said, 'No we will not, we will not move together. We will not break up'. And we were marched up against our elected Squadron Leaders and we were warned that we would be court-martialed when things

sort of settled down ... I mean what stupidity ... I'd got shot up with my mate and I was going to be separated from him? And my mates, the squadron mates, were all going to be separated, because of a nominal roll?

The officers had no choice but to back down, and nobody was court-martialed. In smaller camps with no Allied officers in charge, NCOs would often assume command and take on the responsibility of care for the men. This happened to the remnants of a party of 600 Royal Artillerymen, or 'Gunners', who were transported to New Britain. Following the departure of the rest from Rabaul to Timor, 56 sick men were transferred to the island of Kopoko off Rabaul. Former Gunner Alf Baker, 47 Coast Observation Department (COD), was one of only eighteen survivors from this group. As all their officers had been killed fellow Gunner Joe Blythe had assumed responsibility for the welfare of the men. It seems that even the Japanese respected him. Alf recalled that pre-war Joe

was an insurance man ... a member of St John's Ambulance. He was a Methodist local preacher and that made him our padre and of course because he was with St John's Ambulance he became our doctor, because there was no doctor left. And he was magnificent. He would stand up to the Japs and only once did we see him beaten by a Jap and that was because they were in awe of him. They saw him as a holy man. And he did actual operations, without anaesthetic, one with a razor blade, and that man lived and came back.

Intelligence and secret radios

Senior Allied officers needed Japanese-speaking interpreters, though there were few men with the skill and nerve to take on such a risky job. In Thailand, Captain Charles Ewart Escritt, Royal Army Services Corps and pre-war Oxford scholar, learned both spoken and written Japanese and latterly was interpreter at Nong Pladuk camp. At Tamarkan, Toosey was fortunate to have with him Captain Bill Drower who had learnt Japanese when, after graduating from Oxford in 1936, he had worked as an assistant to the new Japanese Ambassador at the embassy in Portman Square, London. At interview he recalled, 'I did some translating jobs with working parties and that sort of thing for about two months and then I was told that I'd been given the job of interpreter for 'A' Force – in 'A' Force was largely Australians – and that I would be working to Colonel Toosey.'

Interviewee former Lieutenant Gordon Smith, 2nd Battalion Argyll and Sutherland Highlanders (A&SH), recalled how he had shared a cell in the notorious Pudu Gaol in Kuala Lumpur, Malaya, with fellow Scot Lieutenant Oswald Morris Wynd.[3] Born in 1913 in Tsukiji in Tokyo, where his parents were Scottish missionaries, Wynd held dual citizenship which during captivity made him a traitor in the eyes of some Japanese. The family had moved to the United States in 1932. Seven years later, with war imminent he had joined the Scots Guards, was commissioned in the Intelligence Corps and later attached to the 9th Indian Division just before the fall of Malaya. As a fluent Japanese speaker he became the Allied interpreter at both Pudu and later at a camp on Hokkaido, Japan where he exploited his role to the full. Gordon Smith recalled, in his quiet unassuming way, how he and Wynd had operated a radio that Gordon had repaired. Someone had brought into Pudu a damaged radio receiver that had been found.

> [it] wouldn't work ... the main transformer had been damaged ... so I took the transformer out and found the various places where there were shorts and I had to rewind it. In doing so I ... made layers of cotton cloth with candlewax in between the windings (laminations), and this worked quite well. The next trouble we had [was] how we assembled ... the laminations, because it was too big. So what we did was ... one of the other officers who had been doing some work for the Japs ... managed to produce a big file and we had to file the laminations so they reduced in thickness, so finally they'd go in. And we put it all together and ... it did work perfectly well. We used to get mainly [broadcasts] ... from India and it was hidden in our cell ... We made a stool with bits of wooden boxes, and underneath the top we put this thing in and it was left in the middle of the cell. Now the camp commander used to come in to harangue ... Wynd, about various things and ... organised the searches to take place ... [for] anything we shouldn't have, and he sat on this stool all the time ... I don't think we realised how much danger there was then.

Another interviewee who found his skills much in demand and risked all in the quest for information from the outside world was former Corporal Sydney Berkeley, RAF wireless operator mechanic (WOM), who was taken prisoner and initially held on Bangka Island, off Sumatra.

> somebody had brought in a radio ... being a wireless operator wasn't good in those days! Anyway, we go to the kitchen of this place and this radio is up in the attic, so I and the gang, with Jim Wilson ... got [the] radio working. And all the rumours in the camp had been, Yes the Americans had landed in Java! and it won't be long, and we will be released and blah, blah, blah. And of course when I got the radio going ... nothing was happening. I will never forget ... [a] New Zealander Lieutenant Commander who fancied himself as a singer ... we

are up above the kitchen where … they stored tea and we daren't move because it was going to come down. And he started singing, 'One of the little bastard's down here.' … We squatted there for about a quarter of an hour, then he said, 'Come on down.'

Learning how to survive

Gunner Victor Cole 9th Coast Regiment Royal Artillery, had been out in Singapore and Malaya since late 1937. At interview he said how that had helped him to cope initially.

Being out there for three and a half years before, I knew a little bit about the language and you got acclimatised, which is very important. And we survived. A lot of the people who came out on the 18th Div., they were the first casualties … if you were a little person you haven't got a lot to lose, but if you're a 15 or 16 stone person who's a rugby player, y'know you're in dead trouble and, nearly all the big lads in my regiment were the first to go.

From the outset many prisoners of war were quick to realise that they had much to learn from those who knew the tropics well, be they garrison forces like Victor, romusha or members of the local Volunteer Forces. The latter was a colonial equivalent of the Territorial Army. They were the plantation managers, bankers, administrators, engineers and merchants in Malaya, Singapore, Hong Kong and the Dutch East Indies. Working in the tropics for years meant they were used to the climate, understood the language, the flora and fauna, as well as the mores of the indigenous people. They taught the newcomers how to build native huts that were safe, strong and waterproof, which fruit, roots and vegetables were safe and good to eat or had medicinal properties.

Former medical orderly Private Frank Scarr, 198 Field Ambulance RAMC, recalled that in Thailand they were helped by the 'Malay Volunteers, they seemed to … provide us with accommodation and y'know cookhouses … well y'see they'd been working with different people in Malaya that was able to do this y'see, all the workers in these rubber plantations, they had these little huts … more or less in the jungle.'

By mid-1943, as the war began to turn against the Japanese, POW and civilian workers in factories, mines and shipyards across Japan were permanently hungry, sick and exhausted. Tom Jackson spent most of his captivity working in Japanese dockyards.

[W]e worked with Japanese people. The very old ones, like the leader of our gang, he was called Murakami, a wizened, tiny little man … we had a little hut and we took our breaks in this hut with Murakami. And he was a lovely old bloke, he didn't give two tuppenny hoots, the war it just didn't exist, he was just so old he wasn't bothered.

Botanist, academic and RAF Radar specialist, Leslie Audus played a pivotal role in the survival of thousands of men both on Java and later on the island of Haruku which is discussed in Chapter 3. He had led an experimental RAF unit sent to Malaya to establish the first radar station at Johore Bahru. Radar operator Ernest Darch worked in his unit, 512 AMES, Air Ministry Experimental Station and recalled Flight Lieutenant Audus as

> rather academic … he wasn't a disciplinarian … he had a gramophone and he had some classical records and he used to play these classical records to us … give a bit of talk about the way they were made and so on, he was a bit of an expert … Apart from that we didn't see much of him, you operated and he left us alone.

Leslie took his precious gramophone and record collection with him when he, Ernie and the rest of the unit were evacuated first to Sumatra, then to Java and into captivity. In camp in Batavia they separated and Ernie ended up in Borneo. Leslie went to east Java, to Jaarmarkt camp before, in mid-1943, he and 2,000 POW were shipped to the Spice Islands. He left the records and player behind, in the faint hope that they would be looked after. The following year he and the ragged remnants of the working party returned to Batavia. In an article he wrote for the *Java Journals* (later published in the Java FEPOW club's book, *Prisoners in Java)*, Leslie picked up the story.

> In July 1945 I had returned to my starting point on that island, the port of Batavia … [to] Cycle Camp … I was making my way one evening through the camp, when I was brought to a sudden halt, my ears pricking up at a familiar sound. Coming from a distant hut, I heard the somewhat scratchy strains of Brahms' Piano Concerto in B flat Major … In one corner of the hut … was a tall emaciated young British prisoner, winding up a battered portable gramophone. Beside him lay a small pile of records. It was P/O Robinson, a young RAF officer … whom I had known slightly in the Jaarmarkt in Surabaya in 1943. There, on the records was my name, scratched over two years previously. He had rescued the records from my bed space when I left the Jaarmarkt, had been lucky enough to stay on Java and had been able to keep them with him, whenever he moved. Thirty-six records had survived out of the original five dozen or so I had left behind. In addition to the Brahms concert that had brought me to the hut, they included his Third symphony, Tchaikovsky's Pathetique, Mozart's Jupiter,

Franck's Symphony in D and Liszt's Piano Concerto No. 1. Just over a month later we were free. Those surviving records came home with me, complete with their original paper sleeves …

Leslie's return to Java in mid-1944 was a nightmare voyage on the *Taiwan Maru* during which more men died. Aside from the very real and ever-present threat of torpedo attack, life below decks was indescribable; the filthy holds were a squalid, groaning world of dysentery, malaria, vomit and fear. Leslie recalled that when the ship arrived in Java, 'the most seriously ill were straight-away taken to the St Vincentius and Mater Dolorosa hospitals in Batavia.' Nowell Peach was medical officer on duty at St Vincentius Hospital that day.

This draft came into the hospital and they had, we unloaded them from the ambulance, some were bloated with wet beriberi, just like seals, others were absolutely [*sic*] skeletons. Extraordinary the different effect it had on different people. And we put them in beds, we had proper beds in the ward, and it was amazing how quickly they responded to treatment. All we could give them was an improved diet. At the expense of all the rest of the staff they had quite reasonable food. And we had some injections of vitamin B … it's incredible how quickly they responded to treatment, within a week or two some of them.

Lance Bombadier Jim Surr, 242 48th LAA regiment, recalled others arriving at Mater Dolorosa.

A draft came back from Haruku, they'd had a terrible time, it, they were in a dreadful state due to malnutrition and hard labour they'd had to put up with. One lad, who I had to give a daily bed bath, his testicles were the size of a football … Another man was from my home town of Stalybridge … he was blind because of his malnutrition, a condition which affected people in many different ways.

Maurice Kinmonth was medical officer at Mater Dolorosa the day they arrived. 'You couldn't imagine how people could be reduced to such a ghastly, awful state … we had a sort of whip round in the camp and got extra food for them. They picked up quite quickly.'

Working parties

Work was the pivot around which everything else revolved for the prisoners of war. Heavy manual labour could be building railways through jungles or airfields on coral islands; coal or copper mining; working in shipyards or on the docks, in aluminium smelting plants or in steelworks in Indo-China, Taiwan and Japan; or it might be agricultural work, rearing animals, planting rice in paddi fields or harvesting crops of seaweed. Wherever the Japanese needed labourers prisoners of war were put to work.

Allied doctors who had the onerous responsibility of selecting men to go to work each day, faced appalling dilemmas which often brought them into conflict with the Japanese. They had to make life and death decisions and when they chose to make a stand on behalf of a patient they could expect swift and painful punishment. This naturally led to conflict with the men. Irish doctor, Flight Lieutenant Aidan MacCarthy, RAF, medical officer at Bandoeng camp in Java, noted in his book, *A Doctor's War*, that 'the Japanese demanded a fixed quota for outside working parties and inside factory work. As a result we had often been forced to pass unfit men. This put a severe strain on the relationship between the troops and the Medical Officers'.[4]

Australian medical officer Rowley Richards worked in camps in Thailand. In his memoir, coincidentally also entitled *A Doctor's War*, Richards described the effect deciding who should work and who should rest had on him. He felt angry and powerless at the waste of young lives. His sense of fury at the injustice of it made him even more determined to survive. He believed his anger acted as a vital 'self-defence mechanism'

Wherever they were, the daily routine was similar for all: woken between 5am and 6am, on parade for 'Tenko' (roll call), a repetitive and tedious process often necessitating several re-counts. Once the Japanese were satisfied all were present, the men had breakfast then, after lengthy wrangling between medical officers and Japanese officers, those deemed fit enough to go on working parties would line up to be led off by a guard detail by around 7am. It was normal to walk some distance before arriving at the place of work. They did not expect to return until around sunset. At midday there was usually a short break for food which, depending on their proximity to camp, was either delivered or they carried with them. However, men often worked into the night when required.

A vivid glimpse of the daily walk to and from work at the copper mine in the remote hills of Taiwan, was given by Signalman Arthur Titherington, Royal Corps of Signals. To get there they had to

> go down the side of this mountain, down some very roughly made steps ... different heights and there were ... actually 1200, something like that, and when you got in the mine ... went down to the first level where we were working. You did your day's work, you then had to climb out of the mine along the tunnel and climb these damned thousand plus steps to get back to the camp. That was murder because at times, depending on certain circumstances, you probably

Figure 7 Hospital huts at Chungkai
(courtesy of Jack Chalker)

finished getting up the steps on all fours, all the time being harried by guards …
that was Kinkaseki.

Within camps, rotas of jobs provided routine and light work for the sick.
The cookhouse was highly prized as it meant the chance of additional food
during the day. Tending livestock, chickens, pigs, ducks and rabbits, and work
in the vegetable garden were also sought after occupations for both officers
and men. The following description of Chungkai camp, written in 1944 by
Dutchman Frank Samethini, gave a vivid insight into life in this large hospital
camp housing up to 10,000 sick men in Thailand.

> Like Tamarkan, Chungkai is not too bad as far as POW camps go. The Japs
> are reasonable because their commander is humane, the work is not too hard
> and the food is pretty good. There is even a canteen where one may buy fried
> eggs, omelettes, spicy snacks, ginger bread and rice flour doughnuts! Finely
> cut native tobacco, properly cured by former tobacco experts from the British-
> American Tobacco Company in the Indies, is rolled with cleverly constructed
> tools into cigarettes of reasonably thin paper. Scores of men, unfit for manual

work, are being employed by the 'factories', the entire profit of which is donated into the hospital fund.[5]

The mention here of 'factories' within camps highlights the ingenuity of men with engineering, wood and metalwork skills, who conjured up from scrap metal, bamboo, coconuts and rubber, vital medical equipment needed by the doctors and their orderlies. This subject will be explored further in the following chapter.

The beautiful watercolour by Jack Chalker of the hospital huts at Chungkai (Figure 7) looks almost idyllic, so light is his touch; it belies the fact that the huts contained thousands of sick and dying men and exhausted doctors, orderlies and technicians.

Recording the struggle

For the orderlies and volunteers tending the sick, either in huts or tents within working camps, or in the large specially created hospital camps like Chungkai, the daily workload was relentless and hazardous. However, due to the Japanese guards' fear of infectious disease, these were often the places where professional artists like Jack Chalker, Ronald Searle, Philip Meninsky and George Old were asked to work, as there was less risk of detection. Doctors wanted the reality of their battle recorded and these gifted artists could do this as effectively if not better than any news photographer. We shall be returning to the artists later in the book.

For men working in heavy industry in Japan, working hours were the same for both prisoners of war and civilians. Wherever they worked, once back in camp exhausted men slumped on bed spaces often ignoring their meagre rations, few had any energy for chores or leisure activities. In some areas men had a 'yasume', (meaning rest) day every ten days or so; in others months would go by without one.

As Hong Kong was in close proximity to the Japanese islands early on large numbers of prisoners were shipped to Japan's industrial centres to work in factories, mines, shipyards and steelworks. Wherever they ended up, the constant chivvying to work harder, produce more, combined with arbitrary and unpredictable behaviour by guards or overseers, hunger, sickness, neglect and despair, were commonplace to all. But the unpredictability also applied to acts of kindness. Corporal Kenneth Bailey, 5th Suffolks, was one of many men interviewed who felt it was important to record that not all Japanese guards were cruel.

> When I had malaria ... soon after we were taken prisoner ... a friend of mine taking us out to a working party ... had to help me because I had malaria badly

... and the Japanese guard wanted to know from my friend what was wrong. He explained to him and the Japanese pulled from his pocket a little gadget and he had in it a tablet called mepacrin which he said was good for malaria. And so that's one good thing I could say about the Japanese ... No, they weren't all bad I've got to say that. The majority of them were and out on the working parties of course they wielded bamboos. If you stood still for a moment you expected a belt round the shoulders with a bamboo staff and that's generally how it was with most Japanese.

As previously noted, Japan did not observe international agreements embodied in the 1929 Geneva Convention, commonly referred to as the Prisoner of war code, drawn up to protect enemy captives. Although reluctantly agreeing to be a signatory to the Convention relating to the sick of the armed forces, the Japanese (and also the Russians) refused to ratify the Convention pertaining to the treatment of prisoners of war which 'laid down an extremely precise set of instructions as to housing, temperature, food, hygiene, work.' The Japanese felt no obligation to care for the enemy in captivity.

Trading and thieving

Owing to the grossly inadequate rations and medical supplies provided by the Japanese, prisoners of war were forced into clandestine and very risky trading with local natives and merchants and, if discovered punishment was dire for both parties. At Takanun camp in Thailand medical officer Captain Robert Hardie noted in his diary on 15 May 1943 that, 'We know rather better than these new arrivals from Singapore how to make the best of local conditions and know what to try for in local purchases. Angier, who is with No. 7 Battalion ... has already made local contacts to purchase extras which are direly needed.'

When out on working parties POW exploited every opportunity to forage or steal food especially those working on the docks with its potential for rich pickings. Pre-war petty thieves and burglars suddenly found their skills much in demand. Jack Chalker remembered one such man who

was a cat burglar ... he was a very dry little man, quiet little man, used to just tell us about his jobs, used to say, 'I don't do jobs on people who can't afford it, see.' He was a cockney ... and he was like a Robin Hood. And he risked his neck, he used to go out at Nakon Pathom over the wire, knowing very well that he'd be battered to pieces and killed if caught. And he'd bring back 10 ducks' eggs, and a duck's egg will save your life. And he would give five to a bloke who's dying at the end of the hut. Now I just wonder whether I would do that, after risking my neck again and again?

In Tarsao camp in Thailand, Royal Marine Peter Dunstan, a survivor of the sinking of the *Prince of Wales* off Singapore, recalled a theft in camp.

> There were two great big godowns, huts, storage warehouses, and there was a Jap in charge of them ... in the middle of these huts was ... a guard hut, I would estimate about maybe eight foot ... with a half door. Being yours truly, I could look in ... on the back was two boxes, Carnation Milk! Well, that's red rag to a bull, just to even see cardboard boxes with that in ... there was three of us who were a gang and ... a pal who's perhaps five foot six and that, so little George was up, over, in, while we kept cady [army slang for lookout]. And, lo and behold ... Carnation and Condensed Milk ... When we went back to the camp these were hidden in the bottom of the baskets that you used to carry the food up in. And we lived like lords ... get a brick and a tin of Carnation Milk and try and open it. That tin looked like it'd been under a steam roller before it finally burst. And there was us, glug glug glug, glug glug glug.

Derek Forgarty, at Number 3 camp on the Sumatra railway, recalled that the Japanese commander who, unusually, was well-liked, reported that livestock was being stolen.

> Our Japanese commandant, he was a marvellous bloke, looking back in retrospect ... he was only a sergeant but he was a civil man, a civilised man, one Japanese amongst all the Koreans. He complained that somebody was stealing his chickens but Captain Armstrong and Smithy [interpreter] had to explain, 'But our prisoners, the men wouldn't steal your things, they've got more sense they just wouldn't do it, they respect you.' ... had a look around, thinking that something like a mongoose or something like that was stealing. And so another day the sergeant came across and said, 'I've lost my chickens, your men have been stealing them.' Captain Armstrong said, 'They would not do it, I assure you on my honour as a British, and Englishman ... my prisoners wouldn't do a thing like that to you.' ... And they found it was a python was stealing ... the python was caught and the python was killed and we ate the python, for meat, and the skin was put around the post in the kitchen ... true story.

In 1938 at the age of 17 Fergus Anckorn became the youngest member of the Magic Circle of Great Britain. He found a novel way to improve his chances by ruthlessly exploiting the oriental fascination with magic.

> The Japanese camp commandant in the camp was a real devotee of magic. I found this with all the Far East people, they love magic they really do. And he got me into his hut to do magic and I hadn't got anything in those days to do

it with. But what I'd do is I'd borrow a coin off him and then vanish it and then he'd have a tin of fish on his table and I'd open the tin and get the coin out of it, which was good, but he then pushed the tin of fish over to me. They would not touch anything that we'd touched because we were verminous, y'know, so I got a tin of fish ... [I did a] trick with a banana ... he took the four of hearts I think it was, and I asked him to peel the banana and it fell off in four pieces and I got the banana. And then I'd do tricks with cigarettes and I got the cigarettes, tremendous currency ... any food I saw in the place I would immediately do a trick with it ... 'cos I ended up eating it.

By his mid-90s Fergus was the oldest performing member of the Magic Circle. He spent his post-war life honing and perfecting not only his craft but also recollections of his captivity, amazing and fascinating audiences with his dexterity, wit and charm.

Trade with locals in Thailand was not just restricted to 'under the wire' meetings with natives. A clandestine organisation known as the 'V-scheme' ran undetected for nearly three years and saved countless lives, thanks to the courage and tenacity of a small tight-knit group of Thai tradesmen and Far East prisoners of war. Gunner Tom Evans, a volunteer in the Singapore Royal Artillery (SRAV), was directly involved. At interview, he described how pre-war he had worked for the

Anglo-Thai Corporation, they had branches in India, their biggest in Bangkok because they had big teak interests in Thailand, and they were the largest British firm in rice. In fact they were the largest British merchant firm in Thailand, they had the most men interned in Bangkok ... I was general clerk in London, two and a half years, and then when I was sent to Singapore.

By late 1942 he was in Tamuang camp. He explained that

there was an underground system working, whereby money was sent from the firms who had had men interned in Bangkok. The firm I had worked for was the Anglo-Thai Corporation and being the biggest British firm, had the most men interned and two of them were very prominent in sending these monies ... I imagine more money came from Anglo-Thai than it did from say, Shell. ... these men who'd worked for British firms were instrumental in raising the money with the Chinese ... they organised the money from the Bangkok end ... they had to get truck drivers to work for them in secrecy ... when it reached a camp like Tamuang, somebody signed for the money. I signed for Anglo-Thai money for a while. I signed in my own name because I didn't want to implicate the firm. It was put straight into hands at Tamuang of Colonel Lillie.

Essential medicines such as quinine for treating malaria were procured by the 'V-scheme' through a network of Thai traders led by Mr Aw Boon Pong in Kanchanaburi. On 2 September 1943 Weary Dunlop made reference in his diary to one such supply noting that, 'Certain gentlemen have supplied some 72 grains [of emetine] and offer a most hopeful avenue for either free supply of drugs or supplying a cheque for medical purposes.'

David Arkush remembered Mr Boon Pong:

> he did a tremendous lot for us. He, Mr Boon Pong, had a little grocer's shop in Kanchanaburi, which was where we were … a little village … called Chungkai … It was just, walking distance, perhaps a mile and a half, two miles from Kanchanaburi … And the doctors arranged with Dr Nobusawa, the Japanese doctor, to be allowed to go into Kanchanaburi to the chemist shop there, to see if we could buy drugs … and he allowed me to go with them. So I re-established contact with Mr Boon Pong … I managed to buy various things from him.

Medical officers found other ways to take advantage of the situation, for example when Japanese or Korean guards had venereal disease. In the Imperial Japanese Army this could be a capital offence and they were desperate to avoid detection. Pharmacist Harry Hall noted in his diary that Korean guards had a weakness and it was

> women. They were constantly getting VD, and they couldn't go to their own army doctors as the Japs were very strict about the clap, and if anyone of theirs got it, it was up the jungle immediately, which was nearly as bad for the captors as for the captured. So the Koreans used to stealthily approach us, wanting the medicine to cure them. We had a reasonable supply of M&B tablets (the forerunner to antibiotics), as the Japs weren't keen on infectious diseases and though they couldn't care less about our operating and diagnostic equipment, hygiene (oddly), or food, they did worry about contagious bugs … The hapless Korean guard would be obliged to drop his trousers for the diagnosis, while we stared disgustedly at the evidence. Then the bargaining began. 'Biiiiig presento!' intoned our MO solemnly. 'Rice?' offered the afflicted one. 'Biiiiiig presento!' repeated the MO, stretching his arms wide. 'Rice, pineapples?' pleading. It was like shooting ducks in a barrel really, and we only gave out one tablet per present. Since they needed about two weeks' supply, we got quite a bit of useful stuff from them which, presumably, they stole. Our patients would have fared considerably worse had it not been for the randy Koreans.

The successfully treated patient would often continue to repay his debt to the doctor to be assured of his silence. Dentists also exploited the situation whenever possible, exchanging expertise and skill for vital supplies.

From the outset, FEPOW organised leisure activities to keep minds and bodies active and to boost morale. In the early months, before malnutrition and exhaustion took hold, football and rugby involved many and distracted and delighted legions more, especially when playing against their captors. In Java, Lieutenant Wilf Wooler, the Welsh rugby international, trained and played alongside other members of the squad, on the dusty pitch in the centre of Tandjong Priok camp, to the delight of both players and spectators.

Harry Hesp recalled at interview that in Singapore's Changi Gaol, where civilian internees were held, he and the rest of the 148 Merseyside lads, all Merchant Navy crew on the troopship *Empress of Asia* (known as the 'Asia boys'), had organised 'seven-a-side football and we formed a league and we got a thousand folks watching.' These young lads, having survived the bombing of their ship on 5 February 1942, had volunteered as stretcher bearers in hospitals around Singapore immediately prior to the Fall and had witnessed terrible scenes. For some it was to have a profound effect on their lives.

Teaching, researching, learning

Books were shared through libraries or by strict rota systems in many camps. The larger ones, like Changi, had an organised, well-stocked and very busy lending library from the early weeks of captivity. A Major D. R. Mullineux of the 2nd Loyal Regiment was a borrower with a keen interest in education. We know this because his alma mater, Bolton School, published an article in the December 1945 edition of the school magazine written by him just weeks after his return from captivity. In it he noted that early on 'we had obtained permission to bring up from Singapore University and Raffles Library some 1,000 books or more, and with the help of these and the services of the Singapore University lecturers who were with us, we were able to start a "university" in the camp, in addition to many "schools" for more elementary study.'[6]

It is interesting that in many diaries and archives there are often long lists of books, perhaps ones the writer had enjoyed or others listing books he wanted to read. Perhaps this was an inherent belief in survival, that eventually the list makers would not only find these books but also the time and peace to read them?

Despite Japanese regulations forbidding gatherings of men, or the possession of paper, pens and pencils, in some camps education classes were permitted. If so, they flourished, engaging men of all backgrounds and education in teaching and learning all manner of subjects. Even when prohibited, with care and a good warning system to alert teacher and students of lurking guards, those with any specialist knowledge were encouraged to share it with like-minded enthusiasts and the curious, alike. Some men wanted to utilise their time keeping up with pre-war studies, while others took advantage of any form of distraction. Whatever the motivation many gained qualifications during their captivity.

There were several 'universities' established in Far East POW camps. Lieutenant Frank E. Bell, a pre-war Cambridge graduate and linguist, and author of *Undercover University*, established the 'University of Kuching' at Batu Lintang camp in Borneo virtually single-handedly. Courses were run in a wide range of subjects and the experience helped to formulate his plans for the future. After ten years back at Cambridge post-war in 1955 he founded the first Bell Language School there and in 1972 the Bell Educational Trust. The Bell Foundation continues to provide centres of excellence for the teaching of English as a foreign, or as an additional, language.[7]

Most of the academic staff of Singapore University had joined the Volunteer Forces just before the Japanese offensive. They were reunited in Changi POW camp and, guided by fellow academics Guthrie Moir, Henry Fowler and Ian Watt, the 18th Division 'university' was established providing quality tuition in a wide range of subjects. One beneficiary was Stephen Alexander who later in life devoted four pages of his autobiography, *Sweet Kwai, Run Softly*, describing in vivid detail the English Literature classes he attended during his time at the camp, prior to his move to Thailand.

Other professionals utilised their time in captivity to extend their knowledge, many sharing their work post-war, publishing articles, academic papers and books. Doctors, like Indian Medical Service pathologist, Captain Ennis, was one of many doctors who formed medical societies to share knowledge and learn from difficult or puzzling cases. Nowell Peach was a member of the Tandjong Priok Medical Society in Java, and undertook a research study on 'burning feet' syndrome. This was an exquisitely painful and relentless side-effect of vitamin B deficiency which was experienced by men in camps everywhere. Over the winter and spring of 1942/43 he recorded detailed neurological findings from painstaking examinations carried out on 54 men at Tandjong Priok camp. His neatly typed and handwritten notes were recorded on sheets of quarto paper (an old imperial size of paper) purloined from somewhere (see Figure 8).

The case studies, giving full details of his meticulous observations, were nonchalantly produced at interview from the depths of a battered docu-ment case. He had hidden the notes and other records, including a notebook with lists of the minor operations he had performed, through several camp searches and moves before bringing them back with him in 1945.[8] The study sheds light not only on the patients' physical condition but also on Nowell's need to record it, to try to find some way of alleviating the unrelenting pain

Figure 8 Part of front cover of Nowell Peach's Burning Feet study and the top part of one of the records *(courtesy Nowell Peach)*

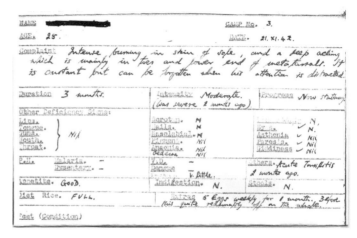

and discomfort so many of them were plagued with, as a result of damage caused to nerves in the feet and legs by malnutrition. Following Nowell's interviews he gave permission for a study to be done into his research and this was published in the *Annals of Tropical Medicine and Public Health* in 2013.[9]

Medical officer Hugh de Wardener made a study of the cholera outbreaks that occurred while in Thailand in 1943. Earlier, while working at Roberts Hospital in Changi camp, Singapore, Hugh had been intrigued by the numbers of patients diagnosed with a severe form of beriberi, known as Wernicke's Encephalopathy. It affected only the central nervous system, characterised by paralysis of the external eye muscles. Until then it had been thought to be related to chronic alcoholism but de Wardener's research, carried out in partnership with RAMC pathologist Captain Bernard Lennox, disproved this theory as the symptoms were clearly apparent in men who had had no access to alcohol for some considerable time. Their research led to the conclusion that it was caused by vitamin deficiency, specifically a lack of thiamine. In his research paper he described it as 'cerebral beriberi' though the name was never adopted. He recalled that,

> eventually I saw altogether fifty-two cases of this disease, and up till then I think the greatest number [that] had ever been published was four, or five ... I saw eight more cases on the railway ... I used to do post-mortems on them and take the hypothalami out ... Bernard Lennox from Newcastle ... a great friend ... kept some samples and I was taking the records. But he had a railway accident, I never quite knew much about that railway accident but he lost the samples. So it was just as well that I had collected some myself on the railway, because I had a sample that I brought back.

Their discovery was to change medical understanding. Both this and Hugh's cholera study were subsequently published in *The Lancet* in 1946 and 1947 respectively, and he was awarded the MBE in recognition of his research work in captivity.[10] Post-war he became Professor of Medicine at Charing Cross Hospital in London and was a leading authority on renal disease.

Entertainments

But it was humour that was often the best medicine, as doctors like Hugh knew only too well. Described by fellow medical officer Captain Patrick MacArthur RAMC, as a 'splendid, pale golden haired Adonis with a delightfully free and easy unaffected manner and plenty of fun and good humour', Hugh was known to friends as 'Ginger'.[11] Hugh had a gloriously deep and ready laugh and it was in captivity, in his mid-20s, that he discovered a natural talent for both acting and comedy. But it was his prowess as a female impersonator in concert parties held in camps along the Thailand–Burma Railway, that Ginger de Wardener was most fondly remembered. Medical orderly Frank Scarr worked alongside him in both Roberts Hospital and at Takanun in Thailand and recalled that he 'took part in [shows] ... used to dress up as a female y'know, did de Wardener ... Oh, he was very good!'

Concert parties and theatricals took place in many areas of captivity, though by no means all. Thanks to diaries and concert posters and programmes which survive, we know that large scale productions such as plays, variety shows, musical comedies, pantomimes and orchestral concerts, took place in Thailand, Singapore, Java, Hong Kong, Korea and Japan. These needed large numbers of men to produce and perform and for stage management, lighting and costumes. Smaller scale entertainments are also recorded, perhaps as few

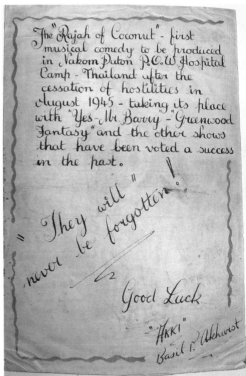

Figure 9 Theatrical poster (with inscription on reverse) painted by Gunner Basil Akhurst, 'AKKI' *(courtesy of Richard Brown and the Akhurst family)*

as a couple of men singing, reciting poetry, doing magic for the entertainment of those in their hut or barrack block. Often after weeks of rehearsals, preparations and growing excitement a production would be cancelled just before curtain up as a punishment for some real or imagined misdemeanour. When allowed to go ahead, the best seats in the house often went to the camp commandant and his officers.

Plays and music were written from memory. On 30 January 1944, at Zentsuji in Japan, *The Duchess Was No Lady*, a musical play, described as 'A plagiaria, fashioned and filched by E. J. Hazel [Lieutenant Colonel Joe Hazel RA], with considerable assistance from John May, George Matthews, Noel Pace, Frank Twiss and others', was performed to an appreciative audience. Captain Duncan recorded in his diary that it was 'very good. The best part about it all was the costumes, particularly those of Wing Commander Mathews and Lieutenant Burke who ... appeared as earls in full regalia, whilst the backless evening gown of Miss "Power" [Lieutenant Norman "Freddie" Power RN] almost produced a riot.' John May was a padre and he wrote some of the music for Hazel's shows. In an email to the author in 2006 he recalled an Australian production of *The Desert Song* for which a British officer, who was a qualified plumber, created the front half of a suit of mediaeval armour from tins from Red Cross parcels!

Sophisticated stage sets, scenery, costumes, programmes and billboards were all designed and created by a host of artists, well-known and anonymous. One example (Figure 9) which survives is from a camp in Thailand. This poster for *The Rajah of Coconut* was painted just after the Japanese surrender by Gunner Akhurst, who used the moniker 'AKKI'. On the reverse he wrote a personal tribute to the theatricals he had enjoyed in captivity. This was one of the comedies that Jack Chalker recalled with great delight when interviewed. He was involved in many productions, both acting and painting scenery and leaflets but he remembered the *Rajah* as being exceptional, not only because it was the first production to be staged after they knew they were free, but also because they made an elephant costume out of woven bamboo and tapioca paste and coloured it using wood ash!

AKKI, or to give him is full title, Gunner Basil Parry Akhurst, 137 Field Regiment, was a prolific cartoonist. His gorgeous watercolour and crayon billboard poster was kept by the show's scriptwriter, Lieutenant Bernard Brown (his son, Richard, on learning of the Tropical School's interest in artwork produced in Far East captivity, donated a colour copy to the study in 2010). We will return to AKKI's work, and his invaluable contribution in raising morale among his fellow captives, later on.

At No. 12 POW camp at Bandoeng, Java in late 1942, following the departure of Weary Dunlop and a large draft destined for Burma, his successor Wing Commander Nicholls, summoned the young Flight Lieutenant Alistair Campbell Hill to see him. Campbell Hill had been a well-known British actor pre-war and was one of the first to organise concert parties and theatricals at Bandoeng. 'It was as if I'd come alive again: back in my element. I still remember my stay in the Bandoeng camp as a ray of sunshine in the three darkest years of my life,' he states in his book *Scenes from Sumatra*. Nicholls told him how much entertainments mattered to the physical and mental health of the camp and added that 'there are thousands of prisoners of war of different races, religions and backgrounds here. I want their minds occupied twenty-four hours of the day.'[12]

In Japan, Sergeant Cyril Jones, a Welshman in the 6th Heavies, Royal Artillery, had ended up at Motoyama coal mining camp on Honshu. At interview he recalled that

> in the early days, we made our own entertainment. We had a little concert party, and very fortunately there was a chap and he had a piano accordion ... he used

to pick up, he just hummed or sang a piece … and there was another Welshman [Ritchie Williams] … he had a beautiful tenor voice and he was the soloist for the male voice choir in Blaenau Ffestiniog … we used to sing duets together, hymns mostly, and they went down beautifully … but, the numbers weren't there, the boys were passing away, bless 'em, … yes we managed to entertain. We had a black and white minstrel show, blacked up, and the Japs used to enjoy it.

This was repeated in camps across Japan, Hong Kong, Korea and Taiwan, where concert parties and entertainments of all kinds were organised. The importance to morale of such events cannot be overstated. In the larger hospital camps, like Chungkai and Nakon Patom in Thailand, Kranji in Singapore and Bowen Road in Hong Kong, theatrical and variety shows were often used as an essential adjunct to medical treatment and care.

All manner of musical instruments were made from the most unlikely materials. Lance Bombadier Jim Surr, 242 48th LAA regiment RA, 'A' troop, always carried a pair of drumsticks with him. He recalled his time working as a volunteer orderly at St Vincentius in Java where he

found a Chinese cymbal off a set of drums and I was always keen on drumming, I was in the Boys Brigade before as a drummer before I joined up in the army … we formed a band for entertainment at weekend and at first I tapped on the, on some wood blocks to keep the time of the band … [then] we made a set of drums by knocking the bottom out of a bucket and stretching a gas cape over the top, pulled down by some cords like you find on the military band … we stretched some wires from one side of the bucket over the top, to make the kettle sound y'know, rattle of a side drum. And with the base drum we knocked the bottom out of a box and … we put gas cape over one side of the box, and to stretch it we put a piece of wood inside the box and twisted it … to push the sides out. And we made a pedal, a foot pedal … when you press your knee there the foot goes down … put a mango on it in a stocking, but we had to keep changing that because the mango got ripe, it got squashed. But it worked very well.

Tom Boardman loved music and was well-known in Changi for going round the huts in the evenings along with Frankie Quinton who played piano accordion, leading sing-songs. This was noted by Tom's friend, journalist Ronald Hastain, author of one of the first post-war Far East POW memoirs, *White Coolie*, published in 1947. Tom is the ukulele player referred to on page 157 when Hastain created this wonderful scene.

There was also a performer on a ukulele, made from an old cigar box and a strand of wire. ('Chinese Laundry Blues,' and 'When I'm Cleaning Windows!').

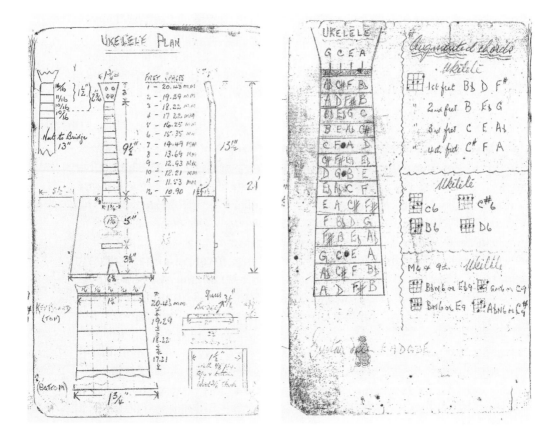

Figure 10 Sketches from Boardman's
notebook with detailed measurements
for the second ukulele
(courtesy Tom Boardman)

With little encouragement volunteers would come forward and sing. Sometimes old sentimental ballards, sometimes the pathetic crooner warbling into a bit of tin on the end of a bamboo stick, to represent the 'mike'. Then there was the raconteur of the risqué story and the determined reciter of 'If' or 'Gunga Din'.

Tom made not one but two ukuleles in captivity, the first while at Changi and the second one in Thailand. He recalled that during the first weeks in Changi he had been sent to the Kranji working camp where they were building a Japanese memorial and

there was this little village close by and amongst the articles that were still around there was a Chinese mandolin and it had gears on [for] tightening the strings, and I'd played a ukulele pre-war so I thought I'd have a go at making one 'cos these are the fundamentals. So I acquired them. And [later] I made my first ukulele in Changi … a very small one. And I took that on the railway and I played it at night time there.

This very small ukulele was the one cited by Ronald Hastain. Due to its small size it did not have much volume and later on when Tom was at Chungkai he gave this ukulele to Corporal Leo Britt, Royal Army Service Corps (RASC) who was a theatrical producer. Pre-war he had been an actor and theatrical impresario and used his skills and flair to organise some of the most professional productions in Thailand, including *Wonder Bar,* starring amongst others Ginger de Wardener. Post-war Britt went on to star in several major films including the 1954 *Dial M for Murder* and *The Charge of the Light Brigade* made in 1968. Tom's second ukulele, made while a patient at Chungkai hospital camp in 1944, was much larger than the first giving it much-needed volume, as by then Tom was playing in the theatre orchestra and needed to be heard by audiences of up to 2,000 men.

The detailed drawings from Tom's notebook (Figure 10) are his working plans. For the sound box he used wood from packing cases in which a Red Cross parcel consignment had been delivered, with rectangular slots burnt through the wood above and below the strings, and

telegraph wires, split and doubled to be the bass string. There's four strings on the ukulele of course and varying tension to produce the note you want for them, which are G C E A and, course you work off the memory of the notes … that's the diagram. Early in Changi … there were some Javanese lads came and they had ukuleles with them at the time and I took the measurements of the frets which determine the notes from the actual [instrument] and I drew it on bits of paper, there's three bits of paper there … I'd no problem making it that shape … it give me some relief really from the, I wouldn't say it was tension, but the demoralising state you were in. It just brightened up my day for me. And it gave me pleasure to work out the chords that were necessary to split, fit to a different tune, because you had different chords for different tunes.

Tom provided additional details later on, describing how

the frets were made from heavy duty galvanized wire which I had to bend repeatedly in order to snap them off into the required lengths. These were then set into the wooden arm of the ukulele at correct intervals, as per the measurements on the plan, by bending the ends round like a staple. Small rounded disks of pale-coloured plastic were cut from an old toothbrush handle to form

Figure 11 *Daily Sketch* photograph, page 8, caption reads: Sergt. T. Boardman, of Leigh in Lancs, coming back with the guitar [*sic*] he made himself. *(courtesy Tom Boardman)*

the 'stops' which were then carefully inlaid to the arm. The stops help you when changing chords to another key.

You can clearly see the stops in Figure 11 above. Both Tom and his ukulele returned, along with over 1,500 FEPOWs on board the SS *Corfu*, the first ship bringing repatriated FEPOW back into Southampton, on 7 October 1945. His arrival was recorded for posterity, as this marvellous photograph of a grinning Tom taken by the *Daily Sketch* photographer testifies.

In 2005 Tom donated his ukulele to the Imperial War Museum North where it can be seen in a display case on the first floor landing outside the main exhibition hall.

Emeritus Professor Sears A. Eldredge, Theatre and Dance Department, at Macalester College, St Paul, Minnesota, has spent over 15 years making a special study of the entertainments produced in camps in Thailand. From the artistes to the artists, the writers, producers, musicians, make-up, lighting and wardrobe technicians, anyone and everyone who not only made magic happen again and again but in so doing kept hope, and men, alive. In 2014 he published this work as an e-book, *Captive Audiences/Captive Performers: Music and Theatre as Strategies for Survival on the Thailand–Burma Railway 1942–1945*.[13] This remarkable piece of work tells an extraordinary story, incorporating oral history, musical extracts and artwork depicting costume design, stage sets, bill posters and programmes. Not only is Eldredge's research compelling, he knows how to work an audience too!

Finding a role

Many of those who volunteered, or were invited, to work with the medical staff found that it gave them a purpose and a reason to survive. Men like Gordon Smith, who while recovering from malaria at Tamarkan hospital camp in Thailand in 1943 was asked by Dr Jim Mark RAMC to stay on and help out with the laboratory work as Jim knew he had been a medical student pre-war. First of all Gordon took on the microbiology work, identifying the different forms of malaria and dysentery, which helped doctors conserve dwindling stocks of medicines by targeting only those in most dire need. Then later he did blood matching for hundreds of blood transfusions which he was also trained to carry out (Chapter 3). At interview he described those days as 'the best part of my life as a POW'. In his book, *A medical student in Malaya*, he was more forthcoming, 'from my own point of view, the existence of the laboratory, and the assistance it gave to the medical staff, was an excellent way of keeping me occupied, and avoided too much fretting about what our future held.'

It did not matter how grim the task was, the fact that they were needed, gave some men a purpose and a reason to live. Arthur Turbutt put it like this. 'It may sound strange to say, the only thing that I found not distressing … was the comfort of knowing that I was doing my job that I had been trained to do.' He went on,

> I enjoyed doing it, not, don't get me wrong I didn't enjoy the methods of treat-
> ment, or the squalor or the horror, it's not a question of being enjoyable. I got
> the satisfaction of knowing that I was doing all that I possibly could. And I think
> Dr Forbes appreciated this. And apart from that, no … it didn't make me feel,
> this is it, this is the end. In fact I think I can truthfully say that at no time did I
> feel that I was going to be next, I was too preoccupied.

This statement, however, belies the true horror of the daily workload for men like Arthur Turbutt, Frank Scarr, Reg Davis, Gordon Smith, George Holland,

Doug Skippen, Harry Hesp and Jim Surr. They were just a few of the thousands of medical orderlies, assistants and volunteers who, no matter how tired or hungry, turned up on shift to work in filth, surrounded by disease and the stench of rotting living bodies, watching their patients die needless, squalid and appalling deaths, day after day after day. Their courage and humanity has barely been acknowledged outside of Far East prisoner of war circles.

The art (and artists) of survival

Notable British Far East POW artists who were at work in Singapore and Thailand include Gunner Jack Chalker (asked by Weary Dunlop to record the medical battle to survive), Gunner Philip Meninsky (who was also enrolled by Dunlop and by another Australian surgeon, Major Arthur Moon), Gunner Ronald Searle, Gunner George Old (who worked for Moon with Meninsky and who was a close friend of Jack's), Gunner Leo Rawlings, Lieutenant Stanley Gimson and Lance Bombadier John 'Jack' Mennie.

As already noted, Jack Chalker had found his métier as an artist in the prisoner of war camps of Singapore and Thailand. But he also volunteered as a physiotherapist in Thailand, having studied anatomy pre-war as he was considering training to be a doctor before finally deciding on a career in art. His understanding of anatomy was put to good use in the battle to rehabilitate so many weak and crippled men. In the early weeks in Singapore, first in Changi and then in Havelock Road camp (Figure 12), Jack bartered for things he needed by drawing dozens of chalk drawings of sexy ladies for the men. In his sketch below, he marked his bed space with an asterisk, on the top tier to the right of centre, above the man standing on the right. Before long the camp guards were trading food for his sketches. He said that the artist in him saw beauty all around and he needed to capture these glimpses of tropical landscapes and later on the jungle with its flora and fauna, as well as the human devastation as it was unfolding. Recording the latter could usually only be done safely when he too was very ill and confined to the sick hut as the guards seldom ventured inside. There he observed and recorded in devastating detail the full horror, sketching hurriedly and in secret.

Some of his medical illustrations are stark, grotesque even, revealing humanity hanging by a thread. They document exactly what he saw, the ravages of cholera, dysentery, horrific tropical ulcers and the appalling effects of chronic malnutrition. In counterbalance he also recorded marvels like successful skin grafts which repaired some of the damage caused by tropical ulcers. There are also detailed studies of the home-made instruments devised by skilled engineers and metalworkers, which were used to perform such intricate surgery.

Figure 12 Havelock Road Camp, Singapore
1942 *(courtesy of Jack Chalker)*

He made many drawings depicting make-do-and-mend medicine, from prostheses, surgical instruments, medical treatments, physiotherapy equipment, home-made stills and everyday utensils to intravenous infusion sets and surgical operations in progress. In 1987 when he attended for TDI screening at the Tropical School, Jack donated a large number of colour photographs of his work to Dr Dion Bell for the School's Far East POW archives as thanks for his care. He remained in touch with the School from then on.

Like Jack, Meninsky and Searle did dozens of studies of medical subject matter amongst other things. There are examples of their work among many other Far East POW artists, in the IWM Art department and other archives.

In addition, a legion of commercial and amateur illustrators and cartoonists painted, sketched and recorded daily life and death in camps right across the Far East, often in glorious technicolour and again mostly in secret.

Figure 13 Cartoon with a serious message warning of the dangers of food contamination, drawn by Geoffrey Barlow Gee[14] (*courtesy of the Gee family*)

The health education poster (Figure 13) from a canteen hut somewhere in Thailand exemplifies this work. Drawn by Glaswegian and former railway clerk, Sapper Geoffrey Barlow Gee of the Royal Engineers, it gets a serious public health message across to hungry, vulnerable and despondent prisoners, in a witty, eye-catching way. Gee also drew portraits of wives and girlfriends from photographs for friends.

These artists were the visual chroniclers of survival in Far East captivity. In recent research many other British artists have been identified from all areas of captivity (see Postscript for further details about this research).

There was a strong need to create things, little tokens to keep and to treasure. Men whittled, carved or engraved in wood, bamboo and aluminium. Nowell Peach prized the four inch high head and shoulders of a Balinese girl that he had carved out of teak in the first months of captivity (Figure 14). A deep warm red colour, it has a smooth glossy patina acquired over six decades. He added the tiny earrings post-war.

Figure 14 Front and back view of the Balinese head carved by Nowell Peach in Java *(courtesy of Nowell Peach)*

Maurice Kinmonth made an exquisite small wooden box with tight-fitting lid (Figure 15) into which he inlaid a brilliant caricature of himself, sharpening his surgeon's knife drawn and then engraved on a piece of aluminium mess tin by New Zealander Sid Scales, a prolific and gifted cartoonist. Scales had studied art pre-war at the London School of Art.[15]

Leslie Audus made a mahjong set which was frequently in use, the tiles cut from one centimetre-thick sheet of perspex. This returned home with him and is treasured by his family. Flight Lieutenant Richard Philps, another RAF doctor on Java and one of many amateur artists, carved a kingfisher out of wood in the early days of captivity in Java. He described in his book, *Prisoner Doctor*, how he

> managed to get hold of a piece of ['bastard' teak] found myself a hacksaw-blade, ground it into a knife blade on a building stone and spent many a happy and emblistered hour whittling out the effigy of an

Figure 15 Maurice Kinmonth's box with caricature by Sid Scales *(courtesy Maurice Kinmonth)*

ordinary European kingfisher to keep me company. I painted it with some of the watercolours I had bought at Tasikmalaya (in Java), gave myself a sharp attack of lead poisoning through licking my brush, and managed to keep it, finally bringing it home.

Captain Henry McCreath 9th Royal Northumberland Fusiliers, engraved each side of his both his Army issue mess tins and a home-made tin mug he had made, with the name, insignia, flags and motto of the regiment (Figure 16). He donated these items to the regimental archives at Alnwick Castle in Northumberland.

Arthur Turbutt kept the small piece of bone he had found in his helping of stew one night on Haruku. It had belonged to a goat which had enhanced the evening meal that day. Arthur treasured it and over 65 years later it was still a very special object to him.

Men etched, engraved, painted and burnt names and numbers on to wooden or metal ID badges, like this one (Figure 17) belonging to Frank Scarr.

Figure 16 Henry McCreath's engraved mess tin (courtesy Northumberland Fusiliers archives)

Figure 17 ID badge with carved numerals and Japanese characters (courtesy LSTM)

He added the red cross (top left), denoting hospital work and the Roman numerals II (top right) indicating he was a member of work group II. The badge measures approximately 2½ inches long by 2 inches deep. There is a piece of thick copper wire threaded through two holes and folded over to form a hook to enable the badge to be hung over a belt or waistband. It had to be worn at all times.

All sorts of things were treasured, hidden away from prying eyes and light fingers. Whether a talisman or a personal item, to the survivors they held great significance. These items cannot be viewed simply as 'souvenirs' of an unwanted sojourn in a foreign place; they are I suggest tangible evidence of survival. As RAF medical officer Richard Philps said of his kingfisher, 'it became one of my talisman possessions … and I think I partly owe my life to it.'

Friends and faith

The British worked alongside Australians, New Zealanders, Americans, Dutch and Canadians, many of whom came from similar working backgrounds. Bonds of friendships were forged some of which lasted a lifetime. Many FEPOW interviewed described these close friendships as being a lifeline. To the British they were 'mates' and to Australians they were 'muckers'; to the Americans 'buddies', and to the Dutch they were 'kongsi-group' (which translated means comradeship), as described by the Dutch author of *Lost Tracks*, Raoul Kramer. Whatever the word was, kinship, having a small group of mates, was essential to survival. As Derek Fogarty poignantly said,

> If you've marched 30 or 40 miles with somebody and you've been through combat with people, you have something which is, you've got a bond … you've been a prisoner for months, shall we say. You've been through troubles together. You've shared your water bottle together. You've got confidences, y'know. A lot of people were frightened, and yes we were all scared in a lot of ways and we had lots of … you talk to people, you bonded like brothers … If a person was sick you took them water, you did their washing. You can never describe the bonding. We were so close and it got closer and closer over the years, people would die for their mates, that's how close things got. And it was lost at the end of the war. And now we haven't got that bonding.

Henry McCreath not only valued close friendship but also doing whatever he could to help his men.

> We [my friend John] were lucky to have been together. He was a stranger to me and I to him but we sort of got on well in the end. And I remember him nursing

me when I wasn't very well and I remember … I had to tell him what to do and he had very bad malaria … it meant a lot. … And it became very strong with me and my, these lads, men of mine, y'know. They gave me an incentive to try because I felt … maybe rightly or not, but I felt I was privileged y'know … I don't think they ever held it against me at all … all I can say is I played my part as well as I could, and that's it.

Bob Morrell remembered the value of mates when they were on Haruku,

We were a small group of four: George, Titch, Derek and I. This means that if one man is ill, stays in camp, you don't get ten cents a day working money, so the others that can work supports the one that is ill … With the ten cents we bought tobacco … which we eased out … the little group of four was ideal … In fact I kept in touch with George and with Titch until the day they died … that was mates.

This life-saving dependence on friends was first highlighted in both Hastain's (1947) and Coombes' (1948) memoirs. However, Gordon Highlander Corporal Alistair Urquhart (who was later attached to the Royal Army Service Corps) said he had preferred to go it alone after the loss of close friends early on in captivity. He vowed to rely only on himself and not get close to anyone else, it was too painful. Alistair returned home to Scotland in late 1945. Over 60 years later when he was in his 90s he published his memoir, *The Forgotten Highlander*, with the help of a journalist.

Some, like Jack Chalker, made lasting friendships with the Australians. But to Fergus Anckorn the 'Aussies' were a liability with a reputation for taking a perverse delight in aggravating their captors whenever possible. Fergus recalled that

if you were an Australian, you stole a lorry, you drove it into the Jap stores and you took two sacks of potatoes and you drove out again, and the Japs assumed you were on a working party … They were real brigands, they would be beholden to nobody … some of our fellows would group themselves together in five or six … the Australians were in bunches of thirty or forty and I just kept out of their way.

For some men faith played a vital part in the struggle to survive. Army chaplains or padres, or in the absence of religious leaders self-appointed lay preachers, ministered quietly often to clandestine congregations. Men like dentist David Arkush, who was the son of a Blackpool rabbi, recalled taking services and officiating at Jewish burials in camps in Thailand. 'I discovered there were ten Jewish soldiers there and one other Jewish officer. And every Saturday I managed to arrange a Jewish service which I took. My father was a rabbi so I had some training. And I had a prayer book, and we were in business.'

Interestingly, David said during his interview that he had found the Japanese respectful of his faith, unlike their Axis partners, there 'never was a word ever said to me, anything derogatory. I'd enough trouble without anti-Semitism, but certainly that was never a trouble, I will say that for them.'

Sergeant John Hugh Edwards had joined the Territorial Army in 1937. He was in the 77th Welsh Regiment, 230 battery, Heavy Anti-Aircraft (HAA) Royal Artillery. Sent to the Far East and captured on Java, Hugh was shipped to the coal mining area of southern Japan in late 1942. He stepped forward when Kamoo (No. 8 camp) was left without a padre.

We were about seven hundred and fifty in the camp there, mainly British, Australian, Dutch, Eurasian, quite a mixture, a couple of Americans as well. And you're looking at the honorary padre of the camp ... Well it was something that had to be done, it's no good ... [just] saying a prayer unless you can show it to other fellows and ... I had to be down to earth, full feet on the ground, but not swearing ... but very much down to the boys' levels ... The work in the mines, was on three shifts ... and we had only two yasume, rest days, in the month ... well what did we do? ... no communication with home, no news coming in, a very dull sort of a life to live. And how could we relieve that dullness? Well by having little service on the two days a month. And if there was any chap who was very ill we would go. And when they were dying we had to go, take the bodies outside the camp where the Japanese monks were and seek cremation, and so on. There was that need that had to be done, at least show a Christian burial.

It was sometimes a great shock when the chap next to you doesn't get up and you know he's died. Men could give up you see, and I think this was part of the battle. I don't pretend that I was 'Onward Christian Soldiers', I didn't mean that at all, but I think to fight the boredom of it all, to fight the horror and the stink and the smell. I have said so many times, that I can talk about the conditions of the camp but I can't bring you the smell of it.

Post-war Hugh became a Baptist minister and was still preaching on his circuit in south Wales up until the last year or so of his life. Former volunteer with the Hong Kong Volunteer Defence Corps, Arthur Hermon White was just 17 years old when he was taken prisoner in Hong Kong. He recalled an extraordinary incident concerning the Bible. On 20 August 1945, with rumours of the end of the war rife in camp, and feeling certain that change was imminent, Arthur sat down with a piece of paper and pencil and worked out from the time he was taken prisoner [25 December 1941] until then, one thousand, three hundred and thirty-four days. There was a chap in my hut with me, he was a religious type he had the Bible, they allowed him to keep the Bible. 'Here,' he said, 'there's something in the Bible about one thousand three hundred and thirty-five days.' Right, the next day, August 21, at quarter to seven in the evening, they called our doctor, he was a Britisher, the one doctor in the camp, he was called to the office. And we were watching and everybody was, the Japs and him were bowing and shaking hands, stuff like that. Something's up? He came out. He said, 'Right lads fall in, don't worry about your caps' (you had to have a cap on, if you didn't you got thumped). Got up and he just simply said, 'The war's over.' Ahh, there were cheers! Went back to the hut and this friend of mine got his Bible out and there, the Old Testament, the Book of Daniel, last chapter, second last verse: 'Blessed is he that cometh and waiteth to the one thousand, three hundred and five and thirty days.'

In April 1943 over 2,000 mainly RAF men with a small contingent of Dutch, were sent from Java to build an airfield on the remote coral island of Haruku. Arriving during the monsoon season, the camp was a quagmire with huts half built and only muddy floors to lie on. Within a fortnight over 1,200 mainly dysentery and beriberi cases were confined to the 'hospital' huts. Four weeks later over two hundred men had died. Arthur Turbutt was one of the medical orderlies trying to cope. He said 64 years later that

we had nothing we could give them. All we could give them was physical, mental and perhaps, I don't know, spiritual comfort. You couldn't do any more for them; they were crying, one fellow … gave me his watch and whatever he had, 'Please give these to Mum when you get home', and that sort of thing. They knew they were dying. And they were dying in agony a lot of them, terrible agony of dysentery. And, all we could do is try and comfort them and make their passing as easy as we could.

Later, Arthur said

The only thing I will say and I know in a way it sounds silly, I got a lot of strength, spiritual strength, mental strength, from two things. One, I prayed every night. Thanked God for my deliverance [long pause] and for the blessings that I had. And the other thing was, Lola. She was my strength … in each camp, I know that I carved her name into the bamboo.

Lola was the fiancée he had left behind and she was there when he returned home.

Leading Aircraftsman Bob Morrell, was with Arthur on Haruku and worked on the airfield. He described in detail what they had to do.

After 48 to 72 hours they wanted men to work on the 'drome and we were dragged up there. I think the first batch was about three hundred men out of a thousand ... And they put us in a line with little hammers and chisels and we looked, and we could see this hill and beyond it was another hill and they told us we were going to level this hill off and we were going to have a nice flat runway [laughs] ... from the four inch chisels and a hammer to long drills about three foot which we hammered and hammered and eventually we put dynamite in ... They tried bulldozers, two of them actually, ruined them. What we did in the end was to dig like a grave ... about four foot long, a foot wide about six foot down, which was bloody hard work, but then they had some bombs ... two fifty pounders ... and by exploding these bombs you had like an ... earthquake effect. Then you could take the huge coral and split it, keep breaking it down until you could move it ... And we did, we took the tops off these two hills eventually and started filling in the hollow ... tamping it down and, oh my, it just went on and on. Then the bloody Yanks came along and blew it up and we had to fill it up again.

Prisoners of war built places of worship wherever materials were available and permission granted by the Japanese. Numerous chapels were constructed in rooms, huts, tents and in the jungle. There were several built in camps in Singapore, with a few of them at the vast Changi POW camp, but St Luke's Chapel in a ground floor room of Block 151 (Roberts Hospital dysentery block) was perhaps the most richly decorated. Early in captivity Padre Frederick Stallard (another fine artist) had asked the Japanese if they could use the room

Figure 18 Block 151, formerly part of Roberts Hospital, Changi. The entrance to St Luke's Chapel was under the first arch at the far end of the ground floor (*photograph courtesy of Changi Murals website*)

Figure 19 Japanese propaganda photograph of St George's Chapel, Tandjong Priok, Java, 12 July 1942, from *Nippon Times* published 23 June 1943 *(A. A. Duncan papers)*

NIPPON TIMES, SUNDA

Chapel in the Open

The considerate treatment of the war prisoners in Java by the Military Administration there may be gauged by the freedom given in religious matters. Prisoners who profess the Christian religion are allowed to hold and attend a service every Sunday. The picture shows a chapel in the open, amid pleasant surroundings, with some of the prisoners in the middle of a service.

(Passed by the War Ministry)

as a chapel and grudgingly they had agreed. His colleagues, Padres Chambers and Pain, knew that Sergeant Stanley Warren, a patient on the dysentery ward above and a devout man, had been pre-war commercial artist and they asked him if he would decorate the walls. Having regarded his recovery from dysentery in the ward above as deliverance, he set to work creating large murals, well-known scenes from the Bible, between September 1942 and May 1943.

He started with the Nativity and then the Resurrection, not knowing when a relapse may halt his work. He carried on until five completed panels were done. The sixth was interrupted by his departure from Changi. The murals were eventually painted over and Warren's work lost until post-war restoration work carried out by the RAF during the 1960s revealed what lay beneath the peeling paintwork. Warren was eventually identified as the artist and although initially reluctant was finally persuaded to return and restore his work. He made three trips in all.

The chapel remains in an unused concrete block, part of what is now Singapore's Air Force base (Figure 18). Looking at the photograph, try to picture the first and second floor verandahs full of men, some out of sight on beds, others standing and leaning on the balustrade, smoking, talking and thinking. The story of the chapel was written up and published for Changi Museum and is also online.[16]

Figure 20 Original windows from St George's Chapel, photographed in Jakarta October 2013 *(author's photograph)*

Post-war, former Army padre Reverend Lewis Bryan, recorded St Luke's chapel in his book, *The Churches of the Captivity in Malaya* published in the early 1950s. Another one that featured, that was not actually in Malaya, was St George's Chapel, Tandjong Priok transit camp in Java. Cyril Jones, Nowell Peach and John Baxter all remembered the chapel. My father too, while not a religious man, did record in his diary what the chapel meant to him at that time.[17] He attended services there until he was moved out. It was a powerful presence and a source of solace and peace in an alien and frightening world. Possibly one of the 'grandest' small chapels ever built by Far East POW (Figure 19), St George's Chapel was made from reinforced concrete and featured a gothic arch, buttresses and even two stained glass windows (they were actually painted glass). Commenced in April 1942 it took three months to complete. Initial designs were drawn up by Australian architects with some British input but when in May, according to Captain Duncan's diary, all the Australians were suddenly moved out of the camp the British took over and completed the work. It was sited in a corner of the camp parade ground under the shade of a small copse of trees. The only known photograph was taken by a Japanese propaganda photographer on the day of the consecration of the chapel, 12 July 1942.

Lieutenant Commander H. C. R. Upton RNR, one of the British architects who assisted with the designing of St George's Chapel, also painted two faux stained glass windows for the wall behind the altar. He used gloss house paints pilfered on working parties from nearby abandoned Dutch houses. His design is not in any way religious, it is blatantly patriotic, displaying the national flags and emblems of the four main groups of POW at the camp: British, Australian, Dutch and American. These remarkable windows, measuring approximately nine inches wide by 30 inches long, survived both the war and the Indonesian uprising of 1945. Today, they are on display at All Saints Anglican Church in Jakarta, where they were taken for safekeeping by a Christian group in 1943 after the last prisoners of war had been transferred to other camps (Figure 20).

Once the camp had been abandoned the chapel windows were vulnerable to attack by local nationalists fighting for independence during the Japanese occupation. In 2005, two six by four inch photographs of the original windows, taken in 1997 and sent to Captain Duncan shortly before he died, were used by Wirral artist David Hillhouse who specialised in painting on glass. With these he created replicas of the two windows which were to form the Java Windows memorial in memory of all Java FEPOW and internees. The windows were to be set into the new FEPOW Memorial Building at the National Memorial Arboretum (NMA) in Staffordshire, due to be officially opened on 15 August that year, marking the sixtieth anniversary since the ending of the Second World War and the release of all Far East captives.

Figure 21 Close-up of the reproduced British Service badge in the replica window (with a little artistic licence) showing detail of the Lion Rampant's face *(author's photograph)*

While examining the photographs with a magnifying glass David noticed the face of the Lion Rampant on the British Service badge looked rather odd. Closer inspection revealed that it was smoking a large cigar! It is quite difficult to see the red cigar in the top left hand window in the photograph on page 89 (Figure 20) but it is visible with magnification. This symbolic and defiant gesture had remained a secret for over 63 years.[18] Sadly, David died suddenly in 2013. He is remembered by many for his exquisitely detailed artworks and memorials and for the care that he took in bringing them to life.[19]

The only known contemporaneous reference to the face of the Lion Rampant came to light about a week after David made his discovery. It appears in a report written after the war by Upton, the original artist, in which he mentions painting Churchill's face on the lion.

> The British were shown with the General Service Badge, ie the Royal Coat of Arms, the Lion of which was shown with the face of Churchill (with apologies) in whose mouth was a very large cigar, the Nips never caught on, I dread to think what would have happened if they had. It afforded considerable amusement to the troops as they passed by or held services there.[20]

This work is yet another vivid and powerful example of how FEPOW artists took enormous risks to keep morale high and defy their captors. It is hard to imagine the outcome had the secret in Upton's artwork been known to the Japanese. Ironically, given the offending visage, the enormous loss of face to their captors would have had swift and dire consequences, not only for Upton but for all Christian worshippers at the chapel.

When there was no cleric available Allied officers led funeral services. Whether men gained or lost faith in God during these experiences, undoubtedly for some faith was the mainstay of their survival. Gunner Alf Baker (who in later life became a Church of England minister) recalled it was not only his faith in one of the ORs that kept him going.

> We got through because of Joe Blythe and a bloody hatred for the Japanese. We were determined, so determined, that they weren't going to get rid of all of us, and I think that's the only thing that kept us going. If we didn't have something to hate badly, there was no point.

Arthur Turbutt was more philosophical and accepting of his fate.

> By the grace of God I didn't get ill there. I don't know, I think he must have been looking down on me, but, of course as an orderly as you are trained, you take utmost precautions, keeping your hands perfectly clean and your body as clean as you possibly could and keeping away from infected material. No you just had to protect yourself in the best possible way ... That, and my prayers gave me immense strength and as I say I never felt at any time that I was going under. I just lived from day to day. I knew that I may not see the next day, I knew that very well, but, I was just thankful that I'd got through another day, seen another sunrise ... every dawn was a blessing. And we just carried on and carried on.

Conclusion

Survival in Far East prisoner of war camps depended on many factors, about which most men had little or no control. They were scattered across a vast region, from the tropics to the most northerly islands of Japan. Large numbers of men were moved around at will, their physical and medical needs deliberately neglected by captors who could not countenance the concept of surrender.

Many of the British forces had had little time to acclimatise to the climate before being captured and they had to learn to adapt quickly to ever-changing circumstances. Early on thousands were transported from Singapore to the tropical jungles of Thailand. Similarly, thousands more were moved from the cooler tea plantations of the central highlands of Java to overcrowded cities like Batavia prior to being shipped away from the island to tropical or more northerly locations such as Korea and Japan. Others lived on coral islands or beside mines, steelworks and dockyards. There were some who encountered all these locations during their captivity.

The Japanese cared little for how the POW were transported or how many survived. Whether herded into the primitive, overcrowded holds of unmarked ships under constant threat of torpedo attack, or tightly packed into railway goods wagons trundling along mile after mile of railway track, prisoners of war had no control or choice. What they did have some choice in was how they adapted to conditions. Having a strong sense of self discipline, basic hygiene, having a purpose or a job, being part of a special group of mates, these were all factors that helped men through these experiences.

Luck was often cited at interview as having played an important part in survival. Friends were separated. Many said that accepting your fate was far better than trying to manipulate it. Initially, owing to the concentration of British troops in Hong Kong and Singapore, camps in these areas held large numbers of trained medical staff. Many were only recently arrived from Europe and had little or no experience of tropical medicine. Doctors and medical staff therefore relied heavily on the local knowledge of both garrison medical staff and those serving with the local Volunteer Forces, many of whom had lived in the region for years.

As large parties of prisoners were dispersed across South East Asia small numbers of medical staff accompanied them, taking with them what they could carry. Men like medical orderly Arthur Turbutt and volunteer Harry Hesp, despite being traumatised by the relentless and barbaric conditions that they worked in, just kept on going. It was not until they were repatriated at the end of the war that the full effect of all they had witnessed surfaced.

What is clear is that Far East POW learned to overcome deficiencies and neglect by drawing on whatever resources and skills they had to hand. To have a purpose, a skill to share, be they botanists or artists, metalworkers or actors, to be needed by your mates, employ humour and sometimes take risks, have the strength, and luck, to overcome infection and disease, were all elements in their survival. The next chapter explores this subject further and in particular reveals how medical staff utilised the skills, ingenuity and inventiveness of a 'citizen's' army in camps across the Far East.

CHAPTER 3

THE CITIZEN'S ARMY

WITHIN THE FIRST WEEKS of captivity Allied doctors began to see the effects of malnutrition due to vitamin deficiency. Malaria and dysentery were endemic. Nowell Peach, when asked over sixty years later what had been used to treat dysentery in the early days in Java, replied, 'nothing really, just a matter of nursing by the medical orderlies. We had no antibiotics or anything, we just had to give them suitable fluid diet.'

One of those medical orderlies was Arthur Turbutt. He remembered nursing men with dysentery on Haruku in the Spice Islands.

> The biggest killer of course was dysentery ... our main job seemed to be trying to lift these poor fellows off the bamboo and, as weak as we were, trying to carry them along to an old cabin trunk, metal cabin trunk, the lid had been taken off and the cabin trunk was lying in the centre of the floor and those that needed had to get to the cabin trunk and put their bottoms over the side and do what they had to do into the trunk. Now that was swimming with filth and slime and blood and, of course, you've got to remember that the place was full of flies, millions upon millions. And these poor fellows, we took them along as best we could and we had to take them back ... some of them were so thin that when they laid on their back you could see their spine, it'd gone, everything had gone.

This chapter looks at how Allied medical teams, the doctors, scientists, trained nursing orderlies and volunteers, struggled to keep men alive in such conditions. With little medicine or equipment, how did they treat, care for and rehabilitate so many sick men? Camps were scattered over a vast region, in towns and cities, on remote islands and in the jungle, with little or no communication between them. Doctors were moved around, working together or alone with only the support of a few exhausted volunteer orderlies.

Using the eye-witness accounts of the men interviewed, together with numerous archive sources, we can piece together a picture of the enormous task that faced both doctor and patient on a daily basis. With the help of the artists in captivity we are able to also visualise this herculean battle to survive.

Medical officers asked artists to record what was happening in sick huts, operating theatres, laboratories and clinics and thanks to their skill the reader is able to glimpse the reality of the conditions that prevailed and medical battle to survive that was fought, relentlessly, for over three and half years. Throughout this chapter there are many examples of this work. Both artist and doctor took huge risks and paid a heavy price if detected. There follows an outline of the scale of the problem, the main medical and surgical challenges and some of the ingenious solutions conjured up by a little known special force within the Armed Services, the 'Citizen's Army'. This was made up of plumbers, carpenters, electricians, engineers, artists, scientists and many others, who brought into camp skills and knowledge that they were ready and willing to share. All of them played a part in solving problems, creating essential items to enable doctors and nursing orderlies to do what they had to do, and in recording it all.

Initially the main priorities for the prisoners of war were to find shelter, sufficient food and a means of taking care of their sick. It was to be a recurring problem as men were frequently moved around, often to new sites where they had to start from scratch once again. In the first weeks after capture most of the seriously ill were battle casualties but within a month or so large numbers of men were showing the signs of gross malnutrition.

Medical facilities

In the tropics, camp hospitals, sick huts, Medical Inspection (MI) rooms, dental clinics and laboratories were housed in buildings, some substantial, others dilapidated huts. In 1943 medical student Gordon Smith was given the job of laboratory assistant at Tamarkan camp in Thailand, initially undertaking microbiology work. He recalled that in 1944 Australian surgeon Major Arthur Moon, who replaced Lieutenant Colonel Toosey as senior officer, let him have 'a small building to use as a laboratory because prior to that I'd worked in the corner of the Medical Inspection room where people could get to all my equipment. But in this new building it was entirely mine, and the other half of it was actually the mortuary which we needed I'm afraid in those days.'

Up country from Tamarkan, and newly arrived at 227 camp just north of Tamaron jungle, was Captain Patrick MacArthur, who during captivity was attached as medical officer to the Argylls. His diary entry for 7 September 1943 notes that, 'the complete framework, all bamboo, of an excellent new MI Room, ward, and sleeping accommodation for self and A. N. Other completed; very good desks, cupboards and beds, as well as two good doors. Alas, no attap for roof and split bamboo impractical.'[1] But three days later he wrote that while the main group had moved on, 'I am staying behind with 43 sick ORs and three sick officers. Have only three fearful tents and tonight I lie in the passageway of officers' tent. Attap has arrived but ... I can get none for my MI Room.' It was to be another two months before it would be completed, just before he was moved off again.

In Singapore most British prisoners of war were initially held at Changi. This vast camp covered an area in the east of the island. Behind the wire were several former British Army barracks and a few scattered villages housing over 50,000 men in all, 30,000 or more being British. All the buildings were hopelessly overcrowded. Men were billeted in tents, native houses, shops and huts made from bamboo tied together with rattan or vines, the 'attap' roofs of overlapping palm frond tiles extending almost to the ground. The walls were open at the sides or made from panels of woven bamboo bark.

Sir Roger Moon, a sapper in the Johore Volunteer Force (JVF), had worked on a Dunlop Rubber Company estate in Johore pre-war. When interviewed he recalled that, in the chaos of the final days before the capitulation, he acquired something that he soon put to good, if somewhat unconventional, use.

The first crate I came across held bottles of salted almonds and the next one, believe it or not, was packets of condoms. And I took a whole packet – not hoping for the best! ... what I used to do, once we got to Changi after the surrender, sleeping on a concrete floor wasn't really very comfortable and I used to blow these condoms up about ten at a time, wrap them up in my shirt and use them as a pillow.

Condoms had many uses, as we shall see later on. The colonial Volunteer Forces were a great help as they shared valuable local knowledge and skills with new arrivals. One of those who ended up in tents at Changi was Captain Henry McCreath. He recalled his battalion, the 9th Royal Northumberland Fusiliers (9RNF), arriving in Singapore just nine days before capitulation on 15 February. On the 17th they marched to Changi, where they were

in the open, just camped in the open area and ... in due course the Japanese wanted, called for working parties ... and each unit was ordered to send ... two officers – my rank and a subaltern and a hundred men down to Singapore. So I went to Singapore, to River Valley Road [camp, near the docks] and I never saw the battalion and the rest of my friends for two and a half years or more.

Another officer in the same regiment, Lieutenant Owen Eva, arrived at Changi leading a different party of 9RNF, where they settled into 'barracks, other buildings and a variety of makeshift shelters.' He recalled how hungry they were initially as they had

> very little food at all ... I think it was May, June, that year [1942] we went down on a working party to the docks at Singapore ... we did odd jobs working mainly on the docks, [a fellow officer and friend] Ken Addy had ... walked out of the dock gates and walked round Singapore ... we used to go in pairs. We always saluted every ... Japanese officer we saw ... we went to the Chinese area, they were so wonderfully good to us, we knew they were short but they insisted we took fruit and things back to the camp with us.

Owen Eva was in charge of a working party on the docks when he sustained a serious injury to his foot and he was sent to Roberts Hospital.

> I was in charge of a party and they were unloading a ship and the Japanese had not done all the safety precautions ... and there were mighty shouts from men, so I went over to see what was happening and ... I went down, a straight fall of thirty feet.

> And I was extremely lucky when I look back, because I landed on my feet. If I'd fallen only a couple of feet away I would have been caught by a load that was waiting to go up and I'd have been on my back ... As it was, because I landed on my feet all I did was major damage to my heel bone, which got broken in three places ... I went back eventually to Changi, they weren't sure if I needed to but then ... the second doctor looked at it, 'Yes, you must go back and have it dealt with.' ... soon as I got back to Changi they looked and ... Dr Rook said, 'That's broken. Let's X-ray it probably in a fortnight's time ...' So, I went in hospital and there I lay on the bed. They decided that rather than attempt to re-set it they'd keep it as it was but I'd have to lie on the bed, I've forgotten now whether it was ten weeks or three months, I had to ... not get up which was a bit difficult, but we managed ... And by the end of it I was so thankful they'd done it that way because I could begin to walk again and it had ... a great big bone sticking out at the side of the ankle ... but it was all right ... I took a lot of the weight on sticks, but eventually I could [walk] ... what amazed me, I'd been certainly less than two months out of hospital and I found myself with a party going up to

Thailand, which I thought was very unfair because I wasn't walking properly at all. But afterwards I was so thankful because [for] the parties that came much later it got worse and worse and I would never have survived.

Former RAMC Captain William 'Bill' Frankland worked at Roberts Hospital initially. Aged 99 when he gave his interview in 2012, Bill was still active and felt that he had been lucky in life, and never more so than during his captivity. Graduating from Oxford in 1936 he felt lucky to do House jobs at St Mary's Hospital Paddington, qualifying in 1938. He joined the RAMC three days before war broke out, transferred to the Tidworth Military Hospital and in October 1941, after undertaking basic tropical medicine training, left on a draft from Liverpool via Greenock on the Clyde, arriving in Singapore in the December.

After a short time attached to an Indian Regiment, on the toss of a coin Bill was once again lucky in being posted to his preferred option, a dermatology job at Tanglin Hospital. His colleague, Captain R. L. Parkinson of 32 Company, lost the toss and went to do anaesthetics at the Alexandra Military Hospital. On 14 February 1942 Parkinson was one of over 200 staff and patients killed when victorious Japanese troops ran amok through the hospital.

One of the medical officers that Bill knew at Roberts Hospital was a Major Richard 'Dickie' Doyle who was six years Bill's senior, an Irishman and Liverpool graduate who had been a light heavyweight boxing champion during his student days. Doyle had joined the Indian Medical Service (IMS) from his job as consultant surgeon at the Royal Southern Hospital in Liverpool. Bill remembered that while Doyle, who was sometimes referred to as 'Paddy' Doyle, was 'not beloved by everyone … he was a personality, a very competent surgeon.'

One unusual surgical case at Roberts that Bill recalled, which concerned Doyle too, took place in mid July 1942 and is recorded in Captain Marshall's diary (*The Changi Diaries*). Apparently, four men escaped in a boat across the Straits to Johore. Two of them managed to evade detection and return to Changi. But the other two, both Gordon Highlanders, bandsman Artie Turnbull and Piper James 'Hamish' Johnson, were turned over to the Japanese. They were taken to an island in the Straits of Johore, Pulau Ubin, to be executed. Turnbull was the first to be beheaded, but just as the sword was poised to strike Johnson, he reared up and made a dash for it into the crowd of watching natives, taking a glancing blow to his left shoulder in the process. He ran and ran, despite the sword having sliced through deep muscle tissue laying bare his left scapula (shoulder bone). Somehow he made it to the nearby creek, tucked his now heavy and useless left arm into his belt and swam for his life. Perhaps the salty water helped staunch the flow of blood as sometime later he floated ashore and staggered to a hut. There he met a Japanese guard who, luckily for Johnson, accepted his story that he'd gone for a swim and been bitten by a shark. The guard patched him before taking him to the hospital where Doyle and others repaired the torn musculature as best they could. Nobody was in any doubt about the lack of shark bite evidence!

Bill's luck held and after a few months working with Doyle and others, he was sent as medical officer to Blakang Mati island (renamed Sentosa) off Singapore, where he remained for the duration, returning to the main island to Kranji Hospital camp, after the Japanese surrender.

Roberts Barracks was the pre-war, newly built regimental headquarters of the Royal Engineers. It had been hurriedly transformed into Roberts Hospital comprising four newly built concrete, three-storey barrack blocks as soon as POW began to arrive there. One block acted as the surgical block where Doyle worked and Johnson had been treated. Block 151 was the dysentery ward (see photograph, Chapter 2 figure 18) which housed hundreds of men on mattresses on the floor (only a few had beds early on), inside and along the long open verandahs on either side of the first and second floors, overlooking semi-jungle. Several of those interviewed had either worked there or been a patient, or both.

When interviewed, medical orderly Corporal Douglas (Doug) Skippen, 196 Field Ambulance RAMC, described his first job as a prisoner in Changi when he was put

in charge of the dhobi-wallahs, or laundry, for about 900 dysentery patients. Each sheet or blanket had to be boiled for at least half an hour and for this I was given five men. Our water had to be carried by hand, wood scrounged and chopped, washing hung out, brought in and folded and then taken to the stores. We had no soap or disinfectant and were allowed no half-days except when it rained. The work was very gruelling under a blazing sun and in front of fires, but it had to be done. Sheets gradually became the colour of brown paper and even mottled with dye from the blankets which were boiled in the same 40 gallon drums ... after about two months of this I was given a welcome change and told to report for duty in a Dysentery Ward. I worked in the wards for about eight to nine months and still found it held some degree of fascination ... must say here and now that a better team of chaps working together on the wards could not be found ... the length of stay for patients varied from about a week to up to three weeks depending on the degree of severity of infection, many unfortunately did not make it. We did our best.[2]

Patients who recovered were discharged. They relapsed and were readmitted, again and again and again. Later on in Thailand, another of the Block 151 orderlies, Frank Scarr 198 Field Ambulance RAMC, remembered how the local reserves helped the British troops, in the early days in Thailand. 'Y'see these attap, these living quarters they were anything up to a hundred feet long and the Malay Volunteers they seemed to take this job over.'

Inside the bamboo huts sloping platforms were built along the length and on either side of a central walkway. Each man had only a shoulder's width of space to call his own, as Arthur Turbutt vividly recalled of the hut on Haruku which had 'a bamboo ledge … two foot off the ground, just long enough … you laid down and your colleague was touching you, that was the amount of space you got.'

The huts were also home to armies of bed bugs, lice and fleas, the scourge of every man's existence and the cause of intense skin irritation and disease. In countless diaries and many of the interviews, men describe how they would sit for hours picking the lice from the seams of their clothing. It was an obsessive and futile occupation; no matter how many they found and killed there were always more. The bedbugs, engorged with blood after a night's feasting, would be easier to catch but smelled foul when squashed. Jack Chalker recalled that in the early days in Singapore 'we made fairly primitive beds from bits of bamboo, old rice sacks, bits of canvas and so on, but they were usually … absolutely riddled with bedbugs and lice and things … eventually we just laid on the wood.'

Drastic measures were employed to rid the huts of these pests with bed platforms dismantled so the wood or bamboo slats could be run through naked flame to burn off the livestock which had taken up residence. It was only ever a temporary solution. By contrast those POW captured in Hong Kong or sent north from the tropics to Taiwan, Korea or Japan were mostly housed in brick or wooden buildings, warehouses, schools or factory dormitories, situated either within or near to coal mines, shipyards, ammunition or steelworks. Conditions there were bleak with hopelessly inadequate heating against the Siberian winters, restrictions on when stoves could be lit and not enough bedding or proper clothing; and bedbugs, lice and fleas abounded there, too.

Food and nutrition

Food was the next essential. Rice was the staple diet in Asia and in many areas supplies were available but the quantity and quality varied greatly, the prisoners being given dirty, weevil-infested polished rice which was minus the outer vitamin-rich husks. Rice is rich in carbohydrates but the Caucasian digestive tract was unaccustomed to an almost exclusively carbohydrate diet being used to a balanced diet of nutrients including fats, proteins and vitamins. Lack of the B complex vitamins quickly resulted in a wide range of unpleasant symptoms affecting primarily the circulatory and nervous systems, resulting in peripheral neuritis (pain in the lower limbs) and tropical diseases such as beriberi.

Despite establishing a system for pooling and rationing the food brought into camps this supply did not last long. Hunger dominated all their daily lives.

Stealing food became a necessity and those working on the docks or in warehouses made the most of the opportunity. While very risky (if caught punishment was swift and harsh) the rewards could be great as food commanded high prices and many a thief stole to fund his tobacco habit. Some men became obsessed with food, making endless lists of favourite dishes, restaurants and recipes, talking incessantly about imaginary meals. Hoarding became a way of coping for others. Hugh de Wardener recalled his batman, a man named Brown, who had collected tinned foods.

> He was a sort of meticulous, pernickety bloke, didn't say much. And while we there in Siam, I lost touch with him. And one day, I saw him in one of the wards at Takanun, he had a terrible sore on his back and he was dying. And he did die. I said to him, 'How did you get that sore?' and he said, 'Oh it was my haversack, walking up here.' I said, 'What did you have in it?' 'Tins of food,' he said. Tins of food! Apparently, he had been buying, for a rainy day, tins of food which he'd packed into this haversack and then carried for the 100 miles up [country]. Now if he'd put them into his stomach and it had given him the strength, he wouldn't have had the sore on his back because (a) he would have been strong and (b) he wouldn't have had the tins to make the hole in the back. So he died because of his personality. He was an obsessionist.

From the outset, efforts by the International Committee of the Red Cross to organise food and medical aid for Far East POW were thwarted by the Japanese. Some camps received occasional distributions of Red Cross food parcels, many rarely received any. What did arrive in camp was usually deliberately withheld by camp commanders, this injustice being compounded by the guards seen openly consuming Red Cross supplies and discarding the tins or wrappers. In late August 1945, following the Japanese surrender and before liberation, US medical officer Thomas Hewlett and others were scouring the city of Omuta in Japan for food when they came across several warehouses packed with Red Cross food and medical supplies. The dates of receipt and storage showed that the consignments had reached Japan prior to August 1943.[3]

In various camps prisoners tended small gardens producing vegetables for the communal pot with the Japanese occasionally supplying seeds and sometimes livestock, such as chickens and rabbits, ostensibly to enhance rations. This provided light work for the sick who were then entitled to full rations (prisoners who could not work were automatically on half rations as were the officers at Zentsuji propaganda camp which was not classified as a work camp). However, once the crops appeared or the chickens and rabbits matured, they would often be declared the property of the Emperor and removed to the guards' cookhouse. Eggs were highly prized. Maurice Naylor recalled a friend's act of generosity at Tamarkan.

> I'd got a very close mate, if you like, a man called John Browne ... from south east London ... he was a very nice chap, very quiet, very introspective, he despaired really. And he went up country, he died in the jungle somewhere ... he was a fellow signaller ... last time I saw him, he came to the hut, the dysentery hut I was in, and stood outside and he said, 'I've brought you these.' And he gave me three eggs ... And I was very touched about it, by it, because it represented a couple of weeks' hard work on the working party. We didn't get paid very much, ten cents a week. Ten cents means nothing, ten cents would buy three eggs, two eggs actually.

Figure 1 'First Egg Ceremony', led by Lieutenant Commander Frank Twiss, drawn by Lieutenant 'Buck' Schacht USN, Zentsuji 1943 *(courtesy of Marcia McInerney)*

At Zentsuji officers' camp in Japan the chicken squad was led by Lieutenant Commander Frank Twiss RN, senior officer on HMS *Exeter*. A great character and humourist, Twiss organised a special parade around the camp one day to mark what he wanted the guards to believe was the laying of the first egg. In fact the hens had been laying for some time with the produce being quietly slipped to the hospital hut. Fearing that the Japanese would become suspicious at the lack of eggs, on 11 November 1943 four of the chicken squad formed up with Twiss at the helm holding the 'first' egg on a cushion, USAC pilot, Lieutenant George Armstrong third and Captain Duncan taking up the rear. The procession was recorded by American naval officer, Lieutenant Kenneth George Schacht USN (known to all as 'Buck'), in a splendid cartoon entitled, 'First Egg Ceremony' (Figure 1) and also by Duncan in his diary.

Peter Dunstan recalled how, in Thailand, he and some friends dealt with something a little larger.

> The chaps used to bring the cattle up on the hoof and leave so many at each camp. And … one chap [at Tarsao] with a sledge hammer would hit the cow on the head and another one would slit his throat and bleed him … I remember more than once collecting a tinful of blood … scrounge fat or oil … and frying that, which turns out like liver.

Snakes, lizards, monkeys, dogs, crickets, slugs and snails were consumed by starving prisoners of war at one time or another.[4]

In mid-1943, for 2,000 half-starved and sick POW landing on Haruku in the Spice Islands from Java, the situation quickly became desperate. They had been sent to construct an airfield in preparation for the Japanese invasion of Australia. The food supply chain was tenuous as Allied submarines were again dominating sea routes and the islands were coral with little land suitable for cultivation. Very soon the guards as well as the POW were suffering from hunger and malnutrition. Flight Lieutenant Leslie Audus and Dutch scientist, Dr J. G. ten Houten knew what was needed and they obtained permission to start manufacturing yeast which is rich in vitamin B and a vital supplement to their reduced diet. Audus was aware that his sight was deteriorating due to the lack of vitamin B. Lack of this vitamin can cause damage to the optic nerves (supplying the eyes) and lead to blindness.

Before he had left Java, while at Jaarmarkt camp in Soerabaya, Audus had been asked by an RAF doctor, Richard Philps, if he could manufacture yeast as it had been found to reverse these visual defects among prisoners at the nearby Malang camp. Audus got together with Malayan Volunteer and plant pathologist, Bill Altson, who pre-war had worked at the Rubber Research

Figure 2 Fl/Lt Leslie Audus at work in the yeast manufacturing laboratory hut, Jaarmarkt camp, Java *(courtesy Audus family)*

Institute in Kuala Lumpur (Figure 2). At the age of fifty Altson was one of the oldest men in camp, and as Audus remembered 'he started looking after the yeast side of it, isolating the yeast, and I started looking after the biochemical side.'[5]

The illustration above, drawn by Audus, is of the lean-to shed behind the hospital which was their laboratory. In his book *Spice Island Slaves*, Audus notes that it was an Australian Radar Officer and do-it-yourself buff, Flying Officer Don Thomas, who fitted it out and made equipment, including the Bunsen burner. Audus was also handy, describing how he made a thermometer, essential in the malt digestion process, from glass capillary tubing, shaped using the Bunsen burner, together with mercury supplied by a Dutch Army pharmacist, Lieutenant van Papenrecht.

Between them they established the process and began to supply the hospital with regular small quantities of high quality yeast. When Audus had been shipped off to the Spice Islands in the Moluccas he took with him some of the yeast culture. Once settled in the camp on Haruku, he and Dr ten Houten began work (Figure 3). The camp commander agreed on condition that they supplied the guards with extract as well as the prisoners and him with alcohol which was a bi-product of the process.

However, it could do nothing for those who were blinded by the unrelenting glare of the sun on the searingly white coral; despite making bamboo-framed spectacles with dark blue cellophane stuck across the slits, their world was to remain irreparably dark.

Producing yeast as a dietary supplement is also recorded in camps in Hong Kong, Thailand and at Changi in Singapore.[6] Sergeant Ken Holland of the 148 Field Regiment, clearly remembered it was Sergeant Harry Hall RAMC at Changi 'making yeast extract … which we used to dish out to the people in my hut, there were about 40 of us in this hut, which was vitamin B actually, which was a help against beriberi.'

Hall had trained as a pharmacist in Nottingham before he joined the RAMC at the start of the war and was based at Roberts Hospital. He kept a detailed diary in a battered brown pocket book in addition to copious notes related to his work, especially his research and experiments to determine the Vitamin B1 content in rice polishings. This was necessary to calculate the correct therapeutic dose to be given to the men. His research using young chicks was written up as a paper in October 1943 entitled, 'The estimation of Vitamin B1 in a rice polishing extract'. His family still has his original diaries and notes.

Figure 3 Yeast manufacturing on Haruku, drawn by Fl/Lt Leslie Audus *(courtesy Audus family)*

In Thailand there were several medical officers making yeast extract. Canadian surgeon Captain Jacob Markowitz recorded trying this at Chungkai, using a concoction of rotting jungle bananas and rice which 'the officers were asked to spit into three times ... knowing that the diastase in the saliva would convert part of the starchy rice into sugar. The result after a few days' fermentation was a vitamin-rich beer worth its weight in uranium.'[7] Further up the railway beyond Takanun medical officer Captain MacArthur was also experimenting with the help of 'Dunlop Rubber Coy chemist, Sapper Barnwell, JVF [Johore Volunteer Force] working for me and we are doing well and will do much more in the new larger MI Room. Already we make 4 gals. daily of a very good vit. B extract from rice polishings – vit. B is water soluble and not destroyed by 130°C for 30 mins.'[8]

Fruits such as mangoes, guava, passion fruit and figs and cashew and peanuts were consumed wherever they were found. Taro, yams, cassava and palm lily, though starchy, relieved the monotony, and greens, known as 'jungle spinach', were found to be quite palatable. More unusual foods like rubber nuts (or seeds) provided protein and vitamins but required either boiling or roasting before being ground up and added to rice pap. Dutch chemist Captain C. J. van Boxtel volunteered to work as a medical orderly for the Dutch medical officer, Henri Hekking, in camps in Burma and played a major part in medical improvisation.

Hygiene and sanitation

The problems of finding a sufficient intake of food were matched by the difficulties encountered in eliminating the little that the prisoners ate. From the outset, overcrowding, lack of water and sewerage systems, sickness, low morale and sheer ignorance, combined with the relentless heat to create huge problems, compounded at times by monsoons. In city areas it took time to re-establish bomb-damaged water supplies and effective drainage to buildings housing thousands of FEPOW; in other areas hurriedly constructed camps had few, if any, services as none had existed previously.

Diarrhoea due to gastro-intestinal infection was endemic. In the overcrowded and basic conditions this presented major sanitation problems. Dysentery (bacillary, or less commonly the more severe form, amoebic), a painful and debilitating disease of the large bowel, swept through camps everywhere. There were few hospital facilities to segregate and care for the sick properly. Hastily dug open pit latrines became filthy as sick men frequently did not make it in time. Some were too weak to move and fouled where they stood or lay. Others who were not sick were either too de-moralised or too lazy to make the effort and simply defecated in any convenient place without thought to the health hazard they were creating. The sight, smell and condition of the paths between huts and tents in the early days in camp quickly deteriorated, as this description by Jack Spittle reveals, 'Particularly nauseating at that time was the all-pervading stench of decomposing organic matter excreta, flesh and other residues of war.' Before long they were dealing with cholera epidemics as well.

Bedbugs, lice and scabies infestations were all part of camp life and created serious health problems which were made worse by men who had given up any pretence at personal hygiene. The intense itching and scratching caused breaks in the skin which quickly became infected. The general lack of discipline saw men discarding food cans wherever the contents were consumed. Both bodily and material waste became magnets to millions of disease-carrying flies. In camps a permanent war was waged on the fly population: they smoked them out, swatted them and collected daily quotas before rations were issued. But whatever they did it was never enough.

Mosquitoes were another major concern. Many men did not have mosquito nets and in the early days those that did often bartered them for food or cigarettes. Before war broke out the British were aware of the mosquito hazard. In November 1941 specialist RAMC anti-mosquito squads were sent to Singapore to tackle the problem, spraying breeding areas with chemicals and oil. Inevitably some of these men became POW, like pre-war sanitary inspector Private Jack Spittle RAMC who was captured on Tekong Island off Singapore in February 1942.[9] An amateur entomologist and keen ornithologist, Spittle made copious and meticulous notes on sanitation and many other subjects throughout his captivity which were illustrated with detailed drawings, diagrams and plans. In 1944 he was moved from Changi to Kranji hospital camp. There, he described the method for digging fly-proof latrines.

These latrines are constructed by boring a vertical hole into the ground 18" in diameter and about 20 ft. deep. A special borer is used for this purpose. A metal cylinder, such as a cut-down oil drum, is then placed over the top of the hole & dug into the ground so as to make it secure. Certain framed wicker chair seats with the wicker work cut away make admirable seats. A fly-proof lid, preferably of metal, must also be provided.

In some camps senior POW officers, under guidance from the medical officers, took control and organised a system for digging latrines, with particular attention given to the siting, rotation and maintenance of same. Men like Spittle were indispensable as they had vital knowledge which had to be implemented quickly in order for things to improve.

Another POW who took fly control and sanitation very seriously was

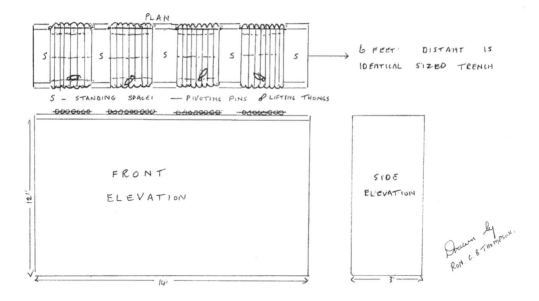

PLAN

S — STANDING SPACES   — PIVOTING PINS ✔ LIFTING THONGS

FRONT

ELEVATION

6 FEET·   DISTANT   IS
IDENTICAL   SIZED   TRENCH

SIDE

ELEVATION

Drawn by
Ron. C. B. Thompson.

12'   14'   3'

Figure 4 Diagram accompanying Harry Howarth's detailed description of a deep trench latrine, Tamarkan camp, Thailand. (*LSTM collection*)[10]

also a member of the 9RNF, Private Harry Howarth. In 1986 he attended the Tropical School in Liverpool for Tropical Disease Investigatons (TDIs). Three years earlier he had published his memoir, *Where Fate Leads*, in which he had described the essential sanitation work he had been responsible for at Tamarkan camp in Thailand. He donated to the School's Far East POW collection a diagram (Figure 4) and written description of the design he used to make fly-proof latrines. Co-opted in 1943 by Lieutenant Colonel Toosey, Howarth was initially dismayed to be asked to dig a series of twelve foot deep latrines. But being given that job meant that he was then on the Japanese payroll at ten cents a day, which to him meant the difference between living and dying.

It was vital work. His diagram shows the dimensions. Two latrines were dug out end to end, the top of one covered with bamboo lids with lifting flaps spaced every couple of feet. After each use the flap was shut tight so flies could not settle on the waste below. Each week a new trench was used, the bamboo cover being transferred to the new one and the used one covered over with soil, cutting out light and air to prevent maggots that had hatched from maturing. Using the latrines like this meant new trenches were only dug every two weeks.

Another of Toosey's ideas was fly swatting; every man in camp, including all but the most sick, had to kill fifty flies a day. The homemade fly swats were made by a platoon of volunteers out of bamboo, wire and leather strips. These simple measures saw the incidence of dysentery sharply decline. In late 1944 at Nakon Pathom in Thailand, men were reportedly paid at the rate of 10 cents per 15,000 flies.

In primitive jungle camps strict rules were laid down to prohibit the fouling of rivers and streams. Elaborate water courses were constructed using bamboo piping. Cut lengthways and with the intersecting discs removed, this made excellent guttering which worked very efficiently when the landscape allowed gravity to be used to deliver a continuous supply of fresh water to different parts of the camp for cooking, ablutions and medical purposes.[11] Water for cooking was drawn from an area upstream from where bathing or cleaning of utensils, bedpans and laundry was carried out.

Later on when cholera epidemics ravaged jungle camps, use of water was strictly controlled. Jack Chalker recalled what happened.

> The onset of cholera ... hits you very quickly and very badly. The body's trying to eliminate ... out of your mouth and your bottom, and ... it's a very, very violent rejection by the body of, of anything in terms of fluids. You are incontinent and ... you produce white stools eventually ... within twenty-four hours sometimes, a patient can become almost unrecognisable ... And also another hideous thing about this was as the body became so dehydrated it produced appalling muscle spasms and cramps, which were absolutely agonising ... and it was pitiful beyond words to see. I remember this so clearly, it broke out in my hut in Chungkai, and we were ... absolutely petrified that we were going to get this because the mortality rate's enormously high with cholera, and we had nothing to help us with it ... that was one of the really terrifying things and almost more terrifying than diphtheria.

Bill Drower recalled in his memoir that

> cholera struck other working parties with whom we had brief contact ... cholera is a terrible disease. The speed with which it dessicates a man is reminiscent of mediaeval descriptions of the plague – in reasonable health in the morning, dead by nightfall. When eventually it struck our camp, the Japanese, fearful for their own skins, quite quickly brought in vaccine, the effect of which may have been as much psychological as biological.

Rainwater was the only safe supply for drinking and cleaning. It was carefully collected and stored and impromptu showers were taken under the eaves of the huts during the rain storms. Procedures were implemented for 'sterilising' all eating utensils, by either dipping them in vats of boiling water or passing through open flame before taking rations. Wood ash was used to clean utensils and a soap substitute was found in the leaves or bark chips of the red ash tree, which when rubbed together, formed a good lather.[12] The fruit of the red ash if crushed and thrown into the river had the helpful effect of stupefying fish, thus making them easier to catch.

Medical challenges and responses

With the Japanese withholding medical supplies, doctors relied on their basic knowledge and sought the help of those who knew the tropics. Men like the Volunteer Forces, drawn from the colonial scientific community and plantation managers who had worked in the region for years, and the native labourers the Malays, Chinese and Eurasians from the Dutch East Indies. These people knew how to survive in the jungle, which plants were medicinal or edible. But the European troops also brought vital skills from 'civvie street'. The carpenters, metalworkers, boilermakers and leather-workers' inventiveness enabled doctors to work more effectively. There follows an appraisal of the main medical conditions prevalent during captivity with examples of lifesaving ingenuity and resourcefulness (see also Chapter 5).

Dysentery

This infective disease of the large bowel is marked by acute pain and the persistent passing of blood and mucous. Bacillary dysentery was the more common form and affected the majority of men. It responded well if sulpha drugs were available which was seldom. In Taiwan, Major Ben Wheeler a Canadian doctor who served in the Indian Medical Service, successfully treated dysentery patients in camps in Taiwan with a diet of rice water followed by ground charcoal.[13] Elsewhere warm tea enemas helped to relieve symptoms.

The more severe form, amoebic dysentery, was much harder to treat. At 55 kilo camp in Burma, the Dutch chemist van Boxtel used distilled water to convert a bottle of extract of ipecachuanha into approximately 150 doses of intramuscular emetine.[14] Having a supply of distilled water was essential for medicinal purposes but mostly it had to be produced by illicit, home-made stills. One gallon guala malacca tin cans and lengths of copper tubing were fashioned into distillation units. Heated by home-made charcoal braziers the stills provided pure water for mixing intravenous (IV) and intramuscular (IM) solutions as well as alcohol, a vital cleaning agent for surgical instruments.[15]

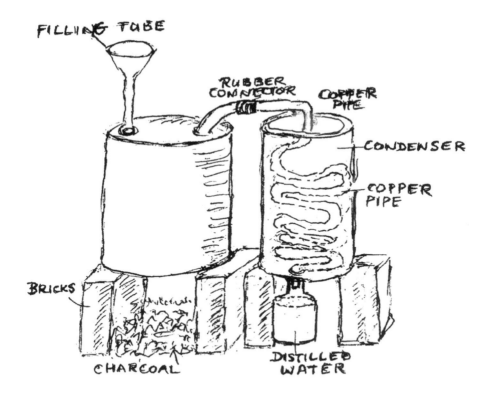

Figure 5 The still made by Lieutenant
Gordon Smith at Tamarkan camp *(courtesy
of Gordon Smith)* [16]

Gordon Smith described how he had made one such still at Tamarkan camp
(see Figure 5).

> I found a bit of copper tubing which came from a Morris 10 car, the engine of
> which was being used as a pump to pump water … this bit of pipe … was put
> inside a tank of water, the ends were soldered in … I found somebody with
> a soldering iron who could do it. And we built a sort of boiler out of an old
> paint can and we connected the two together with a bit of tubing from a steth-
> oscope … only about two inches, and heating the thing with charcoal which
> came up from the cookhouse, we started producing fairly good sterile water
> which I started using for cleaning all my slides and equipment and also could be
> used by the hospital in making various drugs and things such as they had. As a
> by-product I did start to make some alcohol by fermenting some rice and sweet
> potatoes and when it was sufficiently fermented, and after a second distillation,
> I got quite strong alcohol which could be used as … antiseptic. And this was a
> really worthwhile thing.

In his interview Jack Chalker recalled the

> two rather big stills in Nakon Pathom, in the final base camp ... they were a
> couple of Lieber condensers ... and I had a friend who was a geneticist, he
> worked with the pharmacist and they concocted a rice and yeast culture which
> they then condensed and made 90 per cent alcohol. And it was the only cleaning
> agent we had.

In Singapore and Taiwan chronic diarrhoea was relieved by dosing with home-
made Kaolin suspension derived from locally sourced china clay. Dehydration
resulting from prolonged loss of fluid due to enteric disease was sometimes
treated by means of intravenous or rectal infusions by Captain Wheeler in
Taiwan. In the worst cases of chronic dysentery, ileostomies and appendicos-
tomies were also performed (see page 127).

Cholera

Outbreaks could happen anywhere there was an infected water supply but
they were more prevalent in the Tropics. They spread rapidly, in part due
to the lethargy or ignorance of prisoners who ignored the strict regulations
regarding the use of river water. In Thailand the rivers up country were
heavily polluted by the large number of infected corpses of native labourers.
In Burma, Dutch doctor, Lieutenant Gerrit Bras, observed that 'they [natives]
died in droves. You saw dead Tamil bodies floating down the River Kwai,
dead from cholera, all the time.' He tried replacing lost body fluids by giving
patients home-made intravenous saline solution. To be safe to use, river water
had to be filtered several times, boiled and then mixed with rock salt from the
cookhouse.

Clearly visible in Jack's drawing (Figure 6) are the containers for infusions.
These were upturned, suspended Japanese bottles with the base removed. The
neck of the bottle was sealed with a cork stopper; a bamboo spigot inserted
into this with a length of stethoscope tubing connected to either an intravenous needle or bamboo cannula. In autumn 1943 medical orderly Doug
Skippen was nursing cholera patients at Nikki close to the Burmese border.
With no soap they washed with fine river sand and rainwater collected during
daily torrential downpours. Rainwater was their only source of safe drinking
water. In his memoir, extracted from his contemporaneous diary, Doug lists
the many invaluable uses for bamboo:

> Medical use for cholera: cannula [*sic*] or needle for saline infusion.

[Other] medical uses: splints, arm baths, dressing bowels for bathing, containers for tablets, bedpans, urine bottles, disinfecting bowls for hands, spatulas and crutches.

General uses: Making the framework of huts, roofs and even split making flooring. Cut in thin strips and used wet makes useful tying material. Brooms were made from split up pieces, ladders, firewood, latrines, containers for guala malacca, baskets etc.

Food: Bamboo shoots chopped up in the stew make a passing vegetable.

Across the border in Thailand, Captain MacArthur at Tameron north of Takanun noted in his diary for 1 September 1943, 'The cholera case [Bowler] has improved immensely after 3 pints of boiled rain water containing about 1 per cent rock salt.'[17] Further down river at Takanun, Captain de Wardener had tried giving patients large amounts of boiled drinking water despite a dearth of vessels in which to boil sufficient. He later recalled that 'not more than three full water-bottles could be provided each day for the more severe cases.'[18] Together with Captain Benson RAMC, they experimented with saline solution administered by peritoneal infusion, using a trochar (a surgical

Figure 6 Cholera tents at Hintok, Thailand
(courtesy of Jack Chalker)

instrument for introducing a cannula or needle through the abdominal wall) and stethoscope tubing. Anxious not to cause internal injury they practised the procedure repeatedly on a corpse first, to gauge the degree of force necessary to get the trochar through the emaciated abdominal wall. Once they were confident, they gave the peritoneal infusions but the method was abandoned when the fluid intake caused the patients too much discomfort. Weary Dunlop described collecting and boiling rainwater for IV therapy as well as treating a few patients with massive intra-peritoneal saline injections using a Thomson Walker syringe and large needle.[19]

Malaria

There are two main types, benign tertian (BT) which affected the majority of POW and malignant tertian (MT) or cerebral malaria, which was more severe, rarer and often fatal. Quinine and plasmoquine were always in short supply despite the former Netherlands East Indies providing much of the world's supply of quinine. Microbiology, though rudimentary, played a vital role in early diagnosis, which was critical in helping to preserve the meagre stocks of drugs. Large camps like Changi and some hospital camps in Java had established pathology laboratories but these were the exception. A few microscopes existed in smaller camps. Gerrit Bras arrived at Omuta camp in Japan with one he had made in Thailand using bamboo and field glass lens.[20] In an interview in 1986 Bras described another homemade microscope, housed in a section of tail pipe from a Japanese motorcycle, which he had used successfully in Thailand.[21] Recent research revealed that Professor Thomas Wilson (a clinician at LSTM in the 1960s) had been a Far East prisoner of war. In 1943 he undertook detailed and vital malaria research at Songkurai in Thailand using a microscope and other equipment he had carried up from Changi.[22]

Beriberi

This was the commonest form of avitaminosis, resulting from the lack of the B group of vitamins in the diet. 'Wet' beriberi was typified by gross oedema (fluid in the tissues) first of the legs and feet, and then abdomen, face and genitalia which caused weakness, pain and numbness. Skin irritation was common, particularly of the genital area (eloquently referred to as either 'Java', 'Changi' or 'strawberry' balls). Peripheral nerve damage mainly affecting the feet (known as 'happy' or 'electric' feet) was worse at night and lasted for months, resulting in sleeplessness and exhaustion.

Foot drop as a result of beriberi hampered mobility. Nowell Peach recalled among the survivors from the Spice Islands, 'one chap with beriberi had bilateral foot drop, which of course is a frightful impediment to getting around, so I made some bands to go round below the knee and on the foot and sort of threaded string between the two which kept the, kept his feet extended which was a great help for him to get around.'

'Dry' beriberi, the more serious form, was often fatal. Vitamin B deficiency could lead to optic nerve damage and blindness. Doug Skippen recorded a frightening episode, early on when he was working on the dysentery ward in Roberts Hospital, 'I woke up one morning and I said to the chap in the bed next to me, "I can't see." And he said, "Don't talk so daft." I said, "I really can't." And he went and brought Major Gillies over and checked my eyes: vitamin deficiency. I was blind for about seven days, but it came back.' Doug was lucky that with treatment in time he recovered his sight, it did not always happen. Flight Lieutenant Leslie Audus had the same problem in Java and later in the Spice Islands and although not blinded his vision was permanently impaired. His special form of self-treatment was to benefit many hundreds of other prisoners of war (see pages 103–105).

Rice husks, known as polishings or dedek, rich in vitamin B, could sometimes be acquired from natives. In Sumatra dedek was 'brewed' to make a watery extract and given as a daily ration; with further filtering it was given by intramuscular injection in severe cases.[23] This, and yeast extract which has been mentioned earlier, helped halt or in part reverse some of the symptoms.

Pellagra

This resulted from deficiency in nicotinic acid. It was characterized by diarrhoea, dermatitis and dementia. Riboflavin deficiency caused rash, an inflamed mouth and tongue (angular stomatitis and glossitis respectively) as well as scrotal eczema. It too, responded well to vitamin B supplements. Vitamin A deficiency which caused corneal ulceration or conjunctivitis, could be ameliorated by dosing with red palm oil.[24] Nutritional amblyopia is the partial or complete loss of vision in one eye caused by vitamin deficiency. Australian medical officer, Major Alan Hazleton, constructed a rudimentary ophthalmoscope to assist diagnosis of eye conditions at Nakon Pathom in Thailand. Certain types of grass, when harvested and crushed, were found to produce riboflavin extract.[25] In Sumatra the clandestine collection of the native cottela grass leaves provided a rich source of vitamin B.[26]

'Nutritional' or 'famine' oedema

This resulted from protein deficiency and caused gross swelling. By 1945 prisoners in Singapore were starving and in a desperate effort to boost protein intake a snail farm was considered though the sudden Japanese capitulation obviated the need.[27] Latterly, the giving of blood transfusions for the worst cases of malnutrition was found to be beneficial and this is discussed further on.[28]

Diphtheria

Epidemics occurred fairly frequently and without drugs and medication little could be done to relieve the symptoms. In Changi, from September to November 1942, an outbreak affected over 840 men causing needless loss of many lives due to lack of serum.[29] One lucky patient who was treated with the serum was medical officer Hugh de Wardener.

> I got a diphtheritic ulcer of my foot, because I played goal at soccer, we played soccer and I played goal and got a piece taken off the top of my foot. And at the bottom of the building, in a little side room, we had a few cases of diphtheria and I think the dust emanating from under the door must have been full of diphtheritic organisms. And that was very, very painful ... luckily enough there was a little bit of antitoxin about and I had one shot and the pain just disappeared, it was marvellous.

A while later at Chungkai camp in Thailand, medical orderly Frank Scarr was looking after the diphtheria patients when Captain de Wardener arrived to take over from the previous doctor. As he had recently recovered from diphtheria he was felt to be the medical officer least at risk. Frank recalled that before de Wardener took over, the death rate was high. At interview Hugh outlined how he had tackled the problem.

> All I remembered about reading about diphtheria as a student was that ... the great danger was during the height of the infectious disease you got sudden death, of unknown cause really. It was obviously cardiac, but how? Why? And usually associated with sudden movement of some sort. They'd been having deaths in the ward so when I arrived I said, 'Everybody, lie flat.' Well, it's not all that much fun to lie flat on a piece of bamboo which is filled with bed bugs and mosquitoes at night. I mean, you know, you want to move about and scratch and get away. And most of them, in fact everybody did lie flat, except one bloke. He was the sort of bloke who didn't believe in anything, anyhow. He sat up and died within my first twenty-four hours or something. From then on, everybody thought I, there was something about me. They'd better behave!

Scarr remembered being shown how to extract the antitoxin serum. 'We took blood off those that were getting better, we allowed it to clot and we took off the serum and it was injected intramuscular [*sic*], and the amount they got was about 30ccs'. However, at Kinkaseki camp in Taiwan, with no antitoxin available Major Wheeler swabbed every throat with iodine which significantly reduced mortality.[30]

Tropical ulcers (tropical phagedena)

These developed from infection or scratches and abrasions incurred by inadequate footwear and clothing. Due to general debility, lack of rest and clean dressings, heat and dirty living and working conditions, minor cuts and scratches quickly broke down into festering tropical ulcers which soon affected deep tissue, muscle and bone, often becoming gangrenous. Lieutenant Colonel M. E. Barrett of the Kedah Volunteer Force, a pre-war manager of a Malayan rubber plantation, volunteered to train as a medical orderly. He gave a vivid description of the ulcer huts at Chungkai in a report written after liberation.

> Two huts, known as the ulcer wards, each housed some 400 ulcer cases … The ulcers had to be seen to be believed. Here, it suffices to say, that the majority of these were caused by bamboo scratches incurred when working naked in the jungle, i.e. naked except for a loin cloth. Leg ulcers of over a foot in length and maybe six inches in breadth, with the bone exposed and rotting for several inches, were no uncommon sight. The foulness of these two wards could be smelt a hundred yards away; the sickly stench of the rotting flesh of living men. The dysentery wards were a nightmare of living skeleton forms.[31]

Maurice Naylor was working in the camp office at Tamarkan camp near Chungkai. Major Arthur A. Moon (an Australian gynaecologist) the Senior Medical Officer there, treated his ulcerated leg.

> I got a scratch on my leg, don't know how probably bit of bamboo, quite sharp bamboo can be. And it turned into an ulcer. … [Moon] said, 'What are you doing about it?' And I said, 'I don't know, it's not getting any better.' … And he produced a tablet of M&B … which had been smuggled in, and ground it up and packed the ulcer with it, bound it up and it began to heal then. So I was lucky … tropical ulcers were terrible. We had a whole hut full … people with amputation, ulcers and so on … we must have had two hundred amputees at least in there.

Medical treatment for ulcers varied widely. Home-made salt solution (saline) was dripped through rubber tubing from an old Klim tin (Canadian brand of powdered milk, Klim is milk spelt backwards) which was attached to a bamboo tripod. The saline solution irrigated the area of the ulcer (Figure 7).

Sometimes the deep and suppurating lesions were seared with red hot pokers to stop the spread of the infection,[32] cleaned by curettage (the burning away) or cutting and scooping out the dead tissue using sharpened spoons was also done. By removing the infected or dead tissue and pus allowed the granulation of new tissue to begin.[33] In hospital camps in Thailand, surgeons tried skin grafts on the largest ulcers with some good results. This was also attempted at the primitive camp on Haruku, as one survivor recounted at interview. Able Seaman Harold Lock was one of the younger prisoners, having joined the Royal Navy in 1936 aged 14. In March 1942 he was serving onboard the destroyer HMS *Jupiter* when it was sunk in the battle of the Java Sea and he ended up first in Java then the Moluccas. He developed ulcers from small cuts and one deeply infected one.

> Me and my two friends we kept together all the time … went in the jungle at night … got bananas and coconuts and things. It kept us alive … a Japanese caught me … and he stuck a bayonet in me [his leg] and that turned to gangrene about a week later. So I went to see this [Dutch] doctor, Springer … the most marvellous man … 'All I have got here is a spoon … come back and I will spoon all that dead flesh out. It will take about six days and I will have to take a bit off your thigh. I have got a razor blade and I will have to cut it up and jab it back into that open wound.' I said, 'What is the alternative?' as I didn't like the sound of that … 'You will be dead in about a fortnight.' … so I went to see him every day for six days and he cut the skin off here with a razor blade, he cut it up in long pieces and he got a little stick and jabbed it into the wounds.

In a remote camp on the railway near the Burmese border, Medical Officer Patrick MacArthur described making wound cleaning solutions like Eusol [Edinburgh University solution of lime] and other preparations, such as

> a weak tannic acid solution by extracting chopped up stems of the wild banana tree. Salt has be reprecipated [sic] from rock salt and is very pure. A good eusol emulsion has been made from 5 per cent chloride of lime, 5 per cent boracic acid, 2 oz. coconut oil to make 8oz. with water. We have bought quite a lot of seaweed preparation from Japan [sic] which is said to contain iodine. Have made some excellent ointments, with soap, coconut oil and tapioca – ZnO_2, Salicylic and Boric and Sulphur. We are busy trying to make a still for distilled water and later for alcohol as well.[34]

Many men with tropical ulcers needed physiotherapy to help them to mobilise

Figure 7 Saline irrigation apparatus, pen and wash drawing, Chungkai 1943 *(courtesy of Jack Chalker)*

following months of pain and debility. This crucial therapy was given by volunteers like Jack Chalker, who first learned the rudiments from doctors and then worked with others massaging and strengthening contracted muscles and useless limbs. A wide variety of physiotherapy apparatus was made from bamboo and scrap materials of any kind by carpenters and engineers. However, for some, whose tropical ulcers did not respond to any treatment, the only recourse was amputate the limb. This is explored further in the surgical section further on.

While at Tandjong Priok camp in Java, Nowell Peach had a scalpel, patella hammer and curette made by the Royal Engineers in the camp workshop. The latter was fashioned from a piece of stainless steel car trim and was used to clean wounds and tropical ulcers by scouring out the dead or infected tissue. Following his interview, Nowell made a sketch of the curette with notes (Figure 8).

Both the curette and his patella hammer are in the photograph on page 46. The patella hammer was vital for his detailed study into Burning Feet syndrome (see page 69). Medical orderly, Private George Holland 198 Field Ambulance RAMC, who worked at both Roberts Hospital and later Chungkai hospital camp (and others) in Thailand, demonstrated at interview how they had sharpened scalpels, taking

> a glass, a bottle … and you got a razor blade and you put it inside the glass and kept swinging it half way like that, sharpening … on the inside of the glass … it might take two or three hours to get a nice sharp edge for the surgery … and you put the razor blade in the bottle, with your two fingers and you sit there as you're talking, you're sharpening. So you're going in an arc round the edge, the rim of the glass till it got sharper and sharper. And [Gordon] Vaughan used to come and collect them as they got nice and sharp … it was hours, and you're talking of course, you could be doing it in the dark it didn't matter.

Even livestock helped the healing process. Dressings applied over a bed of maggots placed on to tropical ulcers had quick results. Within a few days the wound would be clean, the tissue granulating and the skin margins healing. Small fish were also put to work in areas where the water courses were not too contaminated. Ulcerated or infected limbs were immersed in river water and the fish removed the pus and dead skin, leaving wounds clean.[35]

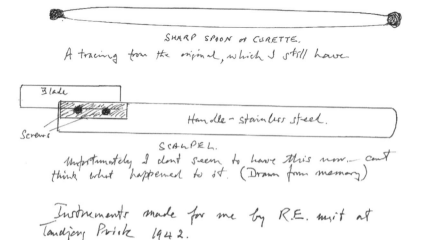

SHARP SPOON or CURETTE.

A tracing from the original, which I still have

Blade

Handle - stainless steel.

Screws

SCALPEL.

Unfortunately I don't seem to have this now.— can't think what happened to it. (Drawn from memory)

Instruments made for me by R.E. unit at Tandjong Priok 1942.

Figure 8 Drawing and description of a curette (top) and a scalpel made for him by Royal Engineers, 1942 drawn by Nowell Peach 2008 (LSTM collection)

Haematology

In camps where they had a microscope doctors and orderlies carried out rudimentary blood grouping and matching using microscopes and home-made centrifuges.[36] The healthier men would queue up outside the MI hut waiting to give blood for routine matching. Glass and metal containers for collecting donor blood, home-made bamboo whisks for thinning it, intravenous needles made from bamboo thorns, tin utensils, bottles and rubber tubing, were all used to carry out blood transfusions which were an effective treatment for gross debility due to malnutrition, dysentery, post-operative recovery and tropical ulcers. The technique was simple and very effective.

At interview Gordon Smith described how, at Tamarkan camp not far from Chungkai, after initially doing the microbiology work, he was asked to take on blood grouping and cross-matching for blood transfusions. After doing this for some time he was then shown how to do the transfusions. Following rigorous scrubbing up, blood was taken from a suitable donor by means of a needle with rubber tubing attached so that the blood dripped into a vessel. If there was no sodium citrate available to prevent the blood from clotting it was gently stirred for a few minutes with a home-made bamboo whisk. Gradually the fibrinogen in the blood (clotting agent) wrapped itself around the whisk. After a few minutes stirring, the whisk and contents were discarded.

This left the now de-fibrinated blood which was then poured into a suspended, upturned bottle suspended above the recipient. The bottle had a stopper with a length of rubber tubing which had a home-made clamp to prevent the blood from flowing freely. A large needle or cannula was needed to open a vein in the recipient's arm. In the absence of a suitable cannula or needle these were fashioned from a bamboo shoot with the centre bored out. These young shoots are typically four to five inches long, very sharp and, crucially, pliable. This was a job for skilled engineers, who could bore out the centre of the shoot making a channel through which liquid could flow. The exceedingly sharp point would then be inserted into the vein of the recipient, the tubing connected to it and the clamp slowly released.[37] This procedure was often repeated several times for one patient.

As well as being a volunteer orderly, Lieutenant Colonel Barrett also trained to give blood transfusions in Chungkai. Unlike Gordon Smith who had been a medical student, Barrett had no previous medical knowledge or training. He was one of four officers who answered a call for volunteers to assist doctors in this work, in August 1943. Describing the benefits to patients in his report, written en route home in 1945, he noted the efficacy of the process.

What was being done was the supplying by means of blood transfusions all those proteins and other essentials in which our diet was so sadly lacking ... transfusions were in the nature of a blood meal, digestible without effort. Stubborn ulcers which would not heal began to mend after two or three transfusions. Chronic cases of malaria gained strength, energy and appetite for even the coarse unpalatable food available. The lives of many dysentery patients were saved.'

A report about this work, written by Barrett, is in the Wellcome Library in London, and makes fascinating reading.[38]

A detailed sketch depicting the scene in the transfusion hut at Chungkai camp, and signed in the bottom right hand corner by Private Ashley George Old in 1944, provides a vivid and compelling record of this work (Figure 9). This illustration is remarkable. The attention to detail, the evidence of ingenuity and inventiveness, is brilliant. In the bottom right hand corner there is the home-made charcoal brazier with the steriliser unit on top next to the instrument table. His signature and the date are clear though easily mistaken for the markings from an old wooden crate. You can see the technician at work, the end of the whisk which he is turning clearly visible. The donor, looking relatively relaxed though obviously thin, while the recipient appears restless, tense and skeletal. Both his feet are bandaged, either as protection in lieu of footwear or covering wounds or ulcers; and so too is the right foot of the technician. It is so clear and obvious what is going on. Old was a brilliant documentary artist. In another of his drawings he depicts the queue of men lined up outside this hut waiting to give blood. Most of the known surviving work by Old is now held in the State Library of Victoria in Australia, as part of the Arthur Moon Collection.

All in all, at Chungkai within an eight month period in 1943, over 3,800 transfusions were performed with no deaths attributed to the procedure.[39] Sadly, such extraordinary results were not possible everywhere. There were camps close by in Burma that lacked the basic tools and know-how to undertake such work.[40]

Pulmonary (chest) infections

Pneumonia was a feature of terminal disease in the tropics, though in Taiwan, Hong Kong, China and Japan it was a primary cause of death due to the combined effects of the extreme cold, poor housing, diet, rest and lack of medicines. In Taiwan, one patient with pneumonia had an accumulation of pus in the pleural cavity (empyema) drained by means of a catheter made from an old bicycle tyre.[41]

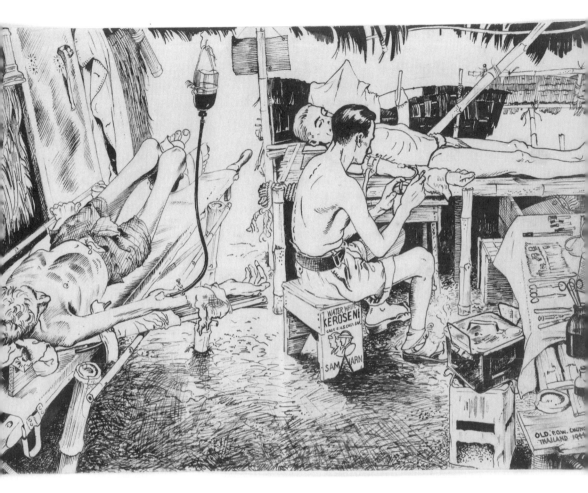

Figure 9 Blood transfusion hut, Chungkai, Thailand drawn by Private Ashley George Old in 1944 *(courtesy Pictures Collection, State Library of Victoria Arthur Moon collection)*

Another POW in Taiwan, Glaswegian accountant Sergeant John Francis 'Frank' Clement, was chronically sick suffering repeated bouts of tuberculosis (TB). He was lucky in that there were hospital huts in several of the camps he was in. While confined for long periods he appears to have used his time of enforced 'rest' away from the prying eyes of the guards (who avoided contact with infectious patients), to make a comic book documentary of life in the camps. He had kept a diary which helped him recall notable events and happenings (see Postscript for more about Clement's work).

Surgical challenges and solutions

In the immediate aftermath of the fighting, war surgery predominated with over 2,500 British wounded in Singapore alone. Roberts Hospital, with its operating theatres and wards, was fairly well-equipped initially. Surgeons were kept busy dealing with injuries sustained during the fighting as well as routine operations such as appendicectomies.

In Java, Lieutenant Colonel Maisey had negotiated with the Japanese to establish a new POW hospital in Batavia. It took some time but eventually two hospitals were created, one at a Catholic boys' orphanage called St Vincentius which was mainly for surgical work and the other, at the Mater Dolorosa Convent, for medical cases. In more remote areas facilities for surgery were almost non-existent, inspiring exceptional feats of ingenuity and improvisation of equipment, instruments and techniques.

Asepis

Australian surgeon Lieutenant Colonel Albert Coates noted in his 1946 paper published in the *Medical Journal of Australia* regarding surgical practice in Burma and Thailand, how difficult aseptic surgery was. The aim was always to try to work as cleanly as possible with all instruments boiled, and in the absence of gloves hands were repeatedly scrubbed in clean water before being washed with alcohol produced in camp. Alcohol was produced by camp stills, sometimes using Burmese brandy, provided both a vital cleansing agent and a means to sterilize syringes. Some surgeons wiped alcohol between the layers of tissue when closing wounds. Coates did not, however, recommend using the naked hand technique in abdominal exploration as sweating palms caused adhesions. His team had gowns, caps and masks which were sterilised in home-made autoclaves.

'Weary' Dunlop in his paper published in the *British Medical Journal* in 1946, advocated the benefits of both well-washed hands and the use of 'a rigid forceps' technique, combined with the use of home-made portable sterilizing units made from large tin cans or mess tins from those who no longer needed them. The sterilisers were heated with charcoal made by the men. Fellow Australian surgeon Albert Coates described how stolen petrol drums were made into large steel sterilisers which could accommodate either surgical cloths or contaminated garments for mass disinfection. At Tandjong Priok in Java, Royal Engineer (RE) craftsman John Baxter helped to make an autoclave from an old army pressure cooker tank which was used to sterilise dressings. He also recalled the hours of laborious cutting required using files or hacksaw blades, to recycle stainless steel and aluminium cooking equipment into scalpels and other instruments. He and other RE craftsmen had a special workshop hut designated within the camp (see Nowell Peach, Chapter 2). In Japan, US Navy surgeon Thomas Hewlett recorded in a report written in 1978 that operations were performed bare-handed and the fingernails of the surgeons were black resulting from the use of bichloride of mercury and iodine during the scrubbing procedure.

Anaesthesia

This was not guaranteed. In 1943, at Chungkai, chloroform was administered via an improvised bamboo mask made by RAMC medical orderly Private Gordon Vaughan 198 Field Ambulance and dental Novocain, procured through black market trade in prisoners' watches, was converted into spinal anaesthesia and used in numerous amputations. However, in Japan it was found that two Novocain tablets dissolved in a small amount of a patient's spinal fluid gave up to 45 minutes of anaesthesia. At 55 kilo camp in Burma, van Boxtel created spinal anaesthetic from diluted Japanese cocaine. In Java, Dutch scientist Major Zaadnordijk, manufactured pure ether in sufficient quantity to provide anaesthetics for both POW and civilian internees.

Like Vaughan at Chungkai, Gordon Smith, who was recovering from a severe bout of malaria at Tamarkan Hospital camp a few kilometres away, found himself making anaesthetic masks.

He was asked to help as they were shorthanded and remembered

quite a number of surgeries were carried out long before the actual hospital came [was set up in the camp] ... you needed anaesthesia. Now the doctors were busy doing what they had to do and so of course I became their anaesthetist, which I had to do in those days with chloroform, which was rather unpleasant. Again, I made a sort of mask of bamboo, little bits of bamboo, covered with thickish cloth and I would sit at the head of the table with his, the patient's head in the crook of my arm from where I could pour the chloroform on to this cloth and also I could, with my thumb, I could open his eyelid when he was in aesthesia to see how, what depth he was, because that's a good, pretty good notice of how deep anaesthesia is.

Captain Jim Mark RAMC, who had been held with Gordon Smith in Pudu Gaol in Kuala Lumpur for the first nine months of captivity, knew Gordon had been a medical student and encouraged him to join the medical team, training him in various techniques. Gordon said at interview that he found the work stimulating, but more importantly having a role, a purpose each day, was lifesaving. He felt it was 'probably the best part of my life as a POW there, doing that ... I used to help in various ways.'

Returning to Private Gordon Vaughan, in addition to his medical training, he brought into camp valuable skills and expertise that were literally life-saving. Born and brought up in Wallasey (across the Mersey from Liverpool), in the mid-1930s Vaughan trained as a telephone engineer with the General Post Office. At the outbreak of war he felt unable to serve as a fighting soldier and so, as a conscientious objector, he volunteered for medical work. He later said that his experiences during the war soon changed this moral stance. Captured at the Fall of Singapore, Vaughan worked first in the dysentery wards of Roberts Hospital before going up country to Chungkai Hospital camp in Thailand. He had contracted dysentery while in Singapore and was very ill at times during the rest of his captivity, as close friend and fellow RAMC medical orderly, Frank Scarr, recalled at interview, 'Unfortunately for Gordon, he went down with dysentery. He had bowel trouble more or less all the time he was POW and he couldn't stomach the rice as it was dished up.'

In 1998, a year before he died, Vaughan was one of the last of the veterans to attend for Tropical Disease Investigations (TDIs – see Introduction and Chapter 5) at the Tropical School. He was a retired dentist, a small, modest man who was seen by Geoff Gill. When asked about his experiences he described working as a medical orderly and offered to donate copies of various documents detailing some of his work. One document, running to three foolscap pages, handwritten by Vaughan, listed the number and types of operations carried out in three jungle hospital camps in Thailand: Tamarkan, Takanun and Chungkai. In all 4,577 operations had been performed, between December 1942 and August 1945, from bunions to brain surgery and everything in between.

Vaughan was involved in many of those operations, first as an orderly and before long as a surgical assistant to several RAMC surgeons. He also made a name for himself designing, making and repairing surgical instruments and equipment along with his friend, RAF Sergeant/Pilot Fred Margarson. Both men were skilled craftsmen; Margarson, from Grimsby, trained as a plumber pre-war and ran the workshop at Chungkai from 1943–1944. In a letter he wrote in June 1975 Margarson quoted the long list of jobs that came through his workshop including

> the repair of false teeth and spectacles to making Paul's tubing [large bore rubber tubing] ... making 200 stretchers in a day and a half ... constructed of rice sacks with bamboo side rails; bed [urine] bottles were made with bamboo and we repaired four gallon oil tins which were used for carrying food, made wooden legs, produced surgical instruments ... modified many pairs of scissors, by means of a charcoal brazier, into forceps.

Together Vaughan and Margarson, using discarded tin cans and other scrap, snipped, crimped and folded metal into watertight seams, wherever possible re-using the solder. They transformed cutlery into surgical instruments, with scalpels made from knives, retractors from forks and curettes, for scooping out infected wounds, out of spoons, the latter being sharpened on stones or with glass to give them a razor-like edge.[42] They made proctoscopes (instruments essential for close examination of the rectum) and a sigmoidoscope for viewing deeper into the bowel, both important in the detection and diagnosis of bowel disease. The latter, Frank Scarr recalled,

> [It] wasn't illuminated which was the unfortunate thing about it. It had two linings, it was entered [into the bowel] and then the inner lining, that's right, the inner lining was removed and there must have been spaces along the side of this otherwise they wouldn't have been able to see what they wanted to see … I wasn't in the camp when it was made, it was shown to me afterwards.'

They also devised an instrument for skin grafting which was done to try to heal damaged tissue caused by tropical ulcers. Scarr again:

> he brought [home] the copper tube with the penny soldered on the end and the reason for that, we were doing pinch grafts and we just had a needle to pick up the skin and it was cut underneath and it was taking hours to cover a small area. And Gordon got this piece of copper tube and he soldered this penny on the end and then he cut slots in the penny with a hacksaw and he put in some hypodermic needles about, I think it was about three inches long. And they were set at a slight angle and I think, I'm not sure, I think there were six needles on that, I may be wrong, but from memory I think there was about six needles on that …

But perhaps the most extraordinary device that Vaughan and Margarson created was one designed to help the very worst cases of dysentery. Men with chronic infection of the bowel were dying and the doctors reasoned that if they could rest the large bowel (where the dysenteric infection is sited) then it might be possible to save some of these patients. They tried a technique called ileostomy. This is when the small bowel is cut in two, the distal or end nearest the large bowel is closed with stitches and the proximal end (nearest the stomach) is brought out on to the surface of the abdomen forming a stoma, allowing liquid faecal matter to flow out.

The main problem was how to manage a constant flow of liquid faecal matter. Water bottles, in particular smaller Dutch issue which were strapped around the abdomen, had worked for colostomy patients but these would quickly fill with liquid effluent. Vaughan and Margarson came up with an

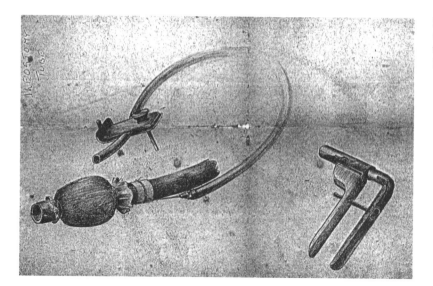

Figure 10 Self-retaining ileostomy tube with clamps (*LSTM collection*)

ingenious solution. They designed a self-retaining ileostomy tube. In 1998 Vaughan donated the original sketch above (Figure 10), together with the typed sheet explaining how it was made and worked, to Geoff Gill for the Tropical School's records.

It works like this. A section of Paul's tubing when passed into the stoma to rest inside the small bowel would not stay in place by itself, due to the peristaltic action of the muscles in the bowel wall which involuntarily squeezed it out. Their solution was to make a balloon at one end, using a condom or the finger of a rubber glove, the end of which was cut off and the rubber sheath slipped over one end of the Paul's tubing and tied into place with thread both top and bottom. Then a hypodermic needle, attached to a piece of stethoscope tubing was carefully run in under the thread at the external end of the tube so that it rested just inside the deflated durex band. The large tube, sheathed end first, was then inserted into the stoma until the sheath could no longer be seen.

Once in place, a syringe with approximately 30cc of air drawn into it, was attached to the small bore tubing with the needle and very gradually the plunger was depressed until most of the air was emptied, inflating the balloon inside the small bowel. This was a process of trial and error, the key being the patient's comfort. If more air was needed the small tube was sealed with a home-made clamp while more air was drawn up into the syringe. The process was repeated until the tube was held firmly in place by the balloon. Providing the patient was not in any discomfort, the needle was then carefully withdrawn. Once liquid was seen to pass through the large bore tubing indicating that the drainage was effective, then the larger clamp could be attached to the Paul's tubing and screwed flat to stem the flow. In this way the patient was able to take care of emptying the bowel as and when necessary. The operation was successfully performed several times. After the war, once the patients were receiving proper treatment, the operation was reversed.

It was evident from the paperwork that Gordon Vaughan donated to the Tropical School that there was one piece of information missing. In the typed description Vaughan had referred to parts of the assembly referenced by letters of the alphabet in brackets, eg (W). However, no such references appear on the drawing. There had to have been a third sheet of paper with some sort of diagram on it. By pure chance, months later on a trip to the IWM to view the diary of Captain Max Pemberton, there at the back of the folder was the missing sheet. It was quite clear what it was but unfortunately it is too faint to reproduce well. Having ordered a photocopy, it was compared to the other two documents to confirm that it was the document in question. The discovery was shared with Rod Suddaby who agreed that this was most likely the missing piece of information. He created a separate file in Gordon Vaughan's name and copies of the Tropical School documents with supporting correspondence were lodged together with a copy of the document found in Pemberton's file.

In June 1946 Dr Markowitz (Figure 11) paid tribute to Vaughan and his fellow orderlies in an article in the Canadian Reader's Digest. Describing his arrival at Chungkai in May 1943, Markowitz told how he found himself the sole surgical officer for 7,000 patients and realised that there were few surgical instruments with which to work. He recalled that

Vaughan offered to go to work right away. 'I've done a bit of tinkering at mechanics,' he said. 'If there's anything you need I could try and make it.' ... Gordon Vaughan's talents as an instrument maker were developing fast. He fashioned a rectal speculum, a rib cutter ... a tracheotomy tube and several spinal and hypodermic needles ... Private Vaughan had a hand in practically every important operation performed ...'

Vaughan also made Markowitz an amputation saw, a simple and effective instrument, it was simply a hacksaw blade with a wooden frame attached to it. Markowitz performed hundreds of amputations in a desperate attempt to save the lives of men dying from tropical ulcers. Hundreds more were done in camps across the tropics. Mostly it was feet and legs that were affected, minor scratches quickly becoming infected, developing into deep penetrating and suppurating ulcers, which if left resulted in fatal septicaemia (infection in the blood). Jack Chalker recalled how he too was involved in this work: 'Marko was designing, or trying to design, new flaps for thigh amputations and ... we were drawing this on little scraps of paper, how they were to be cut and I worked with him in theatre … wouldn't call it theatre, it was the end of a hut, really.'

The pencil sketch opposite (Figure 12) was drawn by trained artist Francis Kenneth Ellwell, a driver in the Royal Corps of Signals. It is significant for three reasons. Firstly, it is a fine example of documentary art, signed and dated 23 December 1943, with a detailed caption on the reverse. Captain Markowitz is clearly identifiable second right, looking across the patient at Private Gordon Vaughan who is assisting at the operation. The caption reads:

Artist's drawing of the scene in the jungle theatre during amputation of the thigh. It then lists the following: The team consisted of (left of patient): Major A.L. Dunlop (anaesthetist) RAMC, Private G. Vaughan RAMC (assisting), Private R. J. Woolridge RAMC; (right of patient): Private W. Tolson RAMC, Captain J. Markowitz RAMC, Sergeant T. J. Steggel SSVF. Patient under spinal anaesthesia.

This shows Markowitz's handpicked surgical team in action. Note the detail the artist has documented: the mosquito net tent hung within the hut to keep out the worst of the insects, the bamboo and wooden furniture, the bottles, tins and instruments, the range of footwear (and amazingly, socks!) and Sgt Steggel holding the operating table light.

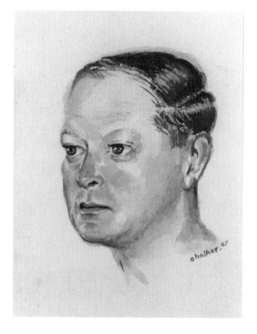

Figure 11 Medical Officer Captain Jacob Markowitz RAMC
(courtesy Jack Chalker)

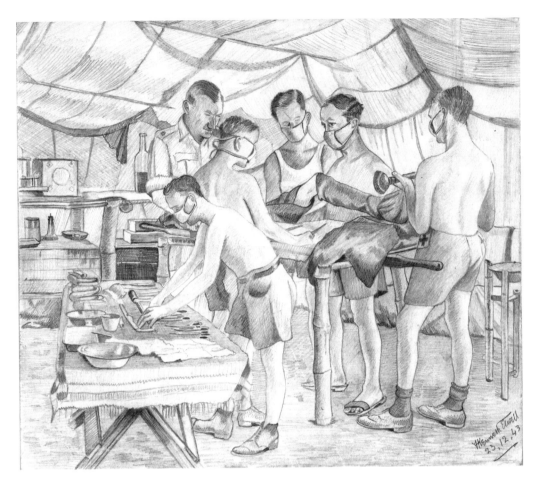

Figure 12 Operating theatre, Chungkai,
signed and dated 23 December 1943.
Markowitz (second right) facing Vaughan,
drawn by F. K. Ellwell
© *Imperial War Museums (Art.IWM ART LD 7189)*[43]

Secondly, this is the only known illustration of Vaughan during captivity. He had been promoted to Operating Room Assistant (ORA) Class III four months earlier, as evidenced by the entry for 25.8.43 in his Army Pay Book (Figure 12). Markowitz came to rely heavily on Vaughan during operations, as is seen in the handwritten testimonial dated November 1943 and signed by Markowitz (Figure 13), which he gave to Vaughan.

Thirdly, Elwell died the following year when he was being transported to Japan. The unmarked ship he was on was torpedoed and sunk by the Allies off the Philippines with the loss of hundreds of prisoners of war. He also did a sketch of the Chungkai dental surgery where Captain Arkush worked (see

Taken Prisoner of War at Singapore — 15.2.42
Graded N.O. II [illegible] — 20.4.42
Graded No. Cl. I Chungkai P.O.W. Hosp. — 28.5.43
Graded O.R.A. Cl. III Chungkai P.O.W. Hosp. — 25.8.43
Appointed A/Cpl. w.e.f. 1/2/44 Authy. Pt. II Orders No. 2 d. 4/5/44 by Lt Col. E.E. Dunlop – Chungkai P.O.W. Camp Hospital — 7/5/44
Promoted A/Sgt w.e.f. 5/2/45 Authy Part II Orders No 1d 5/2/45 by Maj. Pemberton RAMC Chungkai P.O.W Camp Hospital

He acted as my first assistant in the theatre during most of the Major Surgery. He was as valuable as a House Surgeon to me when we were short of medical officers.
Chung Kai Nov 20. 1943.
J Markowitz Capt RAMC, Surg. Spec.

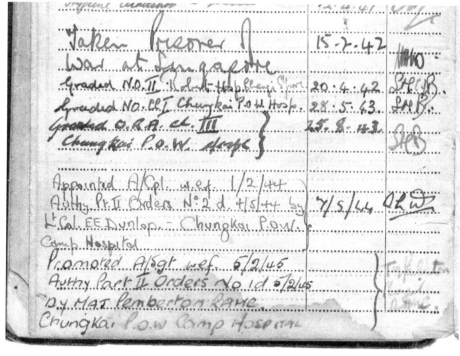

Figure 12 Vaughan's Army Pay Book, Notes of Training, donated by Vaughan family in 2010 (*LSTM collection*)

Figure 13 Extract from Markowitz's testimonial a note that Vaughan donated to LSTM in 1998 *(courtesy LSTM collection)*

page 139). He must have given these sketches to someone before leaving Thailand.

The extract reads: He acted as my first assistant in the theatre during most of the major surgery. He was as valuable as a House Surgeon to me when we were short of medical officers.

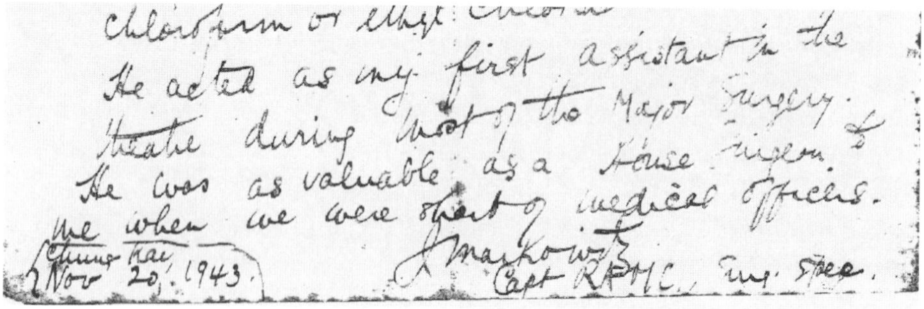

J. Markowitz Capt. RAMC
Chungkai Nov. 20, 1943.

As a footnote, following repatriation Vaughan applied to the University of Liverpool's School of Medicine in 1946 to train to be a surgeon. Sadly, even with Markowitz's glowing testimonial he was unsuccessful in his application for a bursary and therefore unable to take up a place. Undeterred however, he later secured a bursary to study dentistry, qualifying in 1955 and setting up practice in Northwich, Cheshire, where he remained until his retirement.

Jack Chalker worked closely with amputees both as an artist and a physiotherapist and he recalled the spirit of those courageous men.

> They had competitions to see, when the leg was off, as to who could be on crutches first. I mean, once again, this psychology, this mental side of it, played such a huge part in the whole game and, I had such admiration for them … they made a whole series of prostheses, starting first of all with a piece of bamboo which was split into three at the top (Figures 14 and 15). And the buckets [for the stump] were made from army packs … We used to collect the big seeds off the kapok trees when they came off I think in about May, and we collected any kapok we could, to make pads, and you could put that in an odd piece of material and crudely sew it up. We made some of our needles with odd bits of metal, very often taken off army equipment and beaten out. And so you could make pads for somebody who was in agony, to rest their head or their bodies, and also make all the padding for the tops of the buckets for the limbs.

Several other artists did similar studies of prosthetics during captivity, including Ronald Searle, Philip Meninsky and Stanley Gimson. Many of the larger hospital camps in the Far East had workshops where skilled craftsmen, supervised by senior surgical officers, designed, made and fitted artificial limbs made from bamboo, wood and metal. Jack's exquisitely detailed watercolour drawings (Figures 14 & 15) show in extraordinary detail the different designs and construction methods used at Chungkai in Thailand.

A year into captivity in Changi on Singapore Island, Captain R. Bradley 88th Field Regiment Royal Artillery was running a clandestine engineering unit in a small hut, working with a team of 12 Royal Army Ordnance Corps tradesmen. Their tools had been made or else 'acquired' by various means and the workload of repairs and maintenance was constant, though frequently hampered by guard patrols which proved irksome. So, one of the men got chatting to a friendly Japanese NCO after roll call one evening, and feigning a desire to learn Japanese, he carefully noted down the characters for various words: man, dog, tree, house, and workshop. Later he copied the latter on to a piece of wood, waited until the next change of guard and hung the sign on the hut door. The next guard patrol noted a Japanese workshop on their route and just walked on!

Bradley was a qualified engineer. He secretly made a small portable lathe for the workshop which could be taken with them if they were drafted off the

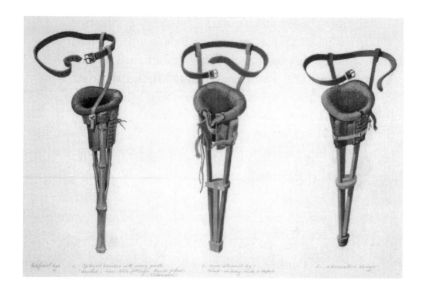

Figure 14 Bamboo and wooden prostheses *(courtesy of Jack Chalker)*

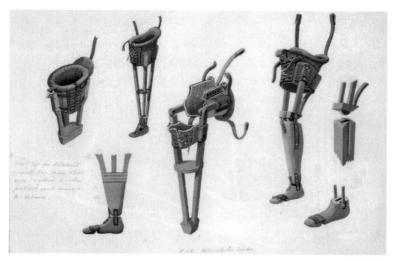

Figure 15 Wooden prostheses including articulating joints, knees, feet and toes *(courtesy of Jack Chalker)*

island. With an overall length of 17" and weighing 30lbs, the 2" back-geared screw cutting instrument lathe was put to good use making the specialist tools needed to produce artificial limbs, as well as a host of other tools and equipment. Bradley brought his lathe back home and it was exhibited at the Machine Tool and Engineering Exhibition held at Olympia in 1948.[44]

Bradley and his team worked closely with Julian Taylor, Consulting Surgeon Malaya Command, who designed many of the artificial limbs produced there. The photograph opposite (Figure 16) is believed to be of one of the limbs made in the Changi engineers' workshop. It is now in the Science Museum's store in London. Constructed from sheet metal taken from crashed aircraft fuselage, and with an articulated knee joint and wooden foot, it weighs in excess of

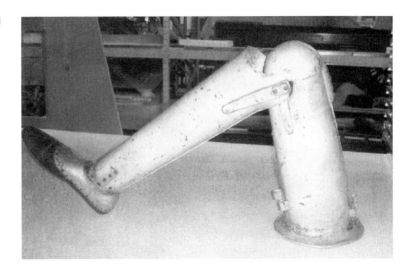

Figure 16 Made in Changi POW camp using aircraft fuselage, designed by Colonel Julian Taylor consulting surgeon, Malaya Command, now in the Science Museum in London *(author's photograph)*

7lbs. According to Bradley's article, the metal was provided by a sympathetic Japanese general. Bradley was keen on astronomy, as was the general, who also spoke good English, and instead of being sent up country Bradley was ordered to remain in Changi to instruct him in the subject. This 'friendly' contact was put to good use. When, later on, and with the knowledge of the Japanese, the Bradley's workshop was relocated to within the hospital area to make artificial limbs and surgical instruments, the general was informed about the work 'during an astronomy lesson ... and the difficulties occasioned by the shortage of tools and materials, with the result that he visited the shop himself, and a week or two later sent in a few hacksaw blades, files, twist drills, a quantity of aluminium rivets, and some light-alloy sheeting removed from crashed aircraft.'

There were many prototypes developed and refined. When the amputees returned home many of them refused to replace their limbs for British standard models, preferring to keep the original.

In Changi there was another large workshop, run by Malayan Volunteers, called Changi Rubber Factory (or Changi Industries Inc. as it was also known). It was the brainchild of Captain John G. Clemetson, a colonial administrator who utilised the skills and expertise of rubber planters, tin miners, engineers and others to manufacture and repair just about anything that was needed in camp. Everything from toothbrushes, paper, spectacles, boots, shoes and bandages to the sandpaper needed in the workshop. They tapped the rubber trees growing in the camp and used the latex. They dug up the laterite clay and ground that into powder for various processes. Sewing needles were made from bicycle spokes and scrap material of any sort was put to good use.

The work of the rubber factory was immortalised by British artist

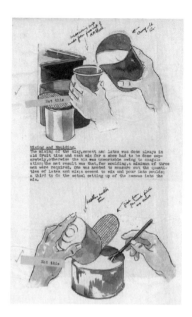

Figure 17 Changi Rubber Factory. Mixing and Moulding latex, drawn and captioned by Lance Corporal Des Bettany *(courtesy Changi Museum. To see more of Bettany's work visit www.changipowart.com)*

Lance Bombardier Desmond Bettany 88 Field Regiment at the time. This example (Figure 17) both illustrates and describes how latex produced from tapping rubber trees was processed to make soles for shoes. His detailed and humorous cartoons were used to illustrate a book, produced in 2005 by Changi University Press for Changi Museum, entitled, *Don't ever say It Can't Be Done* (a play on Clemetson's motto 'Never say, it can't be done!'). Born and raised in Lancashire, Bettany was a prolific artist in captivity. As well as recording the ingenuity of various workshops in Changi, he was also involved with theatrical productions producing dozens of bill board posters, programmes and stage sets. His artwork can be viewed online at www.changipowart.com where his sons have created an excellent tribute to their father's work as a Far East POW artist.

Suture Material

This was in short supply in the more remote camps and again great ingenuity prevailed. In Burma, van Boxtel made suture from animals: livestock for the cookhouse were stripped of skin, bone and sinew and nothing was wasted. He took the peritoneum from pigs or cattle and converted it into 'catgut' by cutting lengths, twisting them on a winder and then drying them. Next it was sterilised and immersed in ether, before being finally stored in alcohol and iodine.[45] Doctors elsewhere used cotton thread and silk from parachute cord for effective suturing. Cushing's haemostatic silver clips were fashioned from silver table forks considerably reducing the risks of haemorrhage.

Red soldier ants had their uses too. Harry Hesp, aged 17 when interned, went on daily woodcutting parties into the jungle collecting firewood for the Changi Gaol cookhouse. One particular incident he recalled vividly. It was when one of the lads had sustained

a very deep cut on his hand caused by a parang (a knife) ... We had nothing to wrap round it but one of the other prisoners ... a Malayan planter, immediately knew what to do. ... we'd been sat on a fallen tree and without knowing it hundreds of red ants, which are about an inch or so long, and were crawling up our arms and legs ... if you let them alone ... they wouldn't bite. ... this planter put [the lad's] hand ... where the ants where, and the ants crawled all over his hand and as soon as there were enough he knocked them off. ... every one of those would bite, bury its head into your skin and nip. ... they'd covered the cut ... the planter then snapped the bodies from the heads which remained and which sealed the wound up enough for us to get him back to Changi – the prison – without bleeding too much.

Figure 18 Red soldier ant showing 5cm wide mandibles

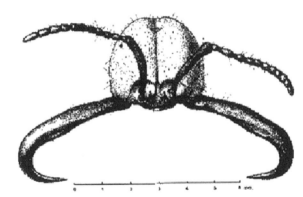

Figure 19 Left: ant clasps skin edges with mandibles. Right: body nipped off leaving mandible 'clip' in place [46]

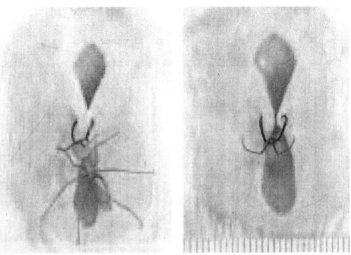

This method of wound suturing is still in use in native communities in South America and elsewhere (see Figures 18 and 19).

Wound management in the Tropics presented many challenges, especially as by 1943 men had few if any clothes left and wound dressing material was almost non-existent. Sometimes leaves were used as wound coverings to keep out flies. Rubber trees were tapped and the latex used in a variety of ways as Doug Skippen recalled, patching his clothes by 'cutting the bark of a rubber tree and rubbing the raw latex which bleeds from the cut on to the clothing, it then sticks very well and a patch can be put over another patch.' This system was adapted by him and others to make adhesive dressings for wounds.

Dentistry

There were not enough dental officers or equipment to go around. In Singapore and Batavia, former civilian dentists serving in the Volunteer Forces were sometimes allowed to transfer equipment from their surgeries into camp. In Thailand most dentists had very little equipment, dental instruments or supplies, such as anaesthetic, 'compo' (the soft material used for making dental impressions) and amalgam for fillings. Captain Eric Smith and his colleague, unofficial rabbi Captain David Arkush, were lucky to keep their smaller dental instruments with them after leaving Changi.

At Chungkai the men made him a fully articulated dental chair from bamboo, complete with adjustable head rest, spittoon, instrument tray and even a footrest, complete with useful bracing bars for his patients (Figure 20). David remembered that with 'some local anaesthetic I was able to do temporary fillings ... zinc oxide and oil of cloves makes a temporary filling which is really not bad at all. It lasts, many of my fillings lasted years, so I was told.'

In the Chungkai workshops Fred Margarson made dental forceps (Figure 21) from scissors and repaired a pair of long dental swab forceps belonging to Captain Smith.

In more remote camps there were often no dentists. At Taihoku in Taiwan, medical officer Major Ben Wheeler, deputised as dentist and used psychology in place of anaesthetic, making great play of filling a syringe with distilled water before undertaking extractions. Men lost teeth due to malnutrition or injury inflicted by guards and dentures were made using vulcanized rubber or aluminium mess tins, with teeth removed from the dentures of dead men. David Arkush also recounted how they repaired dentures, 'you drilled a hole with a broken instrument, holes down each side and with floss silk which we had, you tied it across ... or you took a Dutch mess tin ... and you riveted it over the crack. There were various methods you could use.'

On occasion he also used silver wire, as can be seen in this photograph of

Figure 20 Dental surgery at Chungkai with
bamboo chair made by the engineers.
Sketch by F K Elwell, January 1944
(courtesy Army Medical Services Museum)

Figure 21 Pair of
dental forceps
adapted from
scissors made by Fred
Margarson *(courtesy
of Margarson family)*

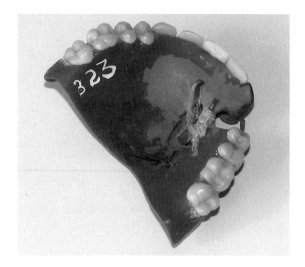

Figure 22 Dental plate made from vulcanized rubber and repaired with wire *(courtesy of the Army Medical Services Museum)*

Figure 23 Sketch of RAF dental officer Clifford Beale's surgery on Haruku, 1943By RAF medical officer Richard Philps *(courtesy Carol Friend)*

a surviving, repaired denture (Figure 22). A sketch of the dental surgery on the island of Haruku has only recently come to light. The illustration (Figure 23) was drawn by an RAF Medical Officer, Flight/Lieutenant Richard 'Dickie' Philps and shows his colleague RAF dental officer Clifford Beale's dental surgery.

Nursing

Basic nursing care was provided by both trained nursing orderlies as well as untrained volunteers and throughout the book there are many examples of their work. Bamboo proved to be indispensable commodity to make the equipment and utensils needed. Doug Skippen described at interview how they had made bedpans. 'Well, we got the largest piece of bamboo that we could get and they're sectionalised so we cut outside the section so that the bedpan was about that length. Then we sawed down and took the top ... if you cut into bamboo you get a very, very sharp edge so you scrape it off.'

Arthur Turbutt recalled that, in the Spice Islands, bamboo was used for coffins. 'The body was taken away to where the undertakers where, the three or four men who were doing nothing but making coffins from bamboo. And the bodies were put into the bamboo coffin and taken away into the part of the jungle where they were buried in shallow graves.'

In Paul Gibbs-Pancheri's book *Volunteer!* Lance Corporal Geoffrey Mowat, Singapore Settlements Volunteer Force (SSVF), an untrained volunteer medical orderly in camps on the Thailand–Burma Railway, described his effective method for cleaning bedpans, where the orderly would 'clean up the patient, take the used bamboo bedpan to the latrine, and if the rain was not adequate to clean it out quickly, he would urinate into it to get rid of the contents, then plough his way back through the mud.'

Those who were nursed back to health night and day, week after week, by men who knew how to care, were then encouraged to play their part. Sick men made bandages, ground charcoal into powder and whittled bamboo into utensils. Kinship, creativity and knowledge were the bywords for survival in Far East POW camps. Even the dead played their part and helped their mates to survive. Post-mortems confirmed or contradicted diagnoses, thereby increasing medical knowledge. Indian Medical Service pathologist, Captain Jack Ennis, performed well over one hundred post-mortems (PM) in Roberts, and later Kranji, hospital camps in Singapore during his captivity. From his diary it appears his first PM was done on Monday 2 March, pulmonary embolism being the cause of death. The following day he notes that he started work as pathologist in the laboratory at Roberts Hospital. On Tuesday 10 March his diary reads: 'An awful night spent in the Lab, faeces, smell, flies and dysentery patients, dropped bedpans. I suppose I shall get used to this eventually. Had Japanese pathologists working in the Lab. Looking at our dysentery cases, took away about 100 cultures. Most were uncommunicative and technique was poor ...' His detailed diary, pathology notes and PM reports, all written up in his small, compact handwriting, were kept hidden throughout captivity and brought home.[47]

Doug Skippen worked on the dysentery wards at Roberts Hospital and may well have worked alongside Captain Ennis in the mortuary, as Doug recalled he had 'had my initiation of post mortems. These took place daily as the medical officer tried to understand the diseases better. Eventually I was to do post-mortems on my own behind only a sacking screen. No apron or gloves were provided, just a scalpel. A gruesome job, which had to be done.'

In Hong Kong at POW Camp 'N', Shamshuipo, the same work was going on. It was recorded on 1 September 1944 by Lieutenant Alexander Skvorzov, a Russian serving with the Hong Kong Volunteer Defence Corps, who drew a pencil sketch of three doctors (one of whom is Captain Arthur William Booth Strachan) undertaking a post-mortem. They can also be seen removing teeth which were used to make dentures. The sketch was kept by Captain Strachan RAMC, and this drawing is now in the collection of Museum of World War II in Boston Massachusetts, USA. Captain Strachan, who was the great grandson of William Booth founder of the Salvation Army, was to become a consultant surgeon in Cumbria post-war.

Figure 24 Sketch of post mortem at Shamshuipo by Alexander Skvorzov, September 1944 *(courtesy Museum of WWII, Boston, USA, by kind permission L. Estes)*

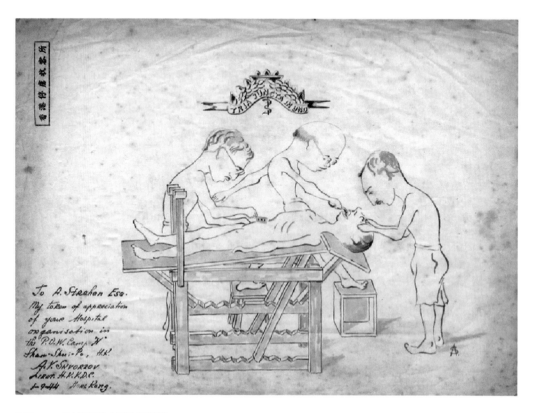

Medical assistant Arthur Turbutt recalled that in Java and Haruku, 'Doctors did carry out PMs just to see what was happening to the bodies and from that they gained a lot of experience. They found what organs had shrunk, that sort of thing.'

Conclusion

Eyewitness accounts of medical care in captivity in the Far East highlight the ingenuity and resourcefulness which enabled many men to survive. Allied doctors, denied the basic necessities to sustain human life, only managed to practise medicine effectively in captivity by marshalling the wealth of talent and skill in their midst. But were these exceptional circumstances or were conditions similar for Allied prisoners of war in Europe? From examination of the comparative death rate statistics (Patrick and Heaf, 1946) it is clear that Allied prisoners in the Far East were five times more likely to die in captivity than those in Europe. Those captured in Europe fared far better than their Far Eastern counterparts in virtually every respect, but in particular with regard to medical care. The Germans observed the tenets of the 1929 Third Geneva Conventions, article 14 of which stated that:

> Each camp shall possess an infirmary, where prisoners of war shall receive attention of any kind of which they may be in need ... It shall be permissible for belligerents ... to retain in the camps doctors and medical orderlies for the purpose of caring for their prisoner compatriots. Prisoners ... whose condition necessitates important surgical treatment, shall be admitted, at the expense of the detaining Power, to any military or civil institution qualified to treat them.

Allied POW in Europe did not have to spend time and energy improvising the basic necessities of medical practice. Their main problem was boredom which for many led to a preoccupation with planning escapes. And in this they at least had a fighting chance of success, being Europeans in European captivity. Not so in the Far East, where western prisoners of war could not hope to merge into the background of Asian civilian life. In Europe prisoners of war were often housed in existing camps (set up during WWI) and there were no appreciable differences in climate, diet or mores to adapt to, whereas in the Far East there was not just the tropical climate to acclimatise to, there was also a gulf in understanding between two cultures, the Orient and the West.

As the Japanese did not accept responsibility for providing more than the most basic level of medical care, FEPOW medical officers came to rely heavily on the expertise and inventiveness of the 'citizens' army' of men from all walks of life who took into captivity with them a vast array of skills and knowledge, as well as innate goodwill. Through this combination of medical expertise and the pool of talents an extraordinary feat was accomplished. Allied doctors slowly overcame seemingly hopeless adversity and prevailed. Some of the sickest men recovered thanks to blood transfusions performed in tents and huts in jungle clearings; blind men stumbling around coral islands regained their sight as a result of regular doses of home-made 'marmite'; and some of those dying, did not, perhaps because a former plumber created a vital instrument out of an old milk tin or table fork. As Jack Chalker said in his interview,

> You put a geneticist and a pharmacist and a tinsmith, all these people together and you've begun to move a bit of the mountain ... this was a kind of corporate effort of survival simply because of all the different skills that we all had. And if you had enough energy and enough guts and enough of a willingness to do it, then it worked. And I think that was pretty magical.

Many men discovered a reason to live by helping others to survive. Again, Jack Chalker summed it up when talking about his work assisting surgeons Markowitz and Dunlop in Thailand.

> It provided me with some survival kit. And this was so important. It was like the others ... they all had something to do, something to try and achieve ... I think that was a privilege to me ... the fact also that I could work with these marvellous people, with Marko, and subsequently with Weary and others, but particularly those two, especially Weary, because you felt you had to support them, you couldn't let them down. I mean these are a godsend, these were magic people to us. And so there was a very happy obligation as well. But it was one's own pride that you daren't let them down somehow. And I think that played a huge part in survival.

CHAPTER 4

REPATRIATION AND HOMECOMING

T HERE WERE JUST OVER 37,500 survivors repatriated from the Far East when the war ended in August 1945. Many had to wait up to five weeks before the camps could be located and medical teams sent to oversee their liberation and the orderly evacuation of the former captives. This chapter examines how captivity ended and liberation of the camps, the repatriation process, how families coped and settling back into family and working life.

Far East war ends

The end of the war in the Far East was swift and decisive. The Allies had fought for over three years against a determined enemy and despite facing invasion of their homeland and certain defeat, the Japanese repeatedly refused to surrender. Many interviewees recalled how the behaviour of the guards became increasingly unpredictable and aggressive during the final months of captivity. Ed Knight recalled his final camp in Japan. When Zentsuji propaganda camp had closed in June 1945, Ed and a hundred other British officers were transferred to Miyata, a coal mining camp in the mountains of Kyushu in June 1945. Conditions there were very harsh when they joined the largely Dutch camp.

> This is where I really got beaten up and y'know you've got no flesh on your body and they go along beating you. Of course, we're now into early August 1945 when they were feeling the pressure. The Americans were coming over with low flying aircraft and strafing them and they didn't like that at all and they were

taking it out on us and beating us. Just the officers not the men, just to please the men; they thought it might please the men. I don't think it did.

What Ed alluded to was not just the usual aggression meted out by the guards, but a specific incident affecting all the British officers who had been transferred to Miyata from Zentsuji. It took place after evening roll call on 8 August 1945 and was described in vivid detail by Flight Lieutenant John Fletcher-Cooke RAFVR, in his book, *The Emperor's Guest*[1] and by Captain Duncan, both of whom were there with Ed. The Japanese sergeant in charge of the camp that night had decided that the newcomers needed to be reminded who was in charge. Duncan later recorded that

> We were lined up on the parade ground ... in two files, given a haranguing by the Jap duty NCO – a sadistic swine by the name of Kurihara – who ended up by telling us about the British misdeeds in India and that he was going to show us what a Jap NCO could do to British officers. For the next forty minutes we had to stand at attention with our arms stretched above our heads while guards, armed with 2" x 4" timbers prowled up and down the files, viciously beating anyone who moved ... we were ordered to assume the prone position and the real beating commenced. Every prisoner was savagely beaten ... the end of the spine and the kidney region being the favourite target areas.[2]

In the month or so before, as bombing raids on Japanese cities, ports and industry intensified, reprisals against the prisoners became more frequent and ferocious. Both Fletcher-Cooke and Duncan also made reference to so-called 'air raid precautions' which took place at Miyata from mid-July 1945 onwards, with prisoners herded into the entrance to a disused mineshaft by young boys, members of a Youth Corps, wielding sticks. There they stood for hours, facing guards with machine guns pointing into the mine.[3] They were in no doubt about the implications of this 'drill' should the Allies have invaded Japanese soil.

Aircraftman Second Class (AC2) Sydney Whitehead RAF, who had arrived in Singapore from Java in spring 1943, recalled at interview that in the closing months a friendly guard gave them a warning. The POW were excavating large tunnels

> in Kranji valley ... three men would build a tunnel two metres square, twenty metres in. Twenty metres away another tunnel would be built, we would then turn left and right, build a big, bigger cavern in the centre. These places would be used by the Japanese to store food and ammunition because they expected the Allies to invade ... On the tunnel Jock, myself and another guy was working, we

had a tall Japanese [guard] ... he was very considerate, he never lost his temper ... so we got on very well with him ... On one occasion ... he drew maps in the sand base, the ground, and he explained that the British were pushing the Japs out of Burma, this would be, I think maybe about June '45. We knew nothing about this ... 'But,' he said, 'You have a problem. The order from the Japanese High Command ... when the Allies invade ... all the prisoners were to be executed.'

In some camps in Thailand, prisoners on working parties were ordered to dig deep trenches with bunds (embankments) right around the perimeter, ostensibly as air raid trenches. In Nong Pladuk where Charles Peall was held, he recalled that 'the Japanese had ... built right round the camp a big ditch and we wondered what the hell that was for.' At Nakom Patom camp, 'Weary' Dunlop noted in his diary on 12 July 1945 that a Korean guard had told him that any invasion would result in a massacre of POW. He believed that was likely especially as guns mounted around the perimeter of the camp faced inwards.

When interviewed Jack Chalker remembered that the same

small Korean guard that used to come in, who loved music ... had never beaten anybody up, he was a funny kind of, little Micky Mouse. And it was he who warned us that we're all, he said, 'All men finiskar.' And he didn't like it ... he was trying to tell us the Japanese order had gone out and all prisoners were going to be shot.

Evidence of the official Japanese order to exterminate all prisoners of war was found by the Allies at Taihoku camp on Taiwan in the Journal of the Taiwan POW Camp HQ in Taihoku, entry 1 August 1944. A photocopy of a document citing this order was given to the Tropical School by Steve Cairns in 2012. It was from a file of documents gathered by British Intelligence for the War Crimes Trials. The second of two points reads:

The following answer about the extreme measures for POWs was sent to the Chief of Staff of the 11th Unit (Formosa POW Security No. 10).

... at such time as the situation became urgent and it be extremely important, the POWs will be concentrated and confined in their present location and under heavy guard the preparation for the final disposition will be made.

Under point (2) The Methods it reads:

(a)   Whether they are destroyed individually or in groups, or however it is done, the mass bombing, poisonous smoke, poisons, drowning, decapitation, or what, dispose of them as the situation dictates.

(b)   In any case it is the aim not to allow the escape of a single one, to annihilate them all, and not to leave any traces.

In the last months of the war, in addition to the Americans' island by island conquests across the Sea of Japan, British-led forces in Burma were regaining ground from the retreating Japanese. A vast multi-national Allied fleet, led by the Americans and including the British Pacific Fleet and Australian ships, assembled in the Pacific in preparation for the invasion of Japan. To the west huge numbers of British and colonial forces had amassed in India and were now moving eastwards to the island of Ceylon (now Sri Lanka) as part of Operation Zipper, the planned invasion of Malaya, Singapore and the Dutch East Indies. By early August, with no sign of the Japanese surrendering despite clear warnings of dire consequences, the Americans unleashed their secret weapon on the population of Hiroshima, an industrial city on the east coast of Honshu Island. On 6 August, the world's first atomic bomb obliterated the city in an instant. Of an estimated population of 350,000, up to 75,000 died immediately, with roughly the same number dying in the next four months. Once more the Allies called for the Japanese to surrender. Japanese military High Command again refused. Three days later the southern port city of Nagasaki on the island of Kyushu experienced the full force of the second atomic bomb. This time out of a population of 270,000 the immediate death toll was approximately 40,000 with a similar number dying in the following four months. After this attack, and with the threat of a third atomic bomb now a reality, the Emperor of Japan took control from the military regime and ordered his forces to surrender to the Allies. In his first ever radio broadcast he told his people that Japan had surrendered. This signalled both the end of both the war in the Far East and the Second World War.

However, it was not only the populations of two large industrial cities who were killed by the atomic explosions. The Allies were unaware that up to 350 Allied POW – American, British, Australian and Eurasian – were in work camps in Nagasaki. At Saiwaimachi, a camp less than a mile from the epicentre of the blast, up to 80 POW were killed. Some had lucky escapes, like Corporal Alistair Urquhart Gordon Highlanders, who was in Omuta camp a few kilometres from Nagasaki. When interviewed over 62 years later he recalled that 'I was in the camp ... I just had a terrible blast of sort of wind you might call it, and it knocked me sideways and I'd no idea what it was. I thought it was one of these typhoons or something.'

RAF Medical Officer Squadron Leader Aidan MacCarthy, in his memoir *A Doctor's War*, recalled being in a nearby coal mine north of Nagasaki when 'a blue flash, accompanied by a very bright magnesium-type flare ... a frighteningly loud but rather flat explosion which was followed by a blast of hot air.

Some of this could be felt even by us as it came through the shelter openings.'

Royal Navy Gunnery Officer Frank Twiss, HMS *Exeter*, which was sunk in the battle of the Java Sea in March 1942, was at Mitsushima camp in Japan when he learned about the atom bombs. 'We got hold of a [Japanese] newspaper … and learned enough to know that a great bomb had been dropped on Hiroshima. This bomb … had disposed of Hiroshima in the twinkling of an eye and was known to us as the 'twinkle bomb'.[4]

The Allies, who had been making plans for the repatriation of Far Eastern captives for some time, had not expected a sudden capitulation and end to hostilities.

Repatriation planning

In 1939, at the outbreak of the Second World War, the War Office was charged with responsibility for prisoner of war issues, the Army being by far the largest of the services. When, in June 1940, over 40,000 men were captured at Dunkirk, the scale of the task of managing the needs of both prisoners of war and their families was fully realised. The Directorate of Prisoners of War was established and placed in overall charge of the various organisations involved.[5] The Royal Navy and the Royal Air Force were encouraged to maintain military responsibility for their own personnel and families as was the Foreign Office Prisoner of War Information Bureaux, the establishment of which had been enshrined in Article 77 of the 1929 Geneva Conventions. Finally, the Prisoner of War Committee of the British Red Cross and the order of St John of Jerusalem, was also closely involved. Inevitably, not all of these organisations worked together harmoniously or efficiently. Often instructions or advice issued by one was later countermanded or negated by the actions of others.

By July 1942, meetings involving all parties had been held at the War Office to draw up plans to deal with the enormous task of bringing home prisoners of war from captivity in both the European and Far East.[6] The War Office was advised by Dr A. T. 'Tommy' Macbeth Wilson, a civilian psychiatrist attached to the department, that careful planning was needed to help and support repatriated POW if they were to prevent the problems faced by ex-servicemen after the First World War. Thousands of men de-mobbed after years in the trenches had been literally abandoned by society during the inter-war years, left without welfare, medical care or support to help them to reintegrate into civilian and family life.[7] No-one accepted responsibility for their care.

Wilson had studied the work of psychiatrists during and after the First World War, men like German psychiatrist Dr A. L. Vischer who, in 1919, published the results of his lengthy study into the psychological trauma caused by captivity during wartime, in which he coined the expression 'barbed-wire disease'.[8] Wilson knew that since publication, little notice had been taken of Vischer's research and had himself undertaken extensive research interviewing former First World War veterans of captivity to identify the specific problems they had experienced. He argued strongly that the government and the Army could not allow such a social and personal disaster to happen again as they had a duty to care for these servicemen. Eighteen months later Major Philip Newman RAMC (a surgeon attached to RAMC) added his analysis of Vischer's work to the debate in an article in the British Medical Journal entitled *The Prisoner of War Mentality*, detailing the psychological and emotional disturbance encountered by the long-term captives. Vischer had been particularly concerned about the state of mind of captive servicemen and the long-term effects of captivity after release. At the start of his article, Newman noted that, 'the number of prisoners ultimately returning to this country alone will be many hundreds of thousands ... it is quite obvious, therefore, that the organization dealing with repatriation of these people constitutes one of our more important post-war problems.' He went on to develop his theory that the situation faced by returned POW was similar to that experienced by deep sea divers who, while adapting to working at great depths had to take great care in their return to the surface. Newman recommended the establishment of a prisoner of war club in all large towns to provide a place where men could meet and talk freely and of one rehabilitation centre for the country, with consultant psychologists and a trained rehabilitation staff.

It was generally accepted that former Far East prisoners of war would need to return home slowly with all the necessary skilled help available to them. A long, slow sea journey would allow time to acclimatise to their freedom and for their physical, psychological and emotional recovery to begin.[9] They needed time to prepare for the changes that had taken place at home, both domestically and politically, to catch up on news and current events. A long sea voyage would be beneficial and would also allow time for preparations to be made at home. When the war ended, South East Asia Command (SEAC), who had controlled Allied operations in the Far East, now spearheaded the work of the various agencies gathering to assist.

The British had established an organisation for the Recovery of Allied Prisoners of War and Internees (known as RAPWI). It had only just completed the evacuation of prisoners of war from camps across Europe when the war in the Far East ended. Staff and resources were hurriedly re-directed and sent to the region. The British Red Cross and St John's War Organisation immediately ordered their personnel, waiting in readiness in Iraq, India and Australia, to proceed to designated centres at Rangoon in Burma, Bangkok in Thailand, Hong Kong and Singapore. The American Red Cross similarly moved their staff to Manila in the Philippines and both Yokohama and Nagasaki in Japan.

Meanwhile, the British Pacific fleet was hurriedly being transformed into a repatriation force. Aircraft carriers steamed for the nearest Australian ports to offload now redundant aircraft and convert the hangars into vast temporary dormitories and wards, before heading north again as part of the repatriation fleet. The Royal Navy's HMS *Implacable* was already in port in Sydney replenishing supplies when the news broke that the war was over. 'The first step was to hold a big meeting on board at which all authorities concerned were represented. This included the Red Cross ... and NAAFI ... it was decided the ship would be able to carry about 150 officers and 2,000 other ranks ... the limiting factors were lavatory and washing facilities.'[10]

In Ceylon, Operation Zipper forces had been on the brink of the invasion of Malaya and Singapore when they were stood down and hurriedly reassigned. Some formed a repatriation force to move immediately into Malaya and Singapore, while the rest were assigned to assist the Dutch in quelling the Indonesian uprising (which had begun in earnest as soon as the Japanese had surrendered and threatened the break-up of the Netherlands East Indies). The transformation happened within a week or two, a remarkable feat of organisation and cooperation involving tens of thousands of Allied servicemen and civilian support staff of different nationalities.

Back in the camps, how the prisoners of war became aware that the war had ended varied widely. In camps with a secret radio or where men were working in factories alongside the local population, news of the Japan's surrender spread rapidly. Not knowing how their former captors might react to the news of defeat, senior Allied officers in camps advised the men to suppress celebrations and rejoicing initially. In parts of Thailand, British and American Special Forces personnel arrived in camps, sometimes within hours of the capitulation. They had been in the vicinity for several weeks, working alongside Thai and Chinese resistance fighters. Elsewhere along the railway, in the more remote camps, men were still unaware more than a week or two after the surrender. Often the first indication was the disappearance overnight of all the camp guards.

In general the first days of liberation were an anxious time and prisoners took great care for fear of reprisals by Japanese guards or, in Japan itself, the civilian population. Where possible Allied senior officers took over control of the camp from Japanese commanders; the first priority was to establish discipline and order to prevent needless deaths or acts of retribution. Some interviewees recalled the rejoicing and celebrations when they finally realised their captivity was over, others a feeling of anticlimax or disbelief.

In the book *Burma Railway*, published posthumously in 1984, medical officer Captain Robert Hardie FMSVF was at Tamuang camp and wrote in his diary: 'It was over. We were free again ... it was almost impossible to grasp ... one just felt rather numb, rather shaky and rather inclined to sob ... one tried to grasp what had happened ... as one thought of friends who had earlier looked forward to the same release but had found a different one.'

Liberation of the camps

While the locations of many camps were known to the Allies some took weeks to find. The men spelt out the letters 'P O W' or 'JAPS GONE' on the roofs of buildings or open ground, to attract the attention of reconnaissance aircraft.[11] As soon as the war ended each Allied nation was allocated specific areas of responsibility for repatriation: the Americans spearheaded the liberation of areas north of Manila (with the exception of Hong Kong which was evacuated by the British). The British, Australian, Canadian and Dutch liberating forces concentrated their efforts on Singapore, Thailand, Burma, Borneo, the Celebes and the Dutch East Indies. The Russians liberated camps in Manchuria with General Chiang Kai Shek's forces responsible for the rest of China.

Once minesweepers had cleared sea routes into Singapore, Rangoon, Batavia, Manila, Yokohama and Nagasaki, ships carrying tons of relief supplies began arriving at these designated evacuation ports. The British Red Cross had stockpiled food, medicines and clothing in India and Australia in preparation for the repatriation.[12] As RAPWI and Red Cross staff, both men and women, arrived in the main embarkation ports to prepare for the sudden influx of thousands of former POW, some were sent out immediately to the camps to assess the needs and liaise with their respective headquarters.

For many former prisoners of war, female Red Cross or RAPWI staff were the first European women they had seen in over three and a half years. Some men recalled how awkward they had felt while others remembered 'these angels' appearing in their midst. Victor Cole recalled in Rangoon that 'the first people we saw were some English nurses, and I never felt so embarrassed in all my life, I felt so embarrassed in their company ... terrible.'

In Japan Geoff Stott was evacuated from his shipyard camp across the bay from Nagasaki by US Naval personnel who arrived in landing craft.

They took cases straight away on the boat back to Nagasaki where there was a brand new hospital ship, its maiden voyage, tied up on the jetty. And later we were told by the sailors that they'd steam hose-piped all the jetty and all the buildings that hadn't been flattened to make them into a reception centre. And when they'd taken the mainly sick away they said, 'We'll be back tomorrow to take you all off.'

Figure 1 Photograph of the streets of Nagasaki prior to evacuating liberated POW, September 1945 *(A. A Duncan collection)*

And the next morning about twenty of these large landing craft came round and the man was there with a large flag waving them in and a man with a whistle and he said, 'Twenty on that one and twenty on that one.' And we steamed back to Nagasaki and went through the reception centre, and we stripped off, went through a shower. If any of the clothing you had on was new from air drops you were given a small kit bag to put it in and put your name on and that was being fumigated as you were going through medical inspection and then you got brand new American blue shirts and trousers and shoes and then you were ... taken out to an American aircraft carrier where you were put in the main hangar deck of the aircraft carrier where they had got all camp bed things.

On 19 September Captain Duncan and the others in Miyata were put on a train to Nagasaki arriving on the same quayside as Stott. He noted that the 'men of the US Navy and Marine Corps cheered us and then led us to a canteen where we were given doughnuts and coffee and where two ladies of the American Red Cross bade us all a welcome.' After the same process as Stott, they boarded a barge and headed out to an American ship, LST 795 (Landing Ship Tanks), his final comment being: 'All this occupied less than three quarters of an hour and is the finest piece of organising I have ever seen.'

The photograph (Figure 1) was taken by US Coastguard officer Lt Richard Nomsen, serving on LST 795. The ship anchored in Nagasaki Bay but there was a delay in the evacuation as a typhoon ripped through the area. Nomsen and a friend spent time ashore, touring what was left of the city in a Jeep. On the two-day voyage south to Okinawa he and Captain Duncan, an avid photographer, shared a cabin. Nomsen gave three of his recent photographs to Duncan, one of the ships' crew which he wrote on the back of, and two of Nagasaki.

In many camps, as soon as the senior Allied officers took control stockpiles of Red Cross stores, some dating back two or more years, were immediately distributed among the men.[13] Airlifts of emergency rations of food, clothing and medicines were dropped into camps within hours of the surrender. But many in more remote areas such as New Guinea, Borneo, Java and Sumatra, or in small unknown camps elsewhere, had much longer to wait for any relief aid.

Reg Davis was one of several men interviewed who recalled the danger of the relief supply air drops. 'There were injuries and even fatalities when parachutes on the large metal drums failed or they crashed into huts, or men deranged by hunger ran into the path of the large metal containers.'

As well as relief supplies men also dropped into camps from the air. Jewish dental officer, David Arkush, vividly and emotionally recalled the moment following the liberation of his camp by Captain Ross (a Special Operations Executive officer who had been parachuted in), when he first learned about the Holocaust.

> He started to tell us about what had gone on, y'know while we'd been imprisoned. He told me about the Holocaust … think I retired to bed in tears when I heard the terrible news. And the people I'm really sorry for are the Dutch Jews because amongst the Dutch prisoners were quite a number of Dutch Jews who, after all we'd been through, had yet to learn that their families in Holland had been murdered.

Medical officers in camp warned against the dangers of over-eating and this was reinforced by strict dietary guidelines supplied with each consignment. RAF medical officer Flight Lieutenant Richard Philps recalled in his book, *Prisoner Doctor*, how in Changi Gaol after the surrender, loudspeakers were fitted throughout the camp so news could be broadcast and 'we learned how dietary experts were to be flown to us to advise on the weaning process we would need to get us back to European food.' This 'weaning' was to prevent what is now known as 're-feeding syndrome', which was first described after the end of the Second World War.[14] Despite all the warnings and being advised to take slow and systematic re-nourishment, regrettably deaths due to over-eating still occurred. In some camps as relief supplies built up former captives distributed excess food and commodities to neighbouring villages were the locals were also starving.

At Hoten camp in Manchuria within a week of the surrender and their liberation by Russian forces, the most senior Allied military personnel (British, Dutch, American, Canadian and Australian, above the rank of colonel) and government officials such as the former Governor of Singapore Sir Shenton Thomas, were starting to be repatriated.

In Major General H. D. W. Sitwell's file in the IWM archives there is an historic photograph of this group of British and Australian Generals, Air Vice Marshals and former Governor Generals, taken en route home at Hsian in China. Sitwell, a First World War veteran and one of the older POW, had been Officer Commanding British Forces in Java. In a long and fascinating letter to his wife Kitty, written on 22 August 1945 while still in Hoten camp, Sitwell detailed what happened when they were liberated and his impatience to get home, ending with this wry comment. 'There is always a chance that generals will be flown out to Chungking ... not banking on it; in any case I'm afraid the American 'Heroes of Bataan' will get precedence over the rest of us.'[15]

Sitwell arrived back in Britain by flying boat, landing in Poole Harbour in Dorset just twenty days after his liberation. His daughter, Mollie Lodder, believed the speed of her father's return home had been detrimental to his mental health and that he would have benefitted from a slower journey home. In the IWM file there is an earlier letter to Kitty, written on 19 August. Sitwell commented, 'I'm afraid my career is wrecked ... apart from being a bit mental probably', though his thoughts soon turned to 'his' men and their future. 'I hope they [the nation] realise the debt they owe the men and will treat them generously when they get back, it won't be my fault if they don't, at any rate.'[16]

Clearly, the welfare of the men was a priority for Sitwell, as it was also for Air Vice Marshall Paul Maltby with whom he had shared captivity. Maltby's diary, transcribed by his daughter in 1997, reveals that on his release he had been very worried that the repatriation of POW would not get the priority it deserved, nor would their sufferings be acknowledged. He felt so strongly about this that he delayed his journey home and on 2 September 1945 he flew to Ceylon to meet with Admiral Lord Louis Mountbatten. During lunch on 5 September Mountbatten listened attentively and, according to Maltby (in a letter to his wife Winifred) afterwards made some very effective moves in the arrangements for POW evacuation.[17]

Repatriation process

The majority of former prisoners of war (and almost all civilians) had to wait several more weeks for repatriation as it took time for sufficient shipping to be fitted out en route to ports of embarkation. HMS *Implacable*, which had been hurriedly refitted in Sydney, steamed straight for Hong Kong and Taiwan where it took on board the British POW and internees who had spent the longest time in captivity, having been captured on Christmas Day 1941 nearly two months before the Fall of Singapore (Figure 2). They were taken to the west coast of the United States after the ship picked up more POW from Manila in the Philippines. One of these was Geoff Stott who had flown down from Okinawa to Manila. He remembered

> the reception centre ... coffee and doughnuts, all sorts. And on one wall of the building there were about 12 doorways and each had a nationality on top of the doorway ... they called out 'All British personnel proceed through the door'. And

Figure 2 Civilian internees from Hong Kong bathing on the flight deck during their repatriation voyage on HMS *Implacable*, with former British prisoners of war in the background *(courtesy of Martin Restorick)*[18]

when you went out there, there were the RAF lorries which were the big long lorries for carrying [aircraft] body parts and wings and they'd put seats along both sides of them. And we were driven out to a camp where all the British were, under canvas ... a British aircraft carrier came in, *HMS Implacable*, and all the British personnel were put on it ... All the British army lads were put on camp beds in the hangar deck. Navy lads were given the hammocks of the crew who weren't there.

During this time British Intelligence officers from MI9 visited camps to begin debriefing officers and men gathering evidence for the War Crimes Trials. This process continued in transit camps and on voyages home. Though not ordered to, all POW were requested to fill in by hand what later became known as a 'Liberation Questionnaire' or Form MI9/JAP. This document was filled out by hand and in pencil or pen by the individual and contains personal information such as the place and date of capture, names and dates of camps including names of the senior Allied officers, information about escape attempts or sabotage.

In a few cases an additional form (Form Q) was also filled out and attached to the MI9 form giving details of specific brutality or torture. For example, former intelligence officer and camp interpreter, Bill Drower, who was interviewed for the study, gave lengthy testimony on his Form Q outlining his final weeks at Kanchanaburi camp in Thailand where he had been tortured. He described the beatings, weeks of isolation, near-starvation and sickness (he contracted black water fever while imprisoned) and was only saved by the war ending unexpectedly.[19] His persecutor, Japanese camp commandant Captain Hideji Noguchi, had pledged that Drower would die in captivity. Noguchi was later hanged for this and other atrocities.

The National Archives at Kew hold in excess of 30,000 questionnaires in 98 files under the reference WO344. For relatives of Far East POW seeing copies of the questionnaire, or better still the real thing by visiting the National Archives, they are a powerful, tangible and evocative connection to that time. Also there, under catalogue reference WO345, are the camp record cards kept by the Japanese (in both Japanese and English languages).[20] These two sets of documents are an invaluable source of information to researchers as they provide contemporaneous details about an individual's captivity, in their own handwriting. Years later, at interview, I gave copies of these documents to the men as most had not been aware that they existed. The documents provided a tangible link for them as well as a useful guide to the dates, names and places that were often so difficult to recall decades later.

Back to the evacuation, and the imperative for RAPWI was to evacuate first those who were seriously ill and get them to the nearest military hospitals. Some were flown to hospitals in Bangkok, Singapore and Rangoon, others stretchered aboard hospital ships which sailed to Australia. RAPWI then arranged transport for the remaining men who were sent to airfields or local ports for transfer to the main designated ports of embarkation for each region. Prisoners in Hong Kong were mainly evacuated by British and Australian ships; those held in Thailand were taken by train and truck to Domuang airfield in Bangkok and flown in Dakotas to Rangoon. On landing there the men were given a leaflet, prepared by the Indian Red Cross and St John War Organisation and entitled *Welcome To Rangoon!!* This reassured them that everything that could be done was being done to speed them on their way home.[21] Most prisoners liberated in Malaya, Indo-China, Borneo, Sumatra and Java sailed or flew to Singapore to await the repatriation ships.

Of those few POW who flew back to Britain from Rangoon, many arrived during September on Sunderland or Catalina flying boats which moored either in Southampton Water or Poole Harbour. At interview Gordon Smith recalled that

> when I got to Calcutta after about three days one of the people from the trans-port company said, 'Would you be prepared to fly back?' The next morning I started on a Sunderland with BOAC staff on board … stayed overnight in Karachi, and a long trip to Cairo where again we stayed the night. And we spent the morning in Cairo trying to get some more clothing … went to Sicily that afternoon. Next day … we set off and had a very good trip right over the battle areas of France and landed in Southampton. We saw Pluto [acronym for pipeline under the ocean, the fuel supply line for the Allied landings in Normandy, June 1944] … which we hadn't even heard about before … French coast, Mulberry harbours [temporary harbour for Allied landings].

While every effort was made to give returning POW a resounding welcome home as shall be seen later, there were problems with the arrival of the first flying boats to land at Poole Harbour in Dorset during early September. Nobody had thought to notify the local authorities that repatriated Far Eastern POW would be on board. Consequently, the first 'planes carrying small numbers of men arrived back to no government, civic or military welcome. The situation was hastily rectified for subsequent arrivals but not until it had been widely reported in the press.[22]

Back in Singapore the numbers awaiting repatriation became so great that many stayed in their camps. Some of the most seriously ill from camps in the Dutch East Indies were evacuated by hospital ship to Australia. In Borneo the Australians set up the 9th Division Field Hospital at Labuan to treat the most seriously ill before repatriation. A watercolour painting by Lieutenant Bagnall

Royal Artillery, which is held in the Art Department of the IWM gives a vivid depiction of hospital conditions under canvas for newly liberated sick men in Borneo with the electric light, iron bedsteads, bedside lockers, white sheets and pyjamas.

In New Britain, eighteen very sick POW, including former Sergeant Alf Baker, were found in a camp on the island of Kopoko close to Rabaul, the sole survivors of a group of 600 Royal Artillery gunners shipped to New Britain from Java in 1942.[23] The Australians evacuated them by boat, first to hospital in Rabaul then to another hospital in Lae before finally airlifting them all to Sydney where they were admitted to hospital. Most recovered sufficiently to be able to sail back to Britain, arriving home before Christmas 1945. Alf Baker and Dai Moore followed on the New Zealand hospital ship *Maunganui*, arriving at Southampton in early January 1946.

The Americans liberated nearly 10,000 British POW (or as they called them, RAMPs – Recovered Allied Military Personnel)[24] from camps in Japan, Taiwan and Korea, evacuating them by ship or plane via Okinawa to the Philippines. In 2007 Peter Barton recalled his departure from Japan.

> We got on an American hospital ship ... the *Constellation*. It was huge, a white ship, red cross on the side, American doctors and nurses ... before, we went in this big hotel on the sea front and the Yanks had fixed up umpteen showers ... we got off the train we got under the showers and a lump of soap and a towel and when we got to the other end, after we'd washed and dried, we had issued American sea-going blue trousers, white shirt, one of them little round white hats ... we went on these landing craft things to the ship and we got on board. And oh the treatment was far superior to what the lads got in Singapore, oh they really went to town on us, man, they couldn't do enough for us.

He went on to describe the sight as they entered Manila harbour a few days later. 'You couldn't get in ... it was filled with sunken ships ... and outside all you could see was funnels, smashed, sticking out of the water.' In addition, the harbour was full of every type of Allied vessel afloat, large and small, either on the move or at anchor. Once ashore the RAMPs were taken to the Fifth Replacement Depot, a vast, multinational tented transit camp established by the Australians, fifteen miles outside Manila. Here, expert medical care and nutrition, leisure activities, re-directed mail and talks about the course of the war and life back home were provided while men waited for up to three weeks or more for passage across the Pacific to ports on the western seaboard of North America or Canada.

Some used the opportunity of time and space to record details of captivity and liberation in letters home or, like Lieutenant Colonel Maisey who on board the *Orontes* from Singapore, wrote a full report on St Vincentius POW Hospital August 1943–April 1945, dated 9.12.45.[25]

The long voyage across the Pacific allowed men time to rebuild mental and physical strength. The ships were met in port by teams of Red Cross personnel ready with gifts and practical help. Those who landed in San Francisco or San Diego were transferred north to Canada by hospital trains to join others who had disembarked in Vancouver. There they boarded transcontinental trains, again with hospital facilities on board, for the five day trip from coast to coast. On arriving in the east of Canada some trains headed for Halifax, Nova Scotia, while others headed south to New York.

The final leg of the journey home was on board one of the great former trans-Atlantic liners converted into troop carriers for wartime service, among them the French ship *Ile de France* from Halifax. The British liners, *Queen Mary* and her sister ship *Queen Elizabeth*, sailed from New York to their home port, Southampton, while smaller ships made for Liverpool. For many men, landing back in Britain marked the end of a five year circumnavigation of the world.

Former Far East POW liberated in South East Asia boarded their homeward bound vessels in either Singapore or Rangoon. Some of the repatriation ships were part of the multinational invasion fleet of British, Dutch, New Zealand and Polish vessels which had been on stand-by to support Operation Zipper when they too were hurriedly reassigned. However, such was the enormity of the task that ships were also sent from Britain, like the former troopship SS *Orbita*. In late August she was refitted in Belfast to serve as a convalescent ship, with large dormitories housing canvas bunk beds instead of the hammocks formerly used by the troops. Former crewmember, Liverpudlian Stanley Buchanan, had joined the Merchant Navy in 1942 aged 16. Stan arrived in Belfast on 30 August 1945 to join the crew of the *Orbita* at the Harland and Wolff shipyard. He recalled at interview his first voyage to South East Asia on the repatriation mission, especially the last few miles of the journey, as the ship made its way slowly up the Irrawaddy River heading for Rangoon harbour. 'As you're sailing up to Rangoon it looks as if you're sailing through their rice fields ... it's all an expanse of water, and you're sailing through on a 15,000 ton ship, and to the right and to the left you've got women planting rice ... it looked so peculiar.' Stan was assigned Troop Deck Steward for the voyage home, and was responsible for the day-to-day needs of between 100 and 200 Far East POW. He recalled that, 'these boys who came aboard now they were really in a bad way, but they could march aboard, y'know ... they were like skeletons some of them. I got my little fatigue party ... those poor lads that had been prisoners of war ... we were going

Figure 3 A group of repatriates and WRENS off the SS *Corfu*, on steps of the British Echelon Barracks, Colombo, September 1945. Corporal Akhurst is standing on the right of central group second step, in shorts and knee socks *(courtesy Akhurst family)*

to slowly come home at probably half speed, to give these lads the chance to acclimatise.'

Hospital ships from Rangoon and Singapore made for Bombay to transfer the sick to hospitals in India. But for the majority, their first port of call was Colombo in Ceylon. Here the men were allowed a brief shore leave. The first repatriation ship to arrive in Colombo on or around 21 September was the SS *Corfu* from Rangoon. Some, like Private Basil Akhurst (AKKI the cartoonist) on board *Corfu*, and later Captain Ronald Horner, on board the Polish liner *Sobieski*, made straight for the British Echelon Barracks at the old fort in the city. Akhurst can be seen, pictured on the steps beneath the arched entrance in the photograph below (Figure 3). Captain Horner, wrote of their reception in his journal on the evening of 2 October. 'Arrive 0800 hours ... back on board 1630 hours. The whole organisation at Colombo was first class, the Dogra pipe band played us into the quay-side and bands were playing continuously at the barracks as well as every facility available for all you could need.'

In 2006 Horner's daughter, Sally McQuaid, published his diaries entitled, *Singapore Diary. The Hidden Journal of Captain R M Horner*, before donating his papers to the IWM. There is a large display centred on his journals and archive at the IWM North in Salford.

Having survived captivity in Thailand, Victor Cole boarded the ship home in Rangoon after a flight from Bangkok. When interviewed he recalled Burma's capital as a 'sight for sore eyes was Rangoon: mile after mile of tanks … you've never seen so much equipment in all your life. I thought then, well no wonder the Japs packed up. But, personally, we were billeted in wooden huts before we went to the docks.' He remembered how he had felt on board ship on the way home. 'We were on this boat called the *Corfu* … for about a fortnight, and I'm looking out to sea and I could *not* understand that I'd been a prisoner of war for three and a half years. It seemed like a bad dream.'

Hugh de Wardener remarked on the splendid welcome his ship, the *Ormonde*, received in Colombo about the same time as the *Sobieski* arrived. Remembering the scene evoked strong emotions. 'When we got to Colombo … there was a warship there, and on the side they'd written in very large letters "WELCOME BACK" … these were the sorts of things that were very moving … somehow or other they caught you on the raw.'

However, for Jack Chalker, despite being unable to recall the name of the ship he had returned on, memories of arriving at Colombo were crystal clear. Their visit was blighted by the senior RAF officer in charge of the repatriated men on board, who had,

for some unknown reason, told us specifically we were part of the contingent [working crew] on the boat and if there were guard duties to be done we should do them. We just couldn't believe this … We arrived at Colombo and he flatly refused to let any prisoners of war go ashore … and so the captain said, one of the crewmembers told me this afterwards, he said, 'The anchor is down. It remains down until those men have gone ashore and have had exactly what these people have been waiting to welcome them.' We had a wonderful welcome.

RAF medical officer Nowell Peach, having stayed behind in Java to assist Dutch civilians in an internment camp near Batavia, was in one of the last parties to leave.

A day or two later I was taken to the airport and put on a Dakota and flown over to Singapore, where we went to the Sea View Hotel, two or three nights of luxury there, wonderful, sheets and things, and then on the motor vessel *Cilicia*, to come home ... And we stopped at Ceylon and I was taken out by a very nice WAAF and entertained and taken shopping, got some nice white shorts.

Another RAF officer on board the *Cilicia* was botanist Leslie Audus. He made the following observations in a private post-war memoir: 'For the vast majority, life on board was dull and boring; everyone was impatient to be back home. Unlike our journey out, there were no amenities for entertainment on board. There was no library ... I played a little bridge ... wrote one or two letters home ... In Colombo I went up to the university to try to contact an old friend.'[26]

Flight Lieutenant Philps, who was the most senior of six medical officers returning home on board the *Cilicia*, wrote in his book *Prisoner Doctor* what happened when leaving Colombo en route to Liverpool. The ship's medical officer informed him that, 'South East Asia Command (SEAC) had sent him a signal ordering us to examine all of the more than a thousand men on the ship and grade them medically before we arrived in Liverpool. For the first time in my life I disobeyed an order ... we were not fit, we were exhausted.'

One of the youngest repatriates to visit Colombo was merchant seaman Harry Hesp. He vividly recalled how he had felt as his ship, the *Nieuw Holland*, arrived in Colombo harbour shortly after the *Corfu*.

> I didn't take too much notice of the journey ... When we got to Colombo, we were all in a state of shock I think, the world was a big place and people, war, was still everywhere. But at Colombo it was absolutely full of naval ships, all the Navy was there, of the Far East fleet. And we'd just come out of being shamed and everything else and felt very low. And all these ships were dressed overall, with flags; all the sailors were dressed in their whites. There were flags on the side of an aircraft carrier: 'Well Done Lads, We're Proud of You.' And I think for the first time in four years, I cried. I wasn't the only one crying. How could they be proud of us? They'd fought to get us out.

Harry was not alone in expressing such profound feelings of disbelief and lack of worth, engendered by his captivity. The post-war lives of so many Far East captives were blighted by an almost corporate sense of shame and guilt after their return home. It was one of the causative factors in the psychological challenge that these men, and their closest families, faced for many decades afterwards. Another factor that many of the interviewees felt had contributed to their inability to talk about their experiences post-war, even to close family, was being ordered not to speak publicly about the circumstances of their captivity when they arrived home.

The original order can be found at The National Archives at Kew, date stamped 1 September 1945, South East Asia Command, issued by HQ ALFSEA (Allied Landing Force South East Asia) to RAPWI and other agencies and individuals, including Lady Louis Mountbatten. It requests that the order be printed as a circular to be handed to Far East POW during the repatriation process. A second, an original typed document containing the same information, appears to be the de-coded message, presumably transmitted at the same time. A copy can be found in P. W. Stevens' file at the IWM. A copy of the final printed circular entitled, GUARD YOUR TONGUE which was handed out to returning POW, is in I. H. Mitchell's file also at the IWM. The text of the circular seems to have been changed slightly making the message more direct. Emblazoned above the title, centred and in red capital letters, is the word: WARNING. Rubber stamped in red ink, italicised and centred at the bottom is the command: You are not to say anything to anyone until after you have written out your statement and handed it in.

Reference was made to the order in the British press at the time of the arrival of the *Corfu*, the first ship home. Undoubtedly, one reason for this order was to seek to protect returning POW from further or undue stress, brought about by the understandable need for information by countless bereaved relatives of dead comrades. It was believed to be bad for the men to be expected to re-live past experiences. Nor did the authorities wish the bereaved, or the general public, to be unnecessarily upset by lurid accounts of conditions in captivity. The prevailing wisdom of the day was to encourage these men to 'forget the past and look to the future' as the best way to re-engage with family life, work and society. Ben Shephard argues that 'reticence went far beyond keeping the details out of the papers.'

However, regrettably, the way in which this order was given, expressed as it is in terse language, the tone condemnatory, threatening even, implied that any POW who spoke out was being irresponsible. This must have upset many men. Surely they of all people did not need to feel they could not be trusted? Although the circular clearly states: 'You are not to say anything to anyone until after you have written out your statement and handed it in' the last part of the instruction seems to have been overshadowed by the first, with the result that thousands of Far East POW felt that it was wrong to share their experiences with anyone at any time. This also helped to create a lasting impression among many of the veterans that the country did not want to know. By being ordered not to talk they felt they were being deliberately ignored.

In the *Liverpool Evening Gazette* on Tuesday 9 October 1945 there is a long article headed, 'Won't Talk But Their Faces Tell,' and underneath it says: 'REPATRIATES "SOFT PEDAL".' It was a report from the Maghull Transit Camp where some of those first to arrive home were getting ready to leave to catch trains back to their home towns. In paragraph five the reporter noted: It was difficult to get them to talk, for they had had instructions not to. I heard an officer tell a group of men: 'If the Press does interview you, keep a soft pedal on the horrors you have seen. If not you will bring untold misery to bereaved parents.'

However, it is clear that while the order was heeded by some, others chose to ignore it, as is exemplified by many eye witness accounts of captivity published in the news reports of the arrival of the repatriation ships, with headlines during autumn 1945 such as:

Liverpool Daily Post:

'It's Wonderful to be Home!' Merseyside Men's stories of Far East Camps (9 October, front page)

RAF Man Was Beheaded, Mad Drunk Japanese (30 October, page 3)

Hospital Ship Arrives in Liverpool, Lancashire Soldier Victims of Japanese Cruelty (22 November, front page)

Blackpool's *Evening Gazette*:

Japs Bayoneted Singapore Hospital Staff (4 October, front page)

Blackpool Welcomes her Sons from Japan, Brutal Treatment (16 October pages 5 and 8)

Southampton's *Southern Daily Echo*:

'The Boys That Could Not be Beaten' So'ton Rotarians Hear Stories of British Prisoners of War (29 October, page 5)

Southampton Officer's Return From Jap Captivity, Old Tauntonian Tells of His Experiences as a Prisoner (29 November, page 9)

Despite an extensive search for this study no evidence has been found yet of servicemen who were formally reprimanded or punished as a result of speaking out.

In the Middle East the ships from South East Asia put in at various ports such as Port Tufik, Port Said or Adabiya in Egypt. At the latter the men were taken to the nearby Ataka Ordnance Depot where the Red Cross had supplies of winter clothing, shoes and other essentials. Shore leave meant that cables could be sent, free of charge, informing families of progress. The British Red Cross distributed a magazine called *News from Britain* to all repatriates which traced events from 1942 to the end of the war to help the men fill in the gaps.[27] Throughout the voyage there were lectures designed to help them plan for the future and to learn about the opportunities to retrain in new jobs or careers. They were given leaflets about the special Civilian Resettlement Units (CRU) which were helping some former European captives integrate into civilian life. Mail was brought on board wherever they made port and each new delivery brought both good and bad news: fiancées planning for a life together, wives remarried with new families, parents or siblings long dead and homes bombed. Some men needed their friends more than ever. The final leg of the journey took them through the Mediterranean where some ships called at Gibraltar briefly before heading out into the Atlantic, north across the Bay of Biscay and homewards to a landing at either Southampton or Liverpool.

At interview, Syd Whitehead recalled his arrival on 11 October 1945 on board the second repatriation ship to dock, the SS *Tegelberg*

> it was a Dutch ship … and we arrived back in Liverpool … to the same quayside that we'd left, four years and four months before … Jock and I were up on the boat davits you know, and we saw crowds of people but you couldn't recognise them from that distance … then Jock said, 'I'm sure I can hear your name.' So we came down on the promenade deck … I could see my wife, mother and father, my sister … Dad, I could just see this, he went and spoke to a policeman … come alongside the ship. So I'm talking down to him and I said … 'Hold your trilby.' And I'd got a kit bag full of … fifty round tins of Senior Service that we got on the ship, and he caught them in his cap … we were allowed off and, well you can imagine the greeting. I started with my wife … I think we were allowed half an hour with them then we were taken to Cosford…

Among the staff waiting to greet them at Cosford was WAAF Corporal Marie Goddard, a clerk in the medical section. She met her future husband there, Fred Freeman, who was one of the returned Far East POW. At interview she recalled that they had just finished sorting out the POW from Germany and Italy when the first of the Far East POW arrived in camp. Did they have much preparation for what they were to deal with?

> Well only what he had when we were down at Sidmouth … how we were going to approach the fellows, what sort of state they might be in … be gentle with them, no sort of shouting at them. If they didn't understand then you just passed on to something else. All in all it was seeing them, probably only one leg or no legs or blind, when you are in your early twenties you don't expect to come face to face with that sort of thing … it was [distressing] … We were just in it. The ones from Germany, not all of them were quite as bad as the Far East ones. … the ones in the Belsen … they were terrible but the others they seemed to have been looked after better than the Far East ones. I mean they had all sorts of food … like snakes and all that sort of stuff out there and then of course there was the heat … Most of them from the Far East were only about five stone something.

Hugh de Wardener remembered the last part of the voyage.

At Gibraltar we got some mail, very well organised. And I discovered that my wife hadn't saved any money. This shook me a bit. I wanted to take my membership. I thought 'Oh gawd, what am I going to do now?' I remember my great friend, Dudley Gotla, laughing like anything. 'Ginger's broke!' Well, she hadn't had much fun either, y'know … anyhow there was no money and this weighed on me all the way home … and when we went into Southampton, the *Queen Mary* was taking American soldiers back [home], passed us in The Roads, not out to sea … and it greeted us [makes sound like ship's hooter] … it was a wonderful noise … the lowest pitch I'd ever heard in my life, it was remarkable … there was a sort of shyness about return. I met my son.'

Whatever the route home, most men experienced some benefit from up to a month at sea, being well fed and cared for, having time and peace to begin to adjust to their long-awaited homecoming. Of those interviewed 64 came back by sea and two flew home. Memories recalled at interview of the welcome they received varied widely, even between men who were on board the same ship. Some differ greatly from the newspaper reports of the day. Newsreels and newspapers carried stories of flag-waving crowds on shore and lining the route to the transit camps, microphones set up on the quayside for greetings to the ship and there were appeals in the *Southern Daily Echo* for garden flowers to brighten up the reception rooms at the transit camp on Southampton Common.

Some men recalled how upset they had been to learn that relatives had travelled great distances to meet a ship and then were not allowed to spend any time with them. Maurice Naylor's account of his arrival in Liverpool on board the *Orbita* is typical of many of the interviewees.

We arrived back in Liverpool during the afternoon. Relatives had been informed in advance and there was quite a big crowd but we were not encouraged to go ashore and meet them. This was a disappointment especially for the relatives, many of whom had come a distance. Nor were they allowed on board. My parents were there and had come from Stockport. Unfortunately whilst I could spot them on the quayside, and although I waved frantically, they could not spot me amongst the great number of soldiers lining the ship's side. In any case I had changed considerably – no hair to speak of and reduced to seven stone or so … we were given a travel warrant the next morning and told to go home on leave … My impression overall was they were only too glad to get rid of [us] … they didn't want to know. In a way I can understand why, we were part of a defeated army … the war was over, nobody was wanting anymore by November 1945 … and so we were just told to go home. And then three weeks later we got a notice to go and be de-mobbed at Blandford in Dorset … I was discharged, demobbed then, and that was it.

Some said there was no welcome party or flag-waving crowds waiting for them on the quayside, no bands, no bunting, 'we were forgotten' and 'nobody wanted to know about us' being typical remarks. Some recalled being hurriedly transferred from ship to bleak transit camps in Huyton or Maghull outside Liverpool or, like Harry Hesp, to Hooton airfield in South Wirral, or up on to Southampton Common, before cursory medical examinations, the issuing of clothing coupons and finally travel warrants for journeys home.

Many said they had gladly accepted 'A1 Fit' stamped on their medical form in order to get home without delay. Their need to get back to families was perfectly understandable. However, in view of the planning that went into organising the repatriation process and the high percentage of men known to have contracted one or more tropical diseases during captivity, it seems extraordinary that in Britain there was no system to refer all returned Far East POW for obligatory follow-up medicals. In both Australia and in America, all returning veterans were automatically registered with the Veterans Administration, entitling them to free medical and welfare care. Those nations would later know how many Far East veterans there were and where they were. But not in Britain, men just scattered and had to fend for themselves. Not one of the men interviewed over 62 years later recalled having had routine or regular medical check-ups once home, though many described persistent health problems.

A former Sapper in the Royal Engineers, Leopold Manning, returned from captivity in Japan to Southampton on board the *Queen Mary*. In his journal he recalled the ship's arrival on 18 November 1945, '[left New York] 13th November arrived in Southampton 18th ... just get off the boat, no welcome, went to a camp in Southampton.'

Alistair Urquhart was also on board *Queen Mary* for that voyage and when asked at interview in 2007 if the ship was welcomed home, replied briefly, 'Not really, not that I could think of.' In Alistair's memoir, *The Forgotten Highlander*, published two years after giving this oral history interview, he went further saying he could not have prepared himself for the disappointment of arriving in Southampton to no welcome, no band or fanfare.

However, these memories seem to be contradicted by the reports in the national, regional and local newspapers of the day. Southampton's *Southern Daily Echo*, on Monday November 19, 1945, recorded the tumultuous reception given to the two repatriation ships which had docked the day before. At the top of page 5 across two columns and under the heading: PIPES AND DRUMS WELCOME SCOTS (in honour of a large contingent of the Argyll and Sutherland Highlanders on board) the report covers the arrival in port of both the *Queen Mary* and the former Italian hospital ship, *Principessa Giovanna*. It reports that not only were the band of the 60th Rifles, together with the pipes and drums of the 11th Battalion Argylls, at Ocean Dock at noon to greet the *Queen Mary* into her berth, but earlier that morning over at Berth 106 in New Docks, the band of the 30th Group Pioneer Corps had welcomed in the hospital ship. One of those on board was Sapper Robert Hucklesby who had needed hospital treatment in Rangoon before boarding a hospital ship to Calcutta. After a few days there he went by train to a hill hospital at Ranchi, then to Poona and from there to Bombay where he boarded the Italian hospital ship bound for Southampton. Civic dignitaries and Armed Forces' representatives were apparently stretched to the limits that day but it was the Mayor who welcomed the men on the *Queen Mary* on behalf of the city.

Why did these men not remember such a welcome? They are not alone in their belief. Similar sentiments are often repeated as 'vivid recollections' in Far East POW club newsletters and magazines, as well as in the memoirs written by men late in life. This example of altered memory became a widespread perception among many former Far East prisoners of war. It reinforced their belief that as a group of veterans they were ignored from the moment of their arrival back to Britain. But it is clear that, at least in this regard, some were mistaken.

While it seems that many men could not wait to be in the arms of loved ones, others struggled with the thought of having to return home. For Stephen Alexander, newly arrived back at Southampton on the *Corfu*, it was too much to contemplate, as he recalled in his book, *Sweet Kwai, Run Softly*. 'From the transit camp I rang up my mother; we found ourselves breaking silences with inconsequential remarks ... I felt reaction setting in ... somehow I didn't feel quite ready for the front door to close behind me again.' From the officers' mess at the transit camp on Southampton Common, Alexander and a few like-minded friends headed straight to London, to 'acclimatise'. He eventually arrived home a few days later.

How families coped

The long night is ended. The grim silence is broken. So begins the opening paragraph on the front cover of the September 1945 edition of *Far East*, which Reverend Hugh Edwards, veteran of camps in Java and Japan, showed to me at his interview. This magazine was the official journal of the Prisoners of War Department of the Red Cross and St John War Organisation produced specifically for the families of Far East prisoners of war.

It seems prophetic that this quote was used in this context, for while the silence of years of captivity and isolation may have been broken by the ending of the war, it was replaced by a new, far reaching and crushing silence for many thousands of these men and their families. In addition to the effect on some men of the orders to *Guard Your Tongue*, relatives at home had also been instructed not to ask questions. Again, this advice was seen to be practical and helpful, the reasoning presumably being, what could be gained by relatives becoming distressed by the details? It had happened, they had returned home so why risk unleashing all sorts of problems? Just go about your daily lives, look to the future was the prevailing wisdom.

Throughout the years of captivity, families had experienced great difficulty in getting reliable information. There were many problems for the authorities: the Japanese did not comply with international law and were slow to notify the Allied nations of the numbers and names of captives. The location of their captivity, over 10,000 miles from Britain, was a huge challenge, as were language difficulties and the censorship of lists, rosters and later mail.

But even more frustrating to anxious families was the plethora of official organisations dealing with Far Eastern POW matters in Britain. In her book, *War and Welfare*, Barbara Hately-Broad details the complex maze and bureaucracy that families had to negotiate. She charts the catalogue of errors and missed opportunities by successive inter-war governments following the publication of the Belfield Report in 1919 which had outlined the confusion and difficulties faced by relatives and POW during the First World War. Belfield's recommendations regarding support for families of captive servicemen in future conflicts were largely ignored. It was a very confusing picture and navigating this labyrinth frequently resulted in increased anxiety for already overwrought relatives.

Not being told anything was perceived by families as evidence of an official 'silence' or the deliberate withholding of information. This was compounded during the early months of 1942 soon after the Fall of Singapore and the Netherlands East Indies, when some families received news of captives from unofficial sources. According to Hately-Broad, when they then made this news public, through announcements in the press informing families still waiting that word was coming through other channels, it resulted in criticism of the government's efforts.

The British Red Cross (BRC) on the other hand seemed more accessible in its work, with local committees keeping armies of volunteers busy doing practical things, like packing comfort parcels for captives in Europe. The BRC responded to public enquiries quickly and in language that was readily understandable and sympathetic, unlike formal government communications which were at best stilted. In 1942 the BRC began publishing a regular magazine distributed free to the next of kin of prisoners of war held in Europe. Entitled, *Prisoner of War* this digest detailed camp reports compiled by the representatives of the International Committee of the Red Cross who made regular visits to prisoner of war camps. The magazine was circulated to public libraries and while descriptions of camp life painted a positive picture the magazine was not afraid to point out difficulties when necessary. In 1943 a letter was published in *The Times,* written by a Far East POW relative, complaining that the *Prisoner of War* magazine was not available to the families of Far Eastern captives. Following discussions between the BRC and the government, it was agreed to issue *Prisoner of War* to relatives of Far Eastern POW as well. Despite there being little helpful information coming from the Far East camps, families appreciated any news as it eased the sense of isolation. The BRC reacted and in February 1944 the first edition of *Far East,* specifically for the relatives of Far Eastern POW, was distributed to families free of charge.

As Hately-Broad notes, in June that year the BRC established Prisoner of War Enquiry Centres across the country encouraging relatives to 'pop in', write or telephone, to alleviate their loneliness and isolation. This was in direct response to the press leaking a story about the government deliberately suppressing information, received as early as 1942, regarding the atrocious conditions in Far Eastern camps. These centres were inundated with callers from the outset. Another organisation, the Prisoners of War Relatives' Association (POWRA), was set up early on with some assistance from the BRC. They too published a monthly magazine for the families of POW in Europe and the Far East as well as detailed maps of camps. However, their magazine was only available to subscribers and the organisation did not have the country-wide presence that the BRC committees and enquiry centres could offer. Hately-Broad noted that these two organisations did not always work well together.

It was during 1944 that some families at last started to receive mail from Far East camps. Once the jubilation had subsided, for some a sense of unease or worse, a rising sense of dread, took hold. It was a very real and understandable fear for what their future lives may hold. Would they recognise their man? How could they help him to recover? Would he ever recover? These were questions that many women were having to now confront, often alone, as to have voiced such sentiments to others was unthinkable.[28] It would have been impossible to voice such concerns. The common link between the women who felt such emotions was that they would wait and cope as best they could.

Despite national rejoicing during the week of 15 August 1945, the date hitherto known as VJ (Victory over Japan) Day, and the press running stories anticipating the return home of Far East captives, by the early autumn of 1945 the time for celebrating was long past. For most Britons the war was over and life now presented many difficulties. At a rough estimate, out of a UK population of 50 million at the time, there were approximately half a million people waiting for a serviceman to return from Far Eastern captivity (based on 50,000 British prisoners of war captured, each having on average eight immediate family members).

In the immediate aftermath of the Japanese surrender, British newspapers ran many stories about the neglect, starvation, sickness and atrocities perpetrated against Far Eastern prisoners of war. For the families this must have been a very difficult time. Wives had waited for husbands and girlfriends for fiancés or boyfriends, some for over five years. In many cases there was no official confirmation that a man was even alive. There had been very little mail to raise hopes. Some women had remarried, believing or having been wrongly informed that their husband had died, and were by then rearing new families and getting on with their lives.

The War Office notified relatives by letter as soon as they knew the names of survivors but not everyone received this information.[29]

Similarly, some men did not know that their wives, children, sweethearts or parents had died during the war. Stan Vickerstaff, a signalman in the Royal Corps of Signals who had spent most of his captivity in Taiwan, recalled when interviewed that he had arrived home unannounced to his parents' house in Long Eaton, Nottingham. 'Well, I went in the house and my brother and his wife were living with my mother. I asked after my father and she said he'd died two years' ago. I didn't know. The news of that had never reached me … and he was only 49, he'd had an inoperable brain tumour.'

For many families, the first indication of the imminent homecoming of a long-lost husband, son or boyfriend, was the arrival of a cable from him during the voyage home. The British national newspapers charted the progress of repatriation ships. The regional and local papers built the story day by day, printing names, photographs and sometimes brief biographies of local servicemen returning home. They also listed those who would not be returning.

The first two ships to leave South East Asia, the *Corfu* from Rangoon and the New Zealand hospital ship, *Monowai* from Singapore, raced each other back to Britain.

The *Corfu* won, reaching Southampton on 7 October, a day before the *Monowai* landed in Liverpool (Figure 4). On board the *Corfu* was Corporal Akhurst, cartoonist and architect's draughtsman. He had played a part in helping to keep spirits high, firstly in Changi POW camp and later in camps along the Thailand–Burma Railway. This he continued to do on board the *Corfu* during the journey home, helping to produce a daily newssheet, *The Corfu Courier*, writing articles both amusing and informative, providing caricatures of personalities on board and cartoon depictions of life back home. His efforts did not go unnoticed by senior officers on board, as a letter, written on Boxing Day 1945 by Major R. A. N. Davidson (Lieutenant Colonel Toosey's adjutant

Figure 4 Crowds on the Pier Head greeting repatriated Far Eastern POW returned on the *Monowai*, the first ship back to Liverpool on 8 October, 1945 *(courtesy Liverpool Daily Post, Liverpool City Library)*

at Tamarkan in Thailand) illustrates well. In his reply to a letter Akhurst had sent him shortly after arriving back home, Major Davidson praised 'AKKI' for his sterling work typing up the *Courier*, and helping to cheer up the men.

The lead article in September's edition of *Far East* had advised relatives not to meet the ships, 'as this would lead to delay in getting the repatriates to their homes.' However, by the time ships docked there seems to have been a change of heart, as instructions to assist the public on the day were published in most newspapers. Liverpool docks had been closed to the public during the war years and the arrival of the *Monowai* was the first time they had been allowed on to the Princes Landing Stage and Pier Head area. Thousands gathered to welcome the men home and Lord Sefton, the Lord Mayor of Liverpool, was joined by civic and military dignitaries to greet the ship, the scenes of rejoicing captured in a two-minute film clip recorded by Pathé News.[30]

One month later 12-year-old Patrick Toosey was waiting on the Liverpool Landing Stage to meet his father, Lieutenant Colonel Toosey.

Patrick recalled what he remembered of that day, in an interview with the *Liverpool Echo* on 10 October 2011, four days before the unveiling of the Repatriation Memorial on the waterfront. 'I was 12 when my father returned on the *Orbita* on November 9, 1945. There was just a sea of people who didn't know whether their loved ones had survived,' he recalled. In addition to Toosey, Maurice Naylor, crew member Stan Buchanan and RAMC medical officer, Harold Churchill were also on board the *Orbita*. He had kept a diary during captivity and in the immediate post-war years wrote a private memoir (published in 2005), in which he recorded the reactions of some of the men as the ship docked.

> The men on the ship hung over the rail, making little reply to this welcome, apparently listless. 'If I open my mouth I shall probably cry,' one of them said to me. I was sad myself as I walked the length of the deck recognising individuals whom I had known, in one camp or another, during our captivity. These men were soon to be lost to me, as completely as their comrades whom we had buried in the jungle; already, as they began to file down the gangway, clad in heavy overcoats and shouldering their kitbags, their look was unfamiliar.

Harold Churchill poignantly highlighted the mutual dependency that grew between some doctors and their patients, borne out of such extraordinary shared experiences. Those men he watched disembarking had needed his expertise in order to survive. Perhaps his own survival had in some measure depended on their need of him?

Men arriving back on later ships into Liverpool remembered being delayed, either due to gales and fog at sea or, like Derek Fogarty, the weather, and because of the national dock strike which was supported by the Liverpool workforce. He was on board the *Antenor* from Singapore, which was held up just hours from the port.

> There'd been a storm, some of the most horrific gales all through England, and it had coincided with this dockers' strike and they wouldn't ... We had to wait off the Welsh coast for, oh well twenty-four hours at least, and then somehow or other the public had persuaded these people that they should do something [became emotional] and they let us in. We got to the quayside...

Once the men were back at home, and the bunting and flags had been taken down, life had to be faced.

Rehabilitation

Repatriated former Far East prisoners of war, like their European counterparts, were offered help to get back on their feet, find a job and integrate into civilian life. In response to the recommendations made by Major Newman in his article in the *British Medical Journal* in 1944, instead of one national rehabilitation centre twenty smaller Civil Resettlement Units (CRU) were opened from early 1945. These voluntary residential communities were established in large houses around the country (including Hatfield House in Hertfordshire, Kneller Hall at Twickenham, Middlesex and later on at Clatterbridge in Wirral). They provided employment training, practical advice, and what would now be termed 'talking' therapy, in a non-militaristic environment. Up to 250 men at a time could be catered for, for a period of four to six weeks. Thousands of prisoners of war from Europe had already benefitted from the CRUs by the time Far East POW came home in the autumn of that year. Widow Emily Smallridge remembered her husband Ken saying that

> when he first came home they sent him to Sherbourne. They had a rehabilitation camp and he was up there ... for a month or six weeks. I remember him saying the officers used to bring them breakfast in bed to start with, but that only lasted a few weeks and then he had to knuckle down and get on with it.

The first such unit, known as No. 1 CRU, was based at Hatfield House. The men were split into groups of twenty or so, known as 'syndicates' and each group had a syndicate sergeant attached. The CRUs were staffed by specially selected Auxiliary Territorial Service (ATS) personnel responsible for the running of the units, working alongside Ministry of Labour colleagues who arranged factory visits and job interviews. Psychiatrists helped lead discussion groups to enable men to talk but there was deliberately no emphasis on medical issues. Former ATS clerk at No. 1 CRU, Edith Neilson from Wirral, recalled how she had volunteered for this work.

> We didn't have any special training ... I was shattered when I saw them, just shells some of them, but they had a great sense of having survived ... there were regulars, Territorials, conscripts ... some had no homes left, they'd been bombed, as had their workplaces, factories. Those we could find jobs for we then had to find a reason under King's Regulations to discharge them immediately [from the Army], we dealt with all the regiments ... We had to sit with them at mealtimes, initially the men were reluctant, they had to learn how to socialise again.

Another former member of staff, Pam Clark, the librarian and Education officer at No. 4 CRU, Middleton Hall, Ilkley and later at Uniacke Barracks, Harrogate, remembered that 'they had seen their families, but the experience of returning to normality was just too much for some of them to handle. They had regained some weight but hair was mainly white and faces haggard and drawn ... We were all as un-military as it was possible to be ... I really think these Resettlement Units helped.' One interviewee who had been encouraged to go was Derek Fogarty. 'I went to Wittering which was a resettlement camp, and they gave us a six week course, which was good food and it enlightened us as to what had happened during the war, the aeroplanes and battles and so on.'

A good diet, carefully thought out, relaxed regime, craft training workshops for the men to practise forgotten skills or learn new ones, as well as unobtrusive trained psychological support were the mainstays of this programme. Former Far East POW were encouraged to take up places on courses which started just a few weeks after returning home. The timing, so soon after homecoming, was an attempt to forestall disillusionment and inertia setting in once the euphoria of their liberation had passed. Mrs Neilson recalled that if a man found a job while at the CRU her job was to liaise with his regiment or unit to accelerate his de-mobilisation to enable him to go straight into work. However, while sixty per cent of all POW took up CRU placements, less than 4,600 of the 37,500 repatriated Far East prisoners of war, roughly twelve per cent, did so. The CRUs finally closed in mid-1946.

The majority of Far East POW, once their 42-day leave was over, returned to barracks to await de-mobilisation. Some men had managed to slip back into family life without too much difficulty and had work to return to, but for many the stress of the change in circumstances was very difficult. For these veterans, scattered across the country, despite the good intentions of doctors like Wilson and Newman, there was no organised club network established for them to go to in their home towns. Many saw this as yet further evidence of having been abandoned.

Psychological struggle

This part of the interviewing was, perhaps, the hardest for the men. Open questions such as, 'What do you remember about the early weeks and months back at home?' elicited a wide range of responses, from the brief 'Not much, I just felt glad to be back' to the moving, and at times emotional, re-visiting of disturbing behaviour and feelings. Many recalled during those early months back home feeling restless, disorientated and alienated from their families, unable to cope with crowds, social occasions or simply family meals. Like Derek Fogarty, who just turned up on the doorstep unannounced. After the initial shock and welcome home, he recalled how adrift he had felt.

I only stayed home for a short time because wherever I went y'know all the, my chums and young people around the place they'd been killed or maimed and my girlfriend had got married. And I couldn't walk, I'd got beriberi and malaria, my nerves were in a shocking state, and I didn't know where I wanted to be … my nerves were shattered … my school chums they came and picked me up and I was frightened to sit in a bus, I was frightened to sit in a car. I couldn't cross the road … you couldn't talk to people. The other point is I some-times forgot the language, y'know where I used Dutch or English or Japanese language in between times, it was a bit embarrassing actually … kept on getting malaria, couldn't walk, my feet hadn't been accustomed to shoes, you had leg pains. Shattered, absolutely shattered. You couldn't sit on a bus for more than about five minutes, you had to keep getting off the bus, you couldn't cross the road … nobody was interested, you just had to get on with it. My mind was strong anyway … it was better to be with your mates, at least you had things in common. Fortunately I was recalled back to camp a week before I should have done and you had a medical, and you had good food. And they pronounced me Fit A1, which was a load of cobblers …

After surviving the very worst of Haruku, having given so much of himself for the benefit of his patients there and in Java, Arthur Turbutt described the elation of finally being reunited with his fiancée, Lola. It was Lola and thoughts of their life together that had kept him striving to survive. However, when feverish plans for their wedding gathered pace within weeks of arriving home, he began to experience feelings of panic and despair. He did not under-stand what was the matter with him, this was what he had survived for, to be with Lola. He just knew beyond doubt that he was not capable of supporting a wife, not yet. So, unable to contain his distress he called off the wedding. Lola was heartbroken. Her parents banished all mention of him from their home. Arthur picks up what happened.

And I went back home, I went up to my room and I sobbed my heart out. But I knew in my heart of hearts that I'd done the right thing, I couldn't have got through. Then began a long period when, I was terribly in love with Lola, deeply in love with her, but I just couldn't take that step of being married. And I used to go out on my own, walk up to the top of the road and sit on the seat outside the Town Hall hoping … to see her again. Occasionally I did and my heart just broke.

Then Lola spoke up.

It was a terrible time. Two years of it … And then one day I was walking past a shop, a wireless shop it was at the top of our road and there was Arthur looking in the window and he hadn't seen me. I could have walked right past without him knowing I was there, but I couldn't do it because you don't just stop loving somebody just like that. So I went up and spoke to him. Well, his jaw dropped and from then on we had to have clandestine meetings. We used to get on a bus and go out to St Albans, there was a lovely church with a churchyard and we used to sit and cry with each other and … nobody wanted us, nobody seemed to understand us … And then eventually I said to Arthur, 'I think I've helped you as much as I possibly can, I think you need professional help.' And you can take up the story from there …

Arthur again.

Yes. Lola twigged it, nobody else did. My parents thought I'd done the wisest thing, that the marriage would never have succeeded, [Lola laughs] that would have been no good. They were delighted really. But anyhow eventually, as Lola said, we met secretly and quite wisely she said, 'I think you need medical treatment.' She could see that it was a mental problem. So eventually I went to the doctor, explained what had happened, I said, 'I think I need psychiatric treatment or something.' And he went, 'Nonsense, nothing wrong with you.' So I said, 'I'm sorry, there is,' I said, 'I want another opinion.' … He said, 'Oh you don't want that.' I said, 'I'm asking you to put me in touch with a psychiatrist or somebody who can help me.'

And eventually I got an appointment with a Dr Gray at the North Middlesex Hospital and I went to see him. … I told him what had happened, where I'd been, my experiences. 'Hmm, yes,' he said, 'so you think you're going mental?' So I said, 'Well it certainly feels like that, doctor,' I said, 'something is wrong.'

So he went across, got up, went across to a filing cabinet, pulled out a drawer of the filing cabinet and ran his finger across a load of files, he said, 'You see those?' He said, 'They're all like you … they are all ex-POWs,' he said, 'they are all in the same boat; they cannot adjust to a normal civilian life. After three and a half years in a prison camp away from normal life and the amenities of life,' he said, 'you just can't come back and pick up the threads like that … it takes time,' he said, 'it has done mental damage.' But, he says, 'For goodness sake don't worry … I'll have you fit in six months.' 'You mean that?' … 'Yes. I want you to take these [tablets].' And quite honestly within six months I was back on my feet, I was back to normal. I could accept what was going on. I was holding my job down, making progress in my job and as a result of that we said, this is it, we can go ahead now, if she'll still have me.

They married, without Lola's parents' blessing, though happily with the arrival of their first child, they were all reunited.

Children who were just babes in arms in 1941 had grown up in matriarchal homes. Some were resentful, jealous and even scared of their newly returned, remote and often rather strange fathers. Even the simple act of sitting in a chair or sleeping in a bed took some men months to get used to, as Stephen Alexander recalled in 2008.

> The other thing one had forgotten to do was to sit on chairs, because in camp you were either lying down and sleeping on the bali-bali or you're squatting like, as the Thais do, and you soon get used to that, what you can't get used to is sitting on a chair. I was not the only person to actually find oneself squatting on a chair like a chimpanzee or something. But this is a very real indication of how you get used to things without noticing it, and it's all part of inexplicable behaviour exhibited to our astonished relations.

Some men recalled how they had felt agitated and needed to be alone for hours or days at a time, sitting, walking or riding a bike. Others admitted to drinking heavily in the early days as a means of coping. Recurrent and persistent nightmares terrorised many for years. Six decades later some men still had nightmares every month or so, and while less severe these were nevertheless unsettling. Wives who were interviewed often amplified or corrected their husband's somewhat understated recollections. They told of being attacked while they slept. When Derek Fogarty remembered having nightmares about being back in the Sumatran jungle, Mary quietly added her own recollection of one occasion, soon after getting married in September 1946, just a few months after she had first met Derek.

> One night in St Andrew's really sticks out in my mind. He used to get terrible nightmares and this particular night he had a hold of me, like you would hold a rag doll and shake it, because I was only little then, y'know tiny little thing, and then he really did. I had to ... tell him where he was. He'd just been having a nightmare this night ... I suppose the first three years we were married he really, in my opinion, was not a well man at all. But understandable, y'know.

She wanted to stress the importance of Derek finally being able to talk about those times. 'I think it's good for him as well to talk about it, it's something I've always thought. I didn't like ... for many, many years, he hardly ever mentioned it, like he was bottling it all up.'

Ken Bailey had nightmares in the early years but he did not mention them during his interview. Not till afterwards, when his wife, Pearl, and his daughter Jane joined us, was the subject even raised, first of all by Jane.

> We were trained as children to wake him up from his nightmares because he used to doze off in the chair ... and when he had nightmares we used to have to wake him up. [He was] crying ... no tears, tearless crying ... groaning and moaning in his sleep, sitting in his chair.

Pearl then interjected, expressing surprise that Ken had not mentioned the nightmares.

> We had those, right from the very first week that we were married ... And I didn't know what to do because I thought he was dying ... it went on and on until he eventually came out of it ... First thing he said to me when he woke up was, 'Don't ever, ever let me have one of those again without you wake me up.' And so ... as he used to go, I used to get hold of his face and I'd be kissing him all over. That was in those days, don't do it now! ... and I'd be saying, 'It's alright darling, it's alright darling. Wake up, wake up, darling wake up.' ... when I look back and I think of the education now that the youngsters have, and I think oh if only I'd have known ... you were on your own in those days and you had to fight for survival really ... used to be so regular in those first few years, I mean I shouldn't think you went a week without you had one ... we never said a word to anyone, did we?

Emily Smallridge married Ken in 1947. She was only 19, he was 26. The early years were not easy.

> He used to get very moody. At times he used to get in real black moods and no matter what ... you could not get him out of it. And usually he was a very cheerful chap, Ken, always smiling, ever so popular he was with the locals. But when he was in those moods ... real black moods, he wasn't nasty or nothing, he would just go quiet and go back into himself and [you] couldn't get him to talk or nothing ... after a while I just knew how to deal with it.

Barbara Wearne was widowed in 1966 when her four children were very young. Her husband was Padre Edwin Charles Cecil Wearne, Chaplain to the Forces who, due to his formidable stature, was naturally known to all as 'Tiny' Wearne. Initially, he had ministered to the troops in Malaya before the Japanese invasion and had subsequently been captured in Singapore. According to Barbara, 'he always said that if he ever had to fight another war, which he hoped he never did, he'd like to go forward, because he'd never been forward!' Tiny Wearne stayed on Singapore Island for the duration and features frequently in the diaries of medical officer, Captain G. K. Marshall (*The Changi Diaries*). Barbara, 21 years his junior, had met Tiny in the 1950s and, despite her natural curiosity and need to understand his war, she respected his decision not to speak.

> He didn't talk very much about it to me. I did once ask a question and he said, 'You don't want to know about that.' And I sensed that he didn't want to talk about it so I never really approached it again. I did overhear sometimes when he met someone and I'd suddenly realised he was talking to someone he'd known in camp somewhere.

As stated earlier on, many Far East veterans were unaware that while they had been ordered not to talk about their experiences, their closest relatives had been told not to ask questions. Not surprisingly some men formed the impression that no one cared. Maurice Naylor was one of those men who reflected on this.

> We did not get a heroes' welcome or anything like that but in fairness we were probably not the first ship laden with FEPOWs to have disembarked at Liverpool, nor the last. Nor were we heroes; just the opposite. We were the remnants and survivors of a defeated army. Apart from our nearest and dearest nobody wanted to know and that was the impression I gained in the weeks that followed [my homecoming].

For some the strain became too much. Marriages broke down, families split up, and men took to drink or, worse still, took their lives. Many men who were in-patients at Queen Mary's Hospital, Roehampton in the early post-war years would have known one nurse in particular, Sister O'Hara, the ward sister who ran Percival Ward. She was Irish and known to all as 'Scarlett' after Scarlett O'Hara in *Gone with the Wind*. According to Emily Smallridge, whose late husband Ken was an in-patient there on several occasions, Scarlett regarded the Far East veterans as 'her boys'. (Ken had strongyloidiasis, a tropical worm infection which was difficult to eradicate at the time).

So, while some men must have resented the re-call to barracks so soon after their homecoming, for many there were benefits in being reunited with comrades once again. Some felt that their mates were the only people who could really understand them. It must have been reassuring to discover that others experienced the same feelings of alienation, the stress and 'odd' behaviour, when trying to reconnect with family life. On the other hand, for exhausted wives and anxious children this enforced return to barracks during the late autumn and winter of 1945–46 must have provided temporary respite from the pressures of trying to keep everything going.

FEPOW Clubs

For many, though not all, Far East POW being back in barracks at that time was like a safe haven, military rules and regulations providing a familiar sense of order. Some decided to stay on in the Forces and signed up there and then, others could not wait to be de-mobilised. Reuniting en masse in this way may have had another consequence too: could it have been a catalyst for the soon-to-be-established FEPOW clubs springing up across the country in early 1946 in village halls and pubs?

Meeting monthly, fortnightly or even weekly, Far East veterans formed clubs so they could get together to talk, to listen and to support one another. In the early years they were strictly just for the men and not their wives. Supporting those most in need, the men, widows and families, was the main-stay of each club. They looked after their own, quietly, independently and with steely determination (see Appendix II for a brief outline of the FEPOW club movement).

Initially it seems to have been mainly the ORs and NCOs who sought comradeship and support in that way, though former officers were welcomed as members too. Some officers took on a leading role, like newly promoted Brigadier and Territorial, Philip Toosey, who in late 1946 was encouraging the men in and around Liverpool to establish one of the first large city clubs. Some were 'his' men from the camps in Thailand and he felt a personal responsibility for their welfare. His post-war role is well documented in *The Colonel of Tamarkan: Philip Toosey and the Bridge on the River Kwai*' written by his granddaughter, Julie Summers and published in 2005.

In Blackpool another senior Territorial officer was also closely involved. Lieutenant Colonel Gill, a local solicitor and former commanding officer of the 137th Field Regiment, gave support and encouragement to the FEPOW club started there. He, like Toosey, used his influence to assist the men. One beneficiary of Gill's was 'AKKI', Basil Akhurst the cartoonist and entertainer from Changi and the railway camps in Thailand, who pre-war had trained as a draughtsman. After his return he married his fiancée Mary in December 1945 and they settled in Blackpool where Akhurst, by then aged 25, set up in business as a building surveyor. Gill gave him an office at a peppercorn rent, at the top of the building in town where he had his legal practice. Business was slow initially and Akhurst supplemented his income selling saucy illustrations to the seaside postcard companies, as well as nightly cartoons to the *Blackpool Evening Gazette*.

Henry McCreath returned to his home town of Berwick on Tweed. He recalled at interview how important the FEPOW club, that he had belonged to for over 60 years, was to him and the other local men who had founded it.

> About 1950 some of us met in the village of Norham … we lost a lot of our men, we didn't know what'd happened to them, y'know … it was through forming these little clubs [like] the Norham and District FEPOW club, unknown to us the same thing was happening throughout the country, we were all forming these little clubs for the same reason … through talking to one another and meeting people we pretty well found out exactly where everybody had been or where everybody had died … and that was what the FEPOW club did, more than anything, the welfare side was very good.

Former Sergeant Bill Brown 9th Northumberland Fusiliers (the same regiment as Henry McCreath) came from Wooler and recalled

> the little club that I joined was called Norham … that's where the chaps had started the club, and that's where they lived. They formed their own little company … the Wooler lads … then the Berwick lads came, and then the Alnwick lads came and Belford lads. So we ended up about sixty … I was Treasurer … there's only four of us left now mind.

These clubs provided a lifeline for men who were struggling to cope, offering a way to continue the unique support systems that had developed in camp and which helped so many to survive. This was as true for officers as it was for the men. However, what may be surprising to learn, is that the total membership of FEPOW clubs never exceeded 16,000, meaning that the majority of the 37,500 survivors actually chose not to join a club.[31] There would be many and varied reasons for this. Perhaps former RAF medical officer, Richard Philps, spoke for some when he wrote the following in his 1996 memoir *Prisoner Doctor*:

> I found myself quite unable to mix with the other men who came back, though we went through so much together. Until now I have shirked reviving these memories and have hardly discussed them (even Emmie [his wife] did not know the details). My reluctance was not from any unsociable motive: it has been the result of my sadness at the loss of so many young men so unnecessarily. I trust that those who may be critical of me for not taking part in these reunions understand my point of view.

When asked at interview whether he had joined a FEPOW club, former Royal Navy officer Bill Bolitho explained that

> I didn't want any reminding ... I wanted to have a normal life and get away from it all. I have to say this was partly due to the official instructions we were given, I was told not to talk about it when I got home. But I was astonished my family never spoke to me about [it] ... and I was hurt, terribly hurt ... not till I wrote this [account] did my wife Heather discover from the family that they were under strict instructions, never to mention the war. And they didn't.

Former Sapper (later Reverend) Raymond 'Ray' Rossiter was, at 87, one of the younger men interviewed. He had been twenty when taken prisoner of war in 1942. Ray reflected on people's discomfort when in his company in the early years post-war.

> I think a lot of people were embarrassed to ask, y'know ... I wasn't questioned or quizzed on it, not at all ... it was a sort of touchy subject they thought ... the talking we did was talking amongst ourselves, FEPOWs, y'know. And I believe the FEPOW movement, for those who joined it was a great thing because we were able to talk these things through amongst ourselves. And I'm sure that's true in my own case. But when the great publicity of the 40th anniversary of the end of the war came [1985] and newspapers were full of it, and radio and television, then my lads started asking questions and said, 'But you've never told us anything about that,' that's when I opened up a bit.

When asked if he felt it was important that the story of Far East captivity was shared, Ray replied

> Oh I do indeed, in all its sordid aspects. Because how can younger people learn and try to avoid these things. We've got to get over to them the horror of war. Because really you go about, young people now they know nothing about the war, nothing at all ... There's no glory in war. It's a sordid business.

Ray officiated at many Far East POW services in Manchester, first as a Lay Reader and then after being ordained in 1976, as Padre to the National Federation.

Former Ordinary Seaman Geoff Stott RN was 17 when he joined the crew of HMS *Exeter* in 1941. His ship was lost in the Battle of Java Sea in March 1942 and after several months in the Celebes he was taken to Japan to a camp near Nagasaki. Geoff knew Ray well, as both were members of the Manchester and District FEPOW club, Geoff being the treasurer from the late 1970s until the club closed in 2005. He and his wife Doreen organised regular monthly meetings in Salford and dinner dances at Buile Hill Hall near Eccles. Geoff described these social events which seem to have resonance with entertainments in captivity.

> We had our motto 'To keep alive the spirit that kept us alive' ... At the dinner dances we did not pay for any entertainment, about ten or twelve of the lads used to get up to something. We did Frankie Vaughans, straw boaters and canes, we did St Trinians' girls. Two of our lady members worked in the rag trade and their bosses said take any stuff you can make use of so they gave us knickers and dresses and things and then ... we did Morris dancers, Doreen went buying all the bells she could get. Oh we did the beauty queens, we all had balloons and ladies' wigs and frocks and one of the ladies did interviews with us. And another one we did like a keep fit class and I had a whistle and the lads were all dressed up in skirts and gym shoes ...

Conclusion

In 1945 they returned home. Many were physically ill, some seriously, as a result of recurrent tropical infections and the effects of long term malnutrition. Despite several POW medical officers and scientists publishing papers relating to disease, injury and malnutrition in professional journals between 1946 and 1948, many family doctors around the country did not possess the specialist knowledge required to accurately diagnose and treat these sick men effectively. If, that is, the men presented with symptoms in the first place. It must be remembered that in those early days a visit to the doctor was expensive for many people; the National Health Service and free healthcare for all was still three years away.

Many Far East POW had been happy to accept 'A1 Fit' status when medically examined at disembarkation transit camps as it meant they could get back home to family without further delay. Some were to find out that when health problems did present this classification later precluded applications for war-related pensions. The FEPOW Clubs and the National Federation lobbied hard on their members' behalf for over 50 years to redress this situation, though not always with success. In Appendix II there is an outline of the background to Far East POW welfare work as well as a tribute to one man, Steve Cairns, who made it his life's work.

The next chapter describes in detail the medical aftermath for Far East veterans in Britain and the work that resulted from the unique collaboration between this remarkable group of patients and the Liverpool School of Tropical

Medicine. The ground-breaking medical research that was undertaken there during the late 1970s to the early 1990s would not have been possible were it not for the help, encouragement and at times financial support of the National Federation of FEPOW Clubs and Associations (NFFCA).

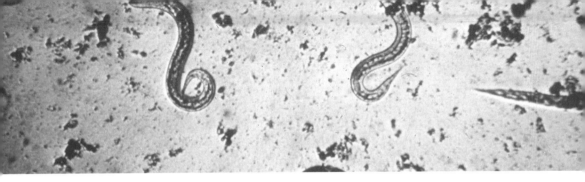

CHAPTER 5

FAR EAST POW HEALTH
POST-1945

THE SURVIVORS OF FAR East imprisonment returned to the UK in late 1945 by varying routes and at different times. Some went straight into hospital but most went home after cursory medicals. A few of the latter went to Civilian Resettlement Units (CRU) where they had medical checks, though these were not specifically looking for tropically acquired infections. Overall, there was a notable and regrettable lack of parasitological screening or psychological debriefing for Far East POW. The general approach was for them to go home, not talk about their experiences, and to get on with their lives.

Very soon, however, some men developed episodes of fever and/or diarrhoea. Retrospectively, these were almost certainly relapses of malaria and dysentery (probably the more chronic amoebic type). This was reported in the correspondence columns of UK medical journals as early as late 1945, and some enlightened doctors called for systematic parasitological screening of these returned POW.

The numbers presenting with these illnesses gradually increased, and by 1946 the military hospital, Queen Mary's Roehampton (in south London), was commissioned as a referral centre for their assessment. The numbers grew to such an extent that a 'FEPOW Unit' was set up, staffed by a combination of military doctors and tropical specialists from the London School of Hygiene and Tropical Medicine. Until its closure in 1968, over 4,000 former Far East POW were seen at Roehampton; following which the Liverpool School of

Tropical Medicine took over the national role as Far East POW referral centre.

The next two sections will describe the Roehampton and Liverpool Far East POW findings. The results are complementary, as the approach to screening and assessment by these two centres differed, and they saw veterans at very different time periods from repatriation – Roehampton 1946–1968, and Liverpool 1968–1999.

The Roehampton Far East POW experience (1946–1968)

Roehampton saw a remarkable 4,686 former Far East POW from 1946 to 1968. The hospital developed a 120 bed tropical department, including a FEPOW Unit, led by Dr J. P. Caplan. Their extensive clinical experience was summarised in a report to the UK Government Department of Health and Social Security (DHSS).[1] Unfortunately, this report was never published, though fortunately the authors did release copies to Far East POW welfare leaders such as Steve Cairns (see Appendix II), and through him and others, the information later became available to the Liverpool Tropical School.

All the veterans seen at Roehampton were admitted for at least a week, for tropical investigation and if necessary treatment. In descending order, the diseases found were:

Psychiatric diseases	41%
Bowel parasites	18%
Liver diseases	17%
Peripheral nerve damage	14%
Peptic ulceration	11%
Tuberculosis	5%

As the POWs were seen between 1946 and 1968, they varied between 1 and 23 years since release from captivity. Some of these problems were therefore very longstanding. Psychiatric problems, essentially a form of post-traumatic stress disorder (PTSD), will be discussed in detail later in this chapter, and also in Appendix I, which summarises the Liverpool-based research project on Far East POW mental health carried out by Dr Kamaluddin (Kamal) Khan. The problem of peripheral nerve damage (neuropathy) will also be discussed later as it was later studied in detail by the Liverpool team.

The intestinal parasites found at Roehampton were mostly *Entamoeba histolytica* (the cause of amoebic dysentery) and the worm *Strongyloides stercoralis* (which caused an infection known as strongyloidiasis). Amoebic dysentery could be treated at the time, usually with emetine and chloroquine, though nowadays there are more effective and less toxic drugs available. There was no very effective treatment for strongyloidiasis during the Roehampton years, but the infection was generally thought to cause at most only minor symptoms. Again, strongyloidiasis will be discussed later, as it was researched in detail as part of the Liverpool FEPOW project.

The high rate of liver disease found (17 per cent) is interesting. The Roehampton report describes such cases as having 'abnormal liver function', 'hepatitis', or in some cases 'cirrhosis'. At the time of the survey the cause of these liver problems was uncertain, but later research in Australia (1987) and Liverpool (1991) demonstrated high rates of serological evidence of past hepatitis B infection.[2] In the Liverpool study former POW were compared with a control group of Burma Star Veterans (BSV), a group who had fought in the same geographical area, but had not been imprisoned. The rate of past hepatitis B infection was 40 per cent in the Far East POW and 13 per cent in the BSV group. At the time, the background rate of hepatitis B infection in the UK was only 2 per cent. It is known that hepatitis B can lead to chronic liver disease including cirrhosis, so it seems likely that the high rate of liver disease found in the Roehampton study was due to hepatitis B infection acquired during captivity.

Interestingly, these observations fit in with some research on post-war Far East prisoner of war mortality patterns, mostly conducted in the USA.[3] These studies showed that ex-Far East POW had an excess mortality compared to prisoners from other theatres of the Second World War. The mortality risk continued to about the mid-1950s, and then returned to normal. The causes of the increased mortality were mainly cirrhosis, suicide and tuberculosis. These very accurately reflect the Roehampton data, with observed high rates of psychiatric illness (particularly depression), and tuberculosis (5 per cent of former Far East POW in the Roehampton study, presumably due to original infection in captivity), as well as of course hepatitis B-related liver disease.

Before leaving the landmark (and sadly poorly publicised) results of the Roehampton study, mention should be made of the high rate of peptic ulceration found (11 per cent). This was confirmed later in the Liverpool survey, where 8 per cent were affected. The reason for this high rate post-release is not known, but it is interesting that dyspepsia was common during Far East captivity. It was often put down to the unusual diet, and was sometimes referred to as 'rice tummy'!

The Liverpool FEPOW Study (1968–1999)

In the introduction to this book the early years of the link between FEPOW and the Tropical School was described. Largely due to the efforts of Phillip Toosey (Chairman of the Liverpool FEPOW Club) and Brian Maegraith (Professor of Tropical Medicine at the Tropical School), sick ex-POWs were seen at the School from 1946. Initially the numbers were small and referrals informal, but as the School's reputation grew larger numbers were referred. From 1968, however, with the closure of Roehampton as a military hospital, the Tropical School took over the role as the main national referral centre for Tropical Disease Investigations (TDIs) and pension claim assessments. The last patient seen was in 1999, and during the total 32 years of fully documented experience (1968–1999) a total of 2,152 Far East POW were reviewed. The numbers referred grew rapidly, with the largest numbers being seen in the 1980s. Table 1 shows the numbers attending in four year blocks. From 1980–1987 inclusive 1,060 men were seen, an average of 132 per year.

Table 1 Numbers of ex-Far East POW seen at the Liverpool School of Tropical Medicine (in 4 year groups)

Years	Numbers
1968–1971	66
1972–1975	266
1976–1979	312
1980–1983	459
1984–1987	581
1988–1991	355
1992–1995	102
1996–1999	9
TOTAL	2152

These peak years were probably because at this time published evidence had appeared clearly demonstrating the link between Far East imprisonment and future ill health. This had been picked up by the lay press, and also disseminated to the Far East POW community by their leaders, notably by their National Welfare Adviser, the charismatic Steve Cairns (see Appendix II).

Not all Far East prisoner of war assessments were carried out in Liverpool. Men from southern areas of the UK were often referred to more local military hospitals. Also, during the peak years of the 1980s in particular, the numbers referred made it impossible for all to be seen in Liverpool. Other assessment centres included military hospitals at Woolwich, Plymouth, Ely and Catterick; as well as the NHS Infectious Diseases Unit at the Edinburgh Royal Infirmary, and the London Hospital for Tropical Diseases.

In Liverpool, men were admitted to the tropical ward from Monday to Friday, though as numbers grew (particularly from 1980) an out-patient system of assessment was adopted. The ex-POW were booked into the Lord Nelson Hotel near Lime Street Station, and would attend the Tropical School or other relevant clinics on a daily basis. At FEPOW Club reunions for many years, men would entertain each other with stories of walking up the hill from the Lord Nelson to the Tropical School with a pot containing a stool specimen in their pocket, destined for the laboratory! Whether seen on an in- or out-patient basis, these TDIs were funded by the UK government, and indeed, the volume of pension claims became such that the Department of Health and Social Security (DHSS) set up a dedicated FEPOW Unit at their Norcross offices in Blackpool.

In Liverpool, most men were under the care of Dr Dion Bell whose pivotal role in the Far East POW story has been outlined in the introduction to this book. He was a superb clinical tropical physician and a very caring doctor. With humble Yorkshire roots (his father ran a lemonade-manufacturing company in Leeds), and a sympathetic and amiable manner, the men who passed through his care held him in huge respect, and he became a legendary figure amongst the Far East prisoner of war community.

The veterans would travel to Liverpool on a Monday morning and have a lengthy and detailed interview and examination with Dr Bell in the School on Monday afternoon. They would then be either admitted to the wards, or check in at the Lord Nelson. During the week, they would have blood tests, provide three separate stool samples for parasite examination, and have any other x-rays, tests etc. as individually indicated. One of Dion Bell's strengths was that he gathered around him a group of other specialists sympathetic to the FEPOW cause. For example, if there were any hearing-related problems (and deafness was quite common – this will be discussed later), the men could be seen at short-notice in the Ear Nose and Throat (ENT) Clinic of Mr Singh, Consultant ENT Surgeon at the Royal Liverpool Hospital. Similar 'fast track' referral systems were nurtured with other specialists – for example orthopae-dics and chest medicine. Perhaps the most important of these liaisons was with Dr Khan, initially Senior Registrar in Psychiatry at Sefton General Hospital and later Consultant Psychiatrist at Arrowe Park Hospital in Birkenhead. The frequency of psychiatric problems led to Dr Khan assessing all former POW referred to Liverpool. His remarkable work will be discussed in more detail later in this chapter, and his unique research on the mental aftermath of the Far East POW experience, is published here for the first time (see Appendix I).

In the mid-1970s Dr Bell was joined by Dr Geoff Gill, a young doctor training in tropical medicine, and shortly to work in Africa. Fascinated by the stories and health problems of these veterans, he led a review of the Liverpool Far East POW records from 1968 to 1978, the first eleven years of the School's official role as a FEPOW referral centre. The experience was of 602 men, with all the clinical records and laboratory results painstakingly examined and analysed. The results were published in three medical papers and an MD thesis between 1979 and 1981.[4] These men had been assessed between 23 and

33 years after release, but despite this long period of time from exposure to the tropics, the following persisting tropical illnesses were found:-

Strongyloides infections	15%
Chronic nutritional nerve damage (neuropathy)	5%
Other tropical conditions	3%

The 'other tropical conditions' above included recurrent malarial attacks, relapsing amoebic dysentery, chronic beriberi heart damage, and unhealed tropical ulcers. In addition to these serious, yet fascinating, conditions, it was apparent that the veterans also had unusually high rates of various non-tropical conditions, presumably related to their POW experiences:

Psychiatric disorders	35%
Osteoarthritis	33%
Chronic Obstructive Pulmonary Disease (COPD)	22%
Duodenal Ulcer	8%
Ear diseases	5%

All of these problems will be discussed in more detail in the next sections of this chapter. The discussion will be based on more detailed analysis of the Liverpool FEPOW project, but also on research from elsewhere. An unexpected but pleasing result of the published Liverpool Far East POW research was that it stimulated doctors in other countries (notably Australia, Holland, Canada and the USA) to investigate their own POW communities for similar problems to those described in Liverpool.

Persistent strongyloidiasis

There are many worm species which can infect human beings, and they can exist in various tissues, the blood, or the bowel. Of those infecting the bowel, perhaps the tape worm is best known; others include roundworms, hookworms and threadworms. Many of these worm infections occurred in prisoners of war held in the Far East, related to polluted food or water or the lack of good footwear, as some worm species infect humans by soil larvae penetrating the skin. Many such worm infections went undiagnosed in the POW camps, but some were detected by makeshift laboratories in the larger camps. Treatments were not very effective in the 1940s, and any potentially effective drugs were largely unavailable to the POW doctors. However, many gastro-intestinal worm infections in humans are asymptomatic or cause only minor symptoms, so overall they were not a major POW health problem.

Undoubtedly, many men returned from the Far East to the UK with worm infections, and some of these were detected and recorded in the early post-war years by the FEPOW Unit at Roehampton. Even without treatment, however, most worm infections disappear naturally. The adult worms literally 'die of old age', and as reinfection is unlikely to occur in the UK, the patient is permanently self-cured. This process may take a few months or perhaps up to two or three years, but only very rarely longer. There was one worm however, which affected Far East prisoners of war in captivity, and in many stayed with them permanently. This was a little-known parasite with no common lay name – *Strongyloides stercoralis*, the causal organism of the human disease strongyloidiasis.

The *Strongyloides* worm is very advanced on an evolutionary basis, and has a unique life cycle. It exists in the soil in several microscopic larval stages, and is mostly found in damp and hot areas of the tropics. The jungles of Thailand and Burma are particularly common areas for infection, and POWs working on the Thailand-Burma Railway were especially at risk. One of the soil larval stages can infect humans by burrowing into the skin of the feet. A break in the skin is not needed for entry, but obviously poor footwear or a lack of footwear will increase the risk of infection. After penetrating the skin, the larvae travel through body tissues to the lungs where they ascend the bronchial tubes and trachea to the throat. The larvae are then swallowed, and finally gain entrance to the bowel. Here, in the upper alimentary tract they develop into adults (though still microscopic) in both male and female forms. The adults reproduce sexually, producing further larvae which pass down the bowel and are excreted in the faeces. If there is a lack of adequate sanitation and sewage removal, the larvae may pass with faeces to the soil, thereby completing their life cycle. Quite uniquely, however, larvae in the lower human bowel can undergo an alternative cycle of 'auto-infection', where they penetrate the mucous membrane of the lower bowel or even the skin around the anus. They then re-enter the tissues and migrate to the lungs and bowel. This cycle of reinfection meant that repatriated Far East prisoners of war in the UK could maintain a *Strongyloides* infection long-term without any external re-infection.

Allied POW doctors on the Thailand–Burma Railway noted that in some patients with strongyloidiasis, a 'creeping eruption' occurred. This was a hive-like linear raised wheal which travelled over the trunk. It was transient and very itchy. The same peculiar rash was noted in the *British Medical Journal* in 1949, in reports of two ex-Far East POW diagnosed with *Strongyloides* infection at Roehampton,[5] and the Roehampton Report (referred to earlier) recorded a further case diagnosed in 1968, though this was not written up in the medical literature. The rash, or creeping eruption, was thought to be caused by migrating larvae under the skin undergoing the auto-infective cycle.

Cases of *Strongyloides* infection continued to be diagnosed when the

Liverpool Tropical School took over FEPOW TDIs, and in 1977, eleven cases were reported in the *British Medical Journal* from one hundred consecutively seen Far East POW. In 1979 a larger series of 602 Far East prisoners of war were analysed, and 88 cases of strongyloidiasis (15 per cent) were found. Interestingly, the prevalence was as high as 20 per cent in the ex-POW who had worked on the Thailand–Burma Railway.[6] These reports from Liverpool included patients diagnosed with this worm infection 33 years after leaving the tropics. In fact, a later summary of the total Liverpool strongyloidiasis experience was of 248 cases, some diagnosed over 50 years since tropical exposure in the Far East. Interestingly, this study showed that 80 per cent of cases were of men who had been imprisoned on the Thailand–Burma Railway.[7]

In some infected patients, there were no symptoms at all, but most had the creeping eruption described previously. This rash is shown in Figure 1. It is a linear red weal travelling rapidly across the trunk, thighs or shoulders. As the eruption comes and goes, it was frequently misdiagnosed in the past as 'hives', 'urticaria', 'nervous rash' or 'allergy'. The term creeping eruption is no longer used, and the rash is now known as 'larva currens'. This term emphasises the faster moving and more transient nature of the rash, compared with other larval skin eruptions.

Infections with *Strongyloides stercoralis* are ideally diagnosed by finding the typical larvae in stool specimens (see Figure 1). However, larvae are not consistently excreted in the stools of infected patients. This is why men undergoing TDIs had at least three stool specimens examined. However, even three negative stools did not exclude the diagnosis, so better tests were needed. This search was led at the Tropical School by Dr Wendi Bailey, a scientist who ran the Diagnostic Laboratory there. She developed a specific serological blood test which greatly improved diagnosis, and in modified forms, remains in use today.[8] An optical scanner was needed and in 1983 FEPOW clubs raised the funds to purchase one (see Appendix II). This greatly facilitated the blood test Dr Bailey had developed and improved diagnosis, especially when stool microscope tests were negative, but the clinical suspicion of infection remained high. Once diagnosed, Far East prisoners of war at Liverpool were treated for their infection. In the early years this was with a drug called thiabendazole – not entirely effective and prone to such side effects that it was used only on an in-patient basis. Later POW were treated with the more effective drug albendazole, which had early trials in Liverpool.[9] From this drug, treatment then moved to ivermectin which is safe and effective, and the drug of choice today.

The Liverpool reports of the remarkable longevity of *Strongyloides* infections in UK Far East POW stimulated research in other parts of the world. Similar chronic infections were initially reported from Australian ex-Far East

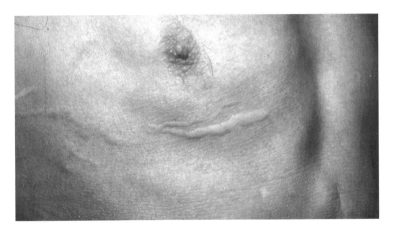

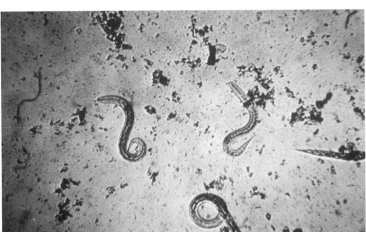

Figure 1 The classical 'larva currens' rash of chronic *Strongyloides stercoralis* infection in an ex-Far East POW, diagnosed over 30 years since primary infection, and a low-power microscope view of a faecal smear of an infected FEPOW showing multiple larvae of *Strongyloides stercoralis*. Reproduced from G. V. Gill & D. R. Bell. Persisting tropical diseases amongst former prisoners of war of the Japanese. *Practitioner* 1980; 224; 801–803. *(By kind permission of the publisher: Practitioner Medical Publishing Ltd)*

POW in 1980.[10] This was followed over the next ten years by other reports from the USA, Canada and Holland. The clinical features of infection were similar to those reported from the UK, though the prevalence rates varied, largely dependent on the original areas of imprisonment in the Far East and south-east Asia.

Adequate treatment of these long-term *Strongyloides* infections proved to be of great importance. For many infected men the infection caused a troublesome rash, and sometimes some bowel disturbance, and all those whose infection was eradicated were grateful for this. However, there is a much more sinister implication of chronic strongyloidiasis. This is known as the 'Hyperinfection Syndrome', which can occur when the infected host's immunity is acutely suppressed. This may be associated with malignancies, chemotherapy or poor nutrition; but most commonly with steroid treatment for other medical conditions. In such cases, hyperinfection involves massive larval migration from the gut, with invasion of the liver, lungs and brain.

Peritonitis and septicaemia often also occur and the syndrome is usually fatal. It was reported in a British Far East POW in 1985,[11] and later enquiries by the Tropical School revealed two further cases in ex-Far East military personnel, one of which occurred in 2010 (over 65 years since repatriation) with the underlying infection entirely unsuspected. Diagnosis of hyperinfection syndrome is very difficult, particularly for doctors with no expert tropical knowledge, so it seems likely that more cases will have gone undetected.

Nutritional nerve damage

The diet in Far East captivity was almost entirely rice-based. This was poor quality 'polished' rice with little vitamin content, and there were also only small amounts of protein, and a shortage of overall calories. There was a particular shortage of the B vitamin group, and this led to a variety of clinical syndromes directly related to B vitamin deficiency:

Wet beriberi
Dry beriberi
Burning feet
Blindness
Deafness
Paraplegias
Scrotal dermatitis

Wet and dry beriberi were previously well described illnesses due to shortage of thiamine. The wet form was due to cardiac damage and heart failure, leading to gross swelling (or 'oedema') of the body, hence the 'wet' terminology. Thiamine deficiency also affected the peripheral nerves (dry beriberi), causing a neuritis (or neuropathy), usually manifest as reduced sensation and tingling in the lower legs and feet. 'Burning feet' was a specific type of lower limb neuropathy where sharp neuritic pains occurred, especially at night. These would interfere with sleep, and men would often stamp around their huts in the dark trying to obtain some relief. It was also known as 'happy feet' or 'electric feet', and was probably mainly due to nicotinic acid (vitamin B6) deficiency.[12]

Various degrees of visual and hearing loss could sometimes occur, known to POW as 'Camp Eyes' and 'Camp Deafness', and was probably due to riboflavin (vitamin B2) deficiency. Spinal cord syndromes could occur, leading to incoordination and/or weakness. A condition known as Wernicke's Encephalopathy was sometimes seen. Outside POW life, it was usually observed in severely malnourished alcohol abusers (clearly not an issue during Japanese imprisonment!). It was due to thiamine deficiency, and involved complex disorders of the stem of the brain, usually leading to damage of some or all of the nerves controlling eye movements. After the war, the charismatic British medical officer, Captain Hugh de Wardener, wrote a paper describing a series of over 50 cases of Wernicke's Encephalopathy.[13] This was a wonderful piece of clinical observation and record-keeping in the most difficult of circumstances (see page 70). De Wardener survived his captivity on the Thailand-Burma Railway and later became a Professor of Medicine in London.

The POW doctors frequently had little or nothing in the way of oral or injectable vitamin supplements. Vitamin extracts from grass, leaves, or yeast were often made; though sometimes the response of these nutritional nerve syndromes to treatment was variable. A general improvement in diet was often helpful – for example buying duck eggs from local traders. Increased numbers of cases of beriberi or burning feet sometimes occurred during outbreaks of dysentery or cholera. The reason was uncertain, but perhaps the infective illnesses put an increased nutritional load on affected men. Finally, skin manifestations of B vitamin deficiency should also be mentioned; these include sore tongue (glossitis), mouth (stomatitis) and eyes (blepharitis), but also a bizarre dermatitis of the scrotum. This was seen soon after capture, and was probably related to riboflavin deficiency. It rapidly became known as 'Changi', 'Java' or 'Strawberry' balls!

It was generally thought that when surviving Far East POW returned to the UK in 1945, any nutritionally related neurological problems would slowly disappear with the return to an adequate diet. However, this did not prove to be the case, and over the immediate post-war years, reports of continuing problems appeared. The Roehampton Survey (investigating over 4,000 Far East POW up to the year 1968) found that 679 of the total 4,684 (14.5 per cent) had persisting syndromes of nutritionally related nerve damage. These were mostly cases of peripheral neuropathy (some with burning feet), optic atrophy (reduced vision due to damage to the optic nerves), sensorineural deafness (reduced hearing due to auditory nerve damage), and spinal cord syndromes.

In 1982, the Liverpool group published a study of 898 consecutively seen Far East POW, up to 36 years since release from captivity.[14] There was evidence of continuing neuropathic disease in 88 (9.7 per cent). In just under half of cases, there were significant symptoms – in particular painful burning feet, visual and hearing loss (sometimes severe), and weakness and inco-ordination of the lower limbs. The overall proportions of these syndromes were:

- Peripheral neuropathy (including burning feet)   60%
- Optic atrophy (leading to visual loss)   24%
- Sensorineural deafness (causing hearing loss)   13%
- Myelopathy (spinal cord syndromes causing
  weakness and/or inco-ordination)   3%

Sadly, at such a long time-period since the period of malnutrition as POW, the nerve damage was permanent and no effective treatments could be offered. The exception was a group of drugs known as tricyclics that could be tried in those with burning feet. Taken at night, these drugs sometimes relieved the pain at least partly (standard pain-killers are not effective in this type of neuritis).

As with strongyloidiasis, the research at Roehampton and Liverpool had shown that some tropical conditions could have potentially life-long effects, even after the subject had permanently returned from a tropical to a temperate part of the world.

Other tropical diseases

Smaller numbers of other tropical diseases were found to persist long-term amongst ex-Far East prisoners of war. In the Liverpool study of 602 men assessed between 1968 and 1979 (up to 34 years after release), the following conditions were found:-

Tropical ulcer	6 cases
Chronic amoebic dysentery	6 cases
Quartan malaria	1 case
Cardiac beriberi	1 case

Tropical ulcer. Most ulcers remaining after release rapidly and permanently healed. However, in six men (1 per cent) their ulcers remained. They were usually on the ankle, and tended to intermittently heal, but then break down again for a period of weeks or months.

Amoebic dysentery. In six patients (1 per cent) cysts of *Entamoeba histolytica* (the causal parasite of amoebic dysentery) were found. Most of these men gave histories of intermittent diarrhoea (sometimes bloody), and several had been misdiagnosed as having ulcerative colitis. At the time of the Liverpool study, treatment was available (usually with the drug metronidazole) and all men achieved a permanent cure.

Quartan malaria. Of the five species of *Plasmodium* that may cause clinical malaria, some are more likely to cause relapses than others. *Plasmodium malariae* is the cause of what is known as quartan malaria, and relapses can occur for decades. One man seen in Liverpool nearly 30 years after release gave a story of recurrent feverish episodes since his time as a POW. By chance, he had a fever whilst being investigated in Liverpool. A blood film was examined in the School's laboratory and *P. malariae* parasites were seen on microscopical examination. Drug therapy gave a permanent cure.

Cardiac beriberi. A Far East POW seen in Liverpool was found to be in atrial fibrillation (AF), a heart rhythm disturbance which is not uncommon in the late- to middle-aged or the elderly. It is often due to disease of the coronary arteries. This particular man had no signs of this, though he had suffered very severe wet beriberi in captivity. Some years later it was found that he died in his home city of Sheffield. At autopsy, his coronary arteries were quite normal, but he had severe myocardial fibrosis (scarring of the heart muscle). This was felt to the due to the effects of severe heart damage from thiamine deficiency as a POW. His death was certified as due to 'chronic cardiac beriberi', and the case was so remarkable that it was reported in the medical press.[15]

Psychiatric disorders

Having described in some detail the persisting tropical conditions seen long-term in ex-Far East POW, we will turn to non-tropical conditions. Mental health disorders were undoubtedly a direct consequence of the experience of Far East captivity which involved not only overwork, illness, fear and malnutrition but also isolation from family and, for many, a loss of hope. Most Far East prisoners of war underwent significant physical and psychological mistreatment, and some underwent actual torture. Many witnessed the deaths of their comrades, and some had to bury their bodies, or even cremate them on funeral pyres during the cholera epidemics on the Thailand–Burma Railway. Such experiences were highly likely to lead to what is now known as PTSD (post-traumatic stress disorder), with features including flashbacks, nightmares, depression and anxiety. PTSD, however, was not recognised until the 1980s, and its diagnosis was only officially accepted in 1992. Returning veterans thus never underwent debriefing, counselling or surveillance for the emergence of psychiatric problems. Most men affected simply kept their problems to themselves and did not seek treatment.

Earlier in this chapter, it has been mentioned that retrospective studies showed an excess risk of suicide in approximately the first ten years after release. These studies, however, were not undertaken until the late 1960s, so the problem at the time was not recognised. The Roehampton Study (1946 to 1968) showed a 41 per cent prevalence of significant psychiatric disease, and the Liverpool Study (1968 to 1979) demonstrated a similar rate of 35 per cent. The actual diagnoses made were either depression, anxiety, or a mixture of both. Nightmares were a common feature, and nowadays it seems certain that the diagnosis made in most cases would be PTSD.

In Liverpool, many ex-Far East prisoners of war were seen by Dr Kamal Khan, a consultant psychiatrist with a specific interest in Far East prisoner of war mental health. As well as making detailed initial assessments, he followed up many men in a unique and dedicated FEPOW Clinic. Former merchant seaman, Harry Hesp was one who benefitted greatly from this referral process. He recalled at interview how he had heard about the TDI tests.

It was on the radio that anyone who'd been a prisoner of war should make an appointment to go to the School of Tropical Medicine for a *Strongyloides* test. So Merle [Harry's wife], Merle had taken over then, that made her into a devil woman! … and she wrote to them and they said do come along … they gave me a wonderful check, they were very, very nice to me. I think his name was Wild [Dr George Wyatt]. And after the examination … he said to me, 'You've no *Strongyloides* … [but] you do have two problems,' he said. 'One is your hearing … and the other, you have a mental problem.' And he said, 'Go and see a Dr Khan at Arrowe Park Hospital who specialises in FEPOW treatment. Will you go?' Well, Merle … [makes a gesture implying, You will!]. So we go to Arrowe Park Hospital, meet Dr Khan who, as his names suggests, is an Indian chap. He was a wonderful man. And this was his job … to talk to people like me. And he talked to me for over an hour, he was wonderful, and he said, 'You are like one of 80 percent [52 per cent as quoted in Khan's research] of all Far East prisoners of war,' he said 'and the only problem is I'm twenty years too late.' But I was able to tell him things I was, couldn't tell Merle. So I went on a regular appointment, there were lots of FEPOWs there when I went, that I knew … and each time he was wonderful.

As well as this clinical work, he went on to undertake a detailed study of Far East POW psychiatric and psychological health, and compare these assessments with a control group of Burma Campaign veterans. His results showed a significant excess of psychiatric disease in former Far East POWs at 52 per cent, compared with 30 per cent in the Burma veterans. The work was written up as a PhD thesis,[16] but not reported in the medical literature (though now published in this book – see Appendix I).

The Liverpool work confirmed features of the illness as low esteem, retardation, low mood, flashbacks and nightmares, agitation, insomnia and sometimes 'survivor guilt'. It was also found that symptoms could be very intermittent, and that in some ex-POW there was a delay in onset of symptoms, sometimes over ten years post-release.

In the late 1980s and early 1990s reports from the USA and Australia confirmed the high rate of long-term debilitating psychiatric illness in ex-Far East POW. The Australian study, like Dr Khan's, compared Far East POW with a non-imprisoned control group, and had similar findings.[17] All these research studies supported the Liverpool findings, and confirmed the appalling long-term burden of mental ill-health caused by the experience of Far East captivity during the Second World War. Sadly, at the late stage at which these psychiatric diagnoses were made, treatment was difficult. However, on Merseyside, Dr Khan's FEPOW follow-up clinic was at least anecdotally enormously helpful to individual men, using a combination of general support, psychotherapy and limited drug treatment.

It is of interest that in recent episodes of warfare, UK military forces are much more aware of the potential for future PTSD in those involved in front-line conflict. Support systems include 'buddy support' in the field, and the availability of counselling and psychiatric/psychological intervention on return.

Other non-tropical diseases

Other conditions of a non-tropical nature appear to have had an increased frequency in repatriated ex-Far East POW, and some have been mentioned briefly earlier in this chapter.

Duodenal ulceration. Dyspepsia (or 'rice tummy') was very common in POW camps, but in many men symptoms continued after release. The Liverpool study of 602 Far East POW (1968 to 1979) showed an overall prevalence of duodenal ulceration in 15 per cent. This figure is well in excess of usual UK rates, and similar high figures have been found in Australian ex-Far East veterans. However, neither of these studies used a control group, so their accuracy is uncertain. One such controlled study was carried out in Canada, looking at a group of former Hong Kong POWs and comparing the frequency of duodenal ulceration with their brothers.[18] This showed a significant excess in the ex-POW group, showing that Far East imprisonment did seem to have a real causal association with future duodenal ulceration.

Ear disease. As well as B vitamin deficiency sometimes leading to auditory nerve damage, and hearing loss, there were other factors in prison life causing a potential for chronic ear disease. Some prisoners worked in very noisy environments (eg copper mines in Taiwan, docks in Japan) and were later found to have chronic noise-induced deafness. Also, the Japanese propensity for sudden and forceful blows to the head sometimes led to perforation of the tympanic membrane (eardrum), which could then allow infection to enter the middle ear cavity. These infections could then sometimes become chronic, with long-term ear discharge and hearing loss. There is some evidence from Liverpool and US studies to support this excess of ear disease in ex-Far East POW, though specific detailed studies have not been carried out.

Osteoarthritis. Repeated beatings and hard physical work for the three and a half years of Far East captivity may be expected to lead to joint 'wear and tear' and subsequent osteoarthritis. There is reasonable evidence from Liverpool, Canada and New Zealand that such an excess of this condition did occur long-term after repatriation.

Chronic Obstructive Pulmonary Disease (COPD). This condition was formerly known as 'chronic bronchitis'. Many POW worked in very dusty or polluted conditions during captivity, potentially increasing future COPD risk. Possibly higher than expected rates were found in the Liverpool studies, but smoking rates amongst Far East POW were very high both during and after captivity, making firm conclusions difficult to make.

Conclusions

The role of the Liverpool School of Tropical Medicine was pivotal in detecting and publicising the long-term health effects of ex-Far East POW. The School's long link with former Far East prisoners of war can be divided into four phases:

1946–1968 This was a period of medical investigation of Far East prisoners of war mostly on an informal and local level. As described in the introduction to this book, this was led at least initially by Phillip Toosey as leader of the local Far East prisoner of war community and Professor Brian Maegraith at the Tropical School.

1968–1979 Following the closure of the military hospital at Roehampton in London, the Tropical School took over national Far East POW screening, and over the next eleven years 602 patients were seen, mostly under the care of Dr Dion Bell. His meticulous attention and note-keeping was to provide the basis for the next phase of the project.

1979–2000 This was the period of clinical research and publication, using initially the cohort of 602 seen between 1968 and 1979, but later extending the numbers studied, finally to a total of over 2,000 POW. During this phase of activity, major papers were published on persisting *Strongyloides* infections, long-term neurological effects of vitamin deficiency, and many other problems related to the long-term health effects of Far East imprisonment.

2000–2014 As referrals of ex-POW to the School declined and eventually stopped, the FEPOW project turned to investigating the history, and particularly the medical history, of the Far East prisoner of war experience. This was stimulated largely by the stories the men had related to medical staff at the School, as well as many diaries and artefacts they had donated. This book is in many ways a summary and distillation of this final phase of the Tropical School's FEPOW project.

The key research message of the Liverpool Far East POW research was to demonstrate the remarkable potential longevity of tropically acquired disease.

In many ways the Far East POW experience was a unique 'natural experiment', where a large group of young Britons were subjected to a prolonged period of exposure to tropical infection and malnutrition, following which they returned permanently to their UK homes. The Liverpool-based research also stimulated other groups around the world to similarly research their own Far East POW veterans.

Finally, tribute should be paid to the work of the POW medical officers. This is not just for their bravery and dedication in treating seriously ill men with little in the way of drugs and equipment, but also for their meticulous record-keeping. Other than the most basic clinical notes, the Japanese did not allow detailed records of camp activities in general and of illness data in particular. At considerable danger to themselves, however, many POW doctors recorded information on illness, mortality (including post-mortem reports), and disease outbreaks. There are many examples in the archives of the Imperial War Museum in London of the most detailed medical documents recorded in what must have been the most difficult of circumstances.

This original clinical information was to lead to many papers in post-war medical journals written by repatriated POW doctors, and some of these reports have been referred to in this chapter and others elsewhere in this book. Five of these doctors also wrote more detailed monologues of their POW camp data, and presented them to their universities of medical graduation, subsequently being awarded MD (Doctor of Medicine) degrees. The work of these doctors, and much later the results of the Liverpool Far East POW research, can be regarded as demonstration of how the most negative of wartime experiences can lead to remarkably positive outcomes, with real messages for future generations of doctors.

CHAPTER 6

LOOKING BACK OVER THE YEARS

T HIS CHAPTER GIVES THE final word to a few of those interviewed. The extracts are mainly in response to the question, *How do you feel, over 60 years on, about what you went through?* I wanted to find out what how they viewed their experiences, and whether there had been any lasting consequences. Here a few speak for themselves.

Bob Hucklesby's response, in his soft Norfolk brogue, was brief and to the point. 'I'm grateful to be alive. I'm grateful that I've had an opportunity to serve others. And I'm grateful that it gave me the experience to know that everyone should be respected.' He also had some words for the young, learning about the FEPOW story for the first time: 'I would want them to know that we left a lot of people behind who gave their lives so that in fact they could have the life they've got … I'm very keen that those we left behind in the Far East, in a totally foreign culture, and having served to the best of their ability, that they're not forgotten.'

Former Leading Aircraftman Fred Ryall was at peace with himself.

My feelings are very positive in this regard. One can't forget what happened during the period of captivity, some of the things were shocking, horrible. One can't forget that. Whether one forgives or not is up to each individual; as far as I'm concerned to … reflect back with horror and so on to the past does nothing at all for the future … What happened is in the past, and I'm quite prepared to accept the Japanese as they are today. And I know that that is not a view which is felt by all the former prisoners, but that's mine.

Above General Percival laying a wreath at Manchester's war memorial in St Peter's Square, VJ Day 1958.

Fred had served with the RAF radio installation and maintenance unit (RIMU) in Malaya and Singapore before being captured in Java in March 1942. Two months later, he and the rest of the inmates of Malang camp had been forced to watch the execution by firing squad of four comrades who had tried to escape. This incident had stayed with Fred as it was 'the very first indication of the approach of the Japanese to the prisoners, and so much which was to follow'. What followed for Fred was his transfer to the Spice Islands to build an airfield for the Japanese before returning to Java along with the remnants of the group. Finally he was sent to Singapore. Fred knew how lucky he was. Remembering the early months back home he said, 'I'm going to use the word "survived." I survived those months after the war, because they weren't easy times.'

Early on he joined the London FEPOW club, the largest in the country, enjoying the 'social element … we had as our sort of headquarters the Union Jack Club in Waterloo, London and we would have functions there, social functions providing perhaps a meal, bingo, raffles, dancing, that sort of thing.' In later life Fred served as vice president of the National Federation 'I was pleased to operate in that capacity because I think I was able to do quite a lot one way and the other.'

Former Merchant Seaman Harry Hesp was a tall, gentle bear of a man from Stockton Heath in Cheshire. At seventeen years old he had been one of the youngest to be taken prisoner in Singapore after his ship the *Empress of Asia* was sunk. He spent much of his interview trying to explain the depths of the struggle that he, and Merle, had had post-war. It was like listening to an account of a slow, relentless breakdown and by the end I felt it was unnecessary to pose the question about looking back, as he had explained it so clearly. He ended with this:

'If I hadn't met Merle I would have been buried thirty years ago … the way I was living … I couldn't have ridden with anyone in a car [or] gone on a bus … I had to do it my way … you became a loner and then you became more into yourself … [when] you're getting asked questions about the fathers, the reason the father didn't want to talk about it [is] not that he'd anything to hide. You'd been humiliated, what had you done in the war, what had a prisoner of war done to help? And you felt that. You'd gone to war to fight to save this country … instead of that you'd done nothing … And that is why these young people, the [sons and] daughters, don't get the answers they're always looking for. I wouldn't have told anybody else all this a few years ago. And I wouldn't have told anyone else but you.

His final remark touched me deeply because I knew that Harry had not talked openly about his experiences; it was a privilege to be invited to listen to his recollections. I knew it was because of his profound sense of indebtedness to the Tropical School, and in particular to Dr Khan.

Former wireless operator in the RAF, Alex Smith from Paisley near Glasgow, was another man who suffered from anxiety problems.

> It took me years to settle down properly. I was too agitated, even many years after the end of the war I was still very nervous. In fact I got into bother once in Babcocks [engineers] for working too many machines at the one time. One machine working wasn't enough for me I had to do more, and the union representative … complained to both me and the boss about it … I was working at umpteen machines all at the one time, all going together … It was dangerous … everything had to be done in a hurry and I am still a bit like that … I can't rest.

Bill Brown's response was typical of several of those interviewed, who by their nature did not feel animosity or anger. He would never forget his pals who had not survived but he had been able to find a sense of peace. 'To be honest … I can't travel through life feeling bitter against anybody. The Japanese? I didn't like the ones we met, or the Koreans, but the current day Japanese I have nothing against them … No, I couldn't go through life bearing a grudge like that. Life is too short for that.'

Derek Fogarty however, felt differently.

> [the experience] made you stronger in mind, made you more determined to survive; more bloody-minded in some respects; more tolerant towards things which you wouldn't understand. I know where I'm going and always have done. I'm very determined and always have been. I don't suffer fools in a lot of ways … I understand my fellow man in a lot of ways … It made me appreciate nature … my love of things like orchids, and colour, and I'm very conscious of smells … I could smell water long before I got to it … I loved the animals and I loved to hear the monkeys. I still hate the Japanese as much as I did then and I don't see why under any circumstances I should have any compassion towards them.

Former Private Eddie Stobbart, Royal Army Service Corps, was quite adamant, 'I don't regret it at all … I'm glad that I didn't miss it to be honest, sounds ridiculous doesn't it? Well some people go through their lives with nothing happening and they go to a job in a bank or something like that and they come home and nothing's happened, but this is something different.'

Jim Wakefield, who had remained in Hong Kong throughout, was positive about his time in captivity. He had taught himself Mandarin and by the end of captivity could speak, read and write it fluently.

> I coped with everything in POW camp … I'll be honest, I enjoyed my time as a prisoner of war … that's why I can remember so much about what happened to

Figure 1 Confucian saying written by Jim Wakefield *(given to the author)*

me and the experiences I had. But I think when I went into camp I was determined to get as much out of it as I could … There were other people who sat around, moaned and groaned the whole time and they could think of nothing else but food, which you couldn't get … I on the other hand felt that I could help, as it were, the life in camp.

After my visit to interview Jim at home near Bournemouth he sent me this lovely example (right) of the exquisite work he did, with Chinese pen, stone and ink.

It is a Confucian saying which I understand translated reads: To have a friend to come from afar to visit, is it not a joyful occasion, indeed! The characters to the right stand for: The master said.

Former Aircraftsman 2nd class Frank Yerbury RAF had stayed on Java throughout. He and Olive, his wife, were married before he went out East. She sat silently in the room for the whole interview. Only at the end did she speak, when Frank, reflecting on it all, said:

Some of them [family] say, 'You should write down,' but I haven't … there it is, I haven't done. But they say, Olive says, it's for … any grandchildren or great grandchildren … there's something for them to read about.

At which point Olive spoke for the first time.

Excuse me, what I insist on, to me I've always been interested in history … I was in London and what I saw there [VE Day event] was manipulated. I thought this is not history, this is not true! And this is what I tell him. What he writes down will be true. So he should write down his memories, even if they are unpleasant, because then I know at least what he writes down will be true, not manipulated history.

When asked then, if Frank had spoken about his experiences when he got back home she replied firmly,

No, no, no, and also even now, this is why I've been listening, 'cos even now I hear things that I didn't know about. You can read between the lines and if you know anyone, you know when they're down, you know when they're up.

Like several interviewees Frank Wyatt, a retired Head teacher and former Sergeant Instructor with the Army Education Corps in Singapore, responded to the question by citing the contrast between the Japanese he met during the war and those he met on a trip to the Far East in later life. The latter proved to be cathartic.

Well, I kind of couldn't understand how they could be like that, so cruel ... You see the thing was the Sino-Japanese war had recently finished and also the Russian war ... the Japanese were told that these people were sub-human and they must be treated like sub-humans. And they tended to treat us in the same way as they'd been taught to treat the Chinese and the Russians ... when I retired ... we went to Japan, Hong Kong, Bangkok and Singapore, took a month, had a week in each. And we found the Japanese so different there to the Japanese soldiers, and it wasn't too difficult to learn to forgive.

Former Royal Engineer John Baxter had this to say:

Well I don't obviously agree with war at all, in any shape or form, and I wouldn't recommend wartime as an experience, except to say that it did reinforce things like human relationships and concern for others. You didn't necessarily class all the enemy in the same groove because whether you believe it or not, there were a few good Japanese. I was fortunate in Japan in having one of the overseers at the mine workshops that was favourably inclined towards us. He wasn't actually a Christian but he had Christian principles.

Emily Smallridge remembered at the end, when her husband Ken was dying, he said to her one day, 'You know they keep on with us for reconciliation with the Japs?' he said. 'Some of them have been out there on the railway and met the Japanese and shook hands with them, but I couldn't do it, Em. I can forgive them, but I can never, ever forget.'

Fred Seiker had served in the Dutch Army, was captured in Singapore and shipped up to Thailand. He described at length the tensions he felt once back in post-war society. In his view much more should be done to support the wives when men return home.

An understanding woman. The love of a woman for a man. To know that it is there, is far more important than anything that science can offer this man, or medical advice. It begins at home, it begins with the person like your wife. She is the one who makes it possible for this man to re-capture his inner self again ... it's the womenfolk who suffer most because the blokes don't know they're making this situation for their loved ones. And if, at the beginning, even now at this late stage, it should be made aware that it's the womenfolk, it's the women-folk who are closely associated with these men, they're the ones that have to be educated to make this man's life possible again. Not all the science in the world can change that, it's all peripheral.

Barbara Wearne, Padre Wearne's widow, was closely involved with the Devon and Cornwall FEPOW Club for many years. In the 1970s she had wanted to encourage the men to open up and share what had happened believing it would help them. Looking back 30 years later she vividly recalled her motivation at the time.

I always wanted to take down a tape recorder and get them to talk about their experiences but there was a reluctance and they didn't want to. And I got tied up with the fact that Tiny had said, 'You don't want to know about that.' They didn't really want to bring it back. And also to put it into language that we who had never experienced it, must have been very, very difficult. So I abandoned the idea but when the 40th-after anniversary came the FEPOW at Plymouth were really upset because there'd been such a celebration for the end of the war in Europe but, when it came to the celebration for the end of the war in the Far East, there was hardly anything official.... And fortunately I think it came home to them then that if they didn't start talking about it nobody was going to know. So gradually they were able to open out about it and for the 50th anniversary Plymouth went to town, they had a wonderful celebration. But by that time unfortunately I'm afraid I didn't get round to recording their stories, I wish I had really because I think but they would certainly have talked to me by then. But I always felt a little not embarrassed, a bit overwhelmed, because I always felt they were being a bit careful as to what they told me because they didn't want to upset anybody. And that of course came from the fact that when they came back, and it is fact, it's not just imagination, they were told, they were given medicals and given clothes and check-ups and ... they were told now don't talk to anybody about what's happened to you because it will upset them ... So they really felt that this was true and they didn't want to upset them anymore. And the idea that we have now, thank God, that you talk about things and you try to experience them and go through them so that it helps psycho-logically, that wasn't there, you just bottled it up and it just disappeared that way. But of course it didn't.

And Henry McCreath had this to say.

I was very anti the Japanese for a long time, and in a way I still am. But I sort of calmed down ... and I realised the younger ones, the Japanese, are not to blame.

I only wish that there'd been a little bit more information made available to the public [there] as to the way they'd behaved. Our public as well, y'know, the way they behaved; because it was pretty grim mind, pretty grim. I mean, it really was.

Stan Vickerstaff reflected on how he learned about the atomic bomb.

On this aircraft carrier [USS *Block Island*] when I'd settled down (they'd got camp beds for us to lay on) they'd got piles of magazines and things, and of course I picked this *Time Magazine* up and there was the mushroom cloud on the front. And I grabbed hold of a Yankee sailor and said, 'Hey what's this?' He said, 'Don't you know?' I said, 'Course not, we didn't have magazines in prison camps.' 'Oh, that's what stopped the war.' I said, 'Good God!' And I read the articles. And that's how I learned what the atom bomb was. And I've been its friend ever since.

Following up a short while later, he commented on the post-war anti-nuclear lobby in Britain and the growth of political and public feeling at what was done to the Japanese civilian population.

I viewed it with contempt to be honest, total contempt. Because, if you weren't out there, and did not experience the Japanese nation at its worst, you'd have never come to any view that they didn't deserve the bomb, because they did. I always say, suppose they'd the bomb, what would they have done with it? Blown us to bits, of course. There's no doubt that sympathy for the Japanese was totally misplaced.

When Stan was asked the question about how he felt about the experience, he was quite emphatic:

I've said it many times, and I think it applies to most FEPOW, being a Far East prisoner of war was a totally character-changing experience. You weren't the man you were when you went out there. You were different when you came back. Analysing that a bit further, I would say that from my point of view I acquired a great deal of confidence, because I was saying to myself subconsciously, if you can get through that lot Stan, there's nothing in post-war life that's going to bother you, hardly at all. It'd be so unimportant or trivial beside it, by comparison, that you're not going to be worried about civilian life at all. I know you have to make your way in life, and it gave me the confidence to do that, because I could treat individuals, even though they were way above me, almost as equals. Because I thought, and this wasn't a conscious thought, but I thought you're no better than me. How would you have gone on if you'd been in my place?

LSTM FAR EAST POW HISTORY RESEARCH STUDIES

THE LIVERPOOL SCHOOL OF Tropical Medicine's Far East POW oral history enquiry forms part of the School's Far East POW social history research. It has led to further research studies, a brief summary of which is given below. This work is still ongoing and we welcome contact from other researchers in this field of Second World War history.

Inventive Medicine and Ingenuity in Far East captivity

A sixteen month study from autumn 2008 to the end of 2009, funded by Thackray Medical Research Trust in Leeds, investigated the range and scope of medical innovation and ingenuity employed in captivity. Further oral history interviews were recorded including a few with doctors and medical orderlies who had worked in camps across South East Asia and the Far East. A few of those already interviewed agreed to further questioning. Private papers, diaries, reports and post-war academic studies in archives, museums and libraries in Britain and elsewhere were consulted, bringing together information on aspects such as food and shelter, hygiene and sanitation, medical challenges and responses and surgical solutions. An exploration of the 'citizen's army' of skills among the men in each camp highlighted ingenious medical, surgical and nursing treatments, instruments and equipment. For example, drawings and detailed notes relating to a self-retaining ileostomy tube for patients suffering chronic dysentery infections; diagnostic and surgical instruments, such as a patella hammer, dental forceps and curettes for cleaning infected wounds; and the use of ants and maggots in wound healing. The importance of bamboo to the survival of Far East prisoners of war was pivotal. Its use in myriad ways, both in everyday life in camp and by the doctors and nursing orderlies, became quite clear.

A 10,000-word report formed the basis for a presentation entitled, *Tins, Tubes and Tenacity: medical ingenuity in Far East prisoner of war camps 1942–1945,* which was delivered at the *Creativity Behind Barbed Wire* conference at the University of Cambridge's McDonald Institute of Archaeology in March 2010. An extended version of the paper was subsequently published as a chapter in *Cultural Heritage and Prisoners of War, Creativity behind Barbed Wire,* published by Routledge in March 2012. Parts of that chapter are also reproduced in Chapter 3.

On 15 February 2010, the 65th anniversary of the Fall of Singapore, the Tropical School hosted a two-day event for a group of former Far East Prisoners of War, funded by the Heritage Lottery Fund's Awards for All scheme. A memorial plaque was unveiled at the Tropical School by Patrick Toosey, son of Brigadier Sir Philip Toosey the British officer at Tamarkan camp where the famous bridge over the River Kwai was built. The plaque marks the unique relationship forged, thanks to Brigadier Toosey's post-war efforts, between the staff and Far East POW and which lasted over six decades.

The following day a round table discussion took place at which eight veterans were present, all of whom had given interviews for the oral history study. They were: David Arkush,[1] Tom Boardman, Steve Cairns, Charles Elston, Maurice Naylor, Charles Peall, John Pratt and Geoff Stott.

The audience comprised clinicians, scientists and administrative staff from the Tropical School, many of whom had worked with Far East veterans over the years, plus historians, researchers, students and relatives of the veterans. The Royal Army Medical Corps' chief of tropical medicine, Major (now Colonel) Mark Bailey, was also present. During discussions, when each veteran gave a brief account of their captivity and health-related issues, Major Bailey commented that lessons learnt from the research undertaken at the Tropical School, in collaboration with Far East veterans, had influenced the way that servicemen and women were now cared for and treated when returning from tropical regions.

Far East prisoner of war history education project

In late 2009 the Heritage Lottery Fund awarded the Liverpool School of Tropical Medicine a £48,000 grant to undertake a two-year study exploring ways of introducing aspects of Far East POW history through the oral history

Figure 1 FEPOW Bamboo Garden,
Conservatory, Ness Gardens Visitor Centre
2010–2012 *(author's photo)*

testimonies, into the secondary curriculum. A further £4,000 donated to the project by the Eleanor Rathbone and the P. H. Holt Trusts in Liverpool has enabled this book to be published.

The Tropical School collaborated with teachers at Pensby High School for Girls in Wirral, an all-girl school teaching from age eleven to eighteen. The Head of English, Mrs Jill Thompson, was the lead teacher co-ordinating the project. Subject teachers in history, English, art, design technology, music, drama and science were also involved, devising special cross-curricular projects for different year groups. Pupils had the opportunity to meet and talk to a veteran of Far East captivity, former Royal Artillery Gunner, and magician, Fergus Anckorn, who visited the school at the start of the project.

An unexpected and exciting collaboration with the University of Liverpool's Botanical Gardens at Ness in South Wirral came about in early 2010. After arranging with the curator, Paul Cook, to supply bamboo trimmings (from their extensive collection) for a Year 9 art/design technology workshop as part of the project, Paul asked the Tropical School if they and Pensby would like to join forces with Ness to design a Far East POW bamboo garden based on the history. He proposed that the design would be put forward as Ness Gardens' entry for the Royal Horticultural Society's Show at Tatton Park in July 2010. Year 7 girls were involved in this project and the finished design incorporated a bamboo medical hut with displays, sections of railway sleepers set into a path in a bamboo grove, symbolising the railway tracks constructed by POW slave labour, together with associated tropical planting. The garden won a silver gilt award at the Show. Creative writing by some of the Year 7 girls was produced as part of an associated English/Art project. Thirty six extracts and quotes from the writing were selected for publication in a booklet entitled, *Taking a leaf... out of history*. The twelve-page booklet, printed on card made from bamboo, was sponsored jointly by Ness Botanic Gardens and Antalis in Leicestershire and copies were sold through the visitor centre shop. After the Tatton Park Show the garden was re-created in the conservatory at the Visitor Centre at Ness. A leaflet, FEPOW FACTS, was available, giving an outline of the Far East POW history and Ness also commissioned a twenty-minute audio guide to give visitors a better understanding of the planting scheme and the artefacts reflecting the history of Far East captivity during WWII.

An important part of the education project was the creation of the *Captive Memories* website (www.captivememories.org.uk) which outlines the Tropical School's six decade-long medical and scientific collaboration with former Far East prisoners of war, has extracts from the oral history interviews and outlines the Education Project pilot study, sharing ideas and resources with teachers and learners.

Medical art behind bamboo

In Chapter 2, page 78, the importance of the work of artists, and the record that they created, kept and returned home with, is highlighted. Their role in the recording of this history is absolutely vital to the historian or researcher providing the only visual imagery. In the absence of cameras (very few contemporaneous photographs exist) the work of these artists allows us, decades later, to visualise something of the reality of their existence, of the life and death aspects of captivity.

The inspiration for this study came in the main from the oral history interviewees as, from time to time while recording interviews, pieces of contemporaneous artwork appeared among the talismanic items and documents treasured by many of them; pencil sketched or painted portraits, cartoons, greetings cards, camp plans, posters and programmes from theatrical productions. Some had been created by famous POW artists like Ronald Searle or Jack Chalker but many were done by other illustrators, amateurs and those professionally or commercially trained, including some of the interviewees. This led me to wonder just how much POW artwork is still unknown and what might it tell us about the conditions and the battle to survive? It raised questions such as 'How many other artists were there recording life in captivity?' and 'What other examples of military medical artwork are there still surviving?' We needed to try to find the answers.

In August 2012, the Wellcome Trust awarded a travel grant for a two-year preliminary exploration of British medical artwork, depicting different aspects of survival, created during Far East captivity. We were primarily interested in the work of servicemen in captivity, many examples of which illustrate the research featured in this book.

The grant funded visits to seek out more of this artwork, held in archives and in numerous private collections across the UK, in Singapore and Indonesia. We were also in touch with the British POW artist, Fred Ransome Smith, and the family of Des Bettany, both of whom settled in Australia post-war, as well as the State Library of Victoria which has a rich collection of George Old's work.

The term 'medical' is used in its broadest context, covering the physical aspects of disease, treatment and the environment in which doctors and patients existed, as well as the psychological aspects of survival, including humour, entertainment and faith; in other words, the 'documentary art' of survival.

The six best-known British Far East POW artists are Jack Chalker, Ronald Searle, Philip Meninsky, Leo Rawlings, Stanley Gimson and George Old. Their work, perhaps with the exception of Old, has been exhibited in this country. Some of Old's work has been published in memoirs but generally it is not as well-known as others. All of them were taken prisoner in Singapore and later transferred to Thailand, and their work reflects the fact that they remained in the Tropics. They all had to work clandestinely, as record-keeping of any sort was prohibited by their captors. They were fully aware of the risks that they were taking, especially those men commissioned by doctors to record the medical battle that was being fought in camps across all areas of captivity. Only occasionally were artists invited by guards or officers to draw or paint pictures or portraits for them.

Examples of Far East prisoner of war art can be found in several major collections in Britain, notably the Imperial War Museum (IWM), the Wellcome Library, the National Army Museum and the National Archives at Kew in London, the National Library of Scotland in Edinburgh and the Mitchell Library in Glasgow. There are also many smaller, local museums, art galleries and libraries around the country that hold one or more examples. The IWM's Art Department holds an impressive collection of artwork from Far East captivity and the Department of Documents has a large archive of Far East POW written material which, owing to scrutiny by a growing number

Figure 1 Notebook sketches, with dated captions, drawn by Frank Clement in Taihoku camp in Taiwan *(courtesy of the Clement family)*

of researchers, was known to contain many illustrations. From 2011–2012 Jenny Wood, curator of the Art Department, together with the Keeper of the Department of Documents the late Roderick Suddaby, carried out the first thorough audit across both collections in order to identify, collate and cross reference all artwork pertaining to Far East captivity.

The preliminary investigation by the Tropical School set out to find, in addition to the known works, examples of unknown and unpublished artworks which have been kept in boxes and suitcases in the loft and on archive shelving around Britain and overseas, in some cases for decades. This growing body of work, much of it previously unseen outside of immediate family circles, we describe as documentary art. Whether amateur or professionally trained, their sketches, cartoons, caricatures, portraits, landscape and fine art studies, in pencil, ink, watercolour, charcoal, chalk and crayon, depict in myriad different ways the monumental struggle to survive, using a combination of portable palettes, homemade charcoal, ground up laterite clay and insects to provide the pigments to document what they saw.

On scraps of paper, in notebooks and exercise books, stolen from their captors or bartered for, men who had a gift for drawing documented in different styles what was happening in front of them.

An example of one of the discoveries made during the study is this illustration above (Figure 1) taken from the Clement collection at the Mitchell Library in Glasgow.[2] The actual size of this notebook page is approximately eight inches wide by three and a half inches deep (in landscape orientation, hinged on the left). This photograph shows just over half of one page. Clement rotated the open notebook through 90 degrees to portrait orientation so that the drawings and captions ran down the length of two pages. As noted in Chapter 3 (page 123) Clement was sick with TB for much of his captivity in Taiwan. His work is largely of a comic-style, each sketch with a caption, dated, on the right hand side of the page. This explains what the sketches refer to, the information taken from his diary which gives more detail. Clement filled sixteen home-made notebooks with this type of illustration, making a visual record of day to day life in the camps he was in Taiwan. Each booklet is meticulously designed and crafted. Two of the smaller ones have two-inch square miniature booklets, complete with camp plans and dated highlights, tucked into the inside back cardboard cover. All were kept hidden. It is an incredibly detailed and visual record which sets out chronologically his day-to-day life and survival in camps in Taiwan. After his repatriation and recuperation, Clement won a place to study at the Glasgow School of Art and qualified four years later becoming a successful commercial artist. In 2012 his wonderful notebooks were donated to Glasgow City Archives by his family.

Some artists were commissioned by medical officers to record the conditions that prevailed, others simply needed to draw or sketched or painted for pleasure. Much of the work is small in scale, on average not exceeding A5 size, as it had to done quickly and in secret and there was seldom access to larger paper or safe places to hide it. The portrait (Figure 2) is an extraordinary example of the craft. The patient is the artist Jack Chalker. He was caught with drawings by a Korean guard, hauled off his bedspace, taken to the guard hut where he was beaten up, resulting in a hole on the bridge of his nose and extensive bruising to his body. Mercifully they stopped at that and eventually he was allowed to return to the hut where medical officers patched him up as best they could. His friend and fellow artist, George Old, deftly captured the scene in front of him, skilfully recording for posterity what artists, doing precisely what he was doing, might expect if caught. It was a most courageous act. The original miniature watercolour portrait, measuring just three and half by four and a half inches, was kept by Jack. He sent this copy to the author in February 2009 together with the pencil inscription on the mount (Figure 3). He treasured this piece of Old's work, they were good friends.

Larger pieces of paper or pads were cut into small booklets for ease of carrying and hiding. Much of this work is fascinating, especially when viewed alongside contemporaneous diaries and reports which often explain otherwise inexplicable detail.

Some of this research is now available via the Captive Memories website. It is our intention to organise an exhibition that will showcase much more of this artwork and the history it documents, to honour the talent and courage of so many unknown artists. Contact us via the Captive Memories website if you have, or know of, artwork produced during Far East captivity that you feel ought to be included in this research.

In 2012 the Captive Memories website was included in the British Library's UK Web Archive of oral history websites (see www.webarchive.org.uk for details).

Sincere thanks go to the Thackray Medical Research Trust, the Heritage Lottery Fund, the Eleanor Rathbone Trust, the P. H. Holt Trust and the Wellcome Trust for supporting the work of the Tropical School in researching Far East POW history.

Figure 2 George Old's watercolour of an injured Jack Chalker, 1943 *(Courtesy of Jack Chalker)*

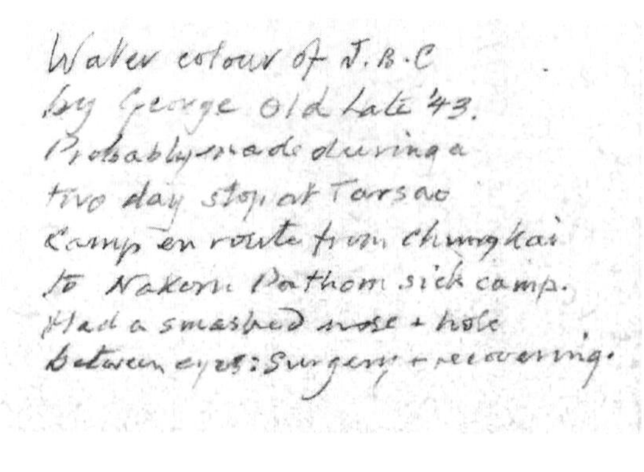

Water colour of J.B.C by George Old Late '43. Probably made during a two day stop at Tarsao Camp en route from chungkai to Nakom Pathom sick camp. Had a smashed nose + hole between eyes. Surgery + recovering.

Figure 3 Caption in Jack Chalker's hand, written in February 2009 when he sent the author a colour copy of the original watercolour above *(author's collection)*

THE LIVERPOOL FAR EAST PRISONER OF WAR PSYCHIATRIC PROJECT 1975–1987

Dr Kamaluddin Khan BSc, MBBS, PhD, FRCPsych, DPM

Introduction

IN 1974 A CHANCE meeting occurred at Sefton General Hospital in Liverpool which was to have far-reaching beneficial effects on the Far East prisoner of war community in Britain. Sefton General was about three miles south-east of the city-centre and in the 1970s it was a busy general hospital with a casualty department and all major medical and surgical specialities. Sadly, it no longer exists, and the former site is mostly occupied by a supermarket.

Uniquely, Sefton General was home to the tropical beds of the Liverpool School of Tropical Medicine (LSTM). These consisted of four protected beds on a medical ward, used by the Tropical School for the investigation and treatment of referred patients with possible tropical conditions. From the early 1970s, these beds were almost always occupied by ex-Far East prisoners of war referred for what was known as a 'TDI' (Tropical Disease Investigation), a right which had been won by the National FEPOW Federation in the late 1960s. These assessments often led to successful war pension claims.

From the early 1970s responsibility for the Sefton Tropical Unit was taken over by Dr Dion Bell, who was Senior Lecturer in Tropical Medicine and an Honorary Consultant Physician in Tropical Medicine. Dr Bell was rapidly gaining an international reputation as a leading tropical expert; he was a man of great drive, ability and compassion. He rapidly became acquainted with many of the ongoing physical problems of the ex-Far East captives referred to Liverpool – in particular long-term infection with the tropically acquired worm *Strongyloides stercoralis*, and the long-term effects of vitamin deficiency (often causing nerve damage to the legs or eyes – see Chapter 5).

Additionally, however, Dion Bell was aware that many of these ex-POW had significant mental health problems, usually anxiety and/or severe depression, clearly related to their experiences in captivity. Realising that these men needed expert help and management, he looked for an interested specialist in the Psychiatric Unit at Sefton General. In early 1975, Dr Bell met with Dr Kamaluddin ('Kamal') Khan, who was Senior Psychiatric Registrar at Sefton General (see Figure 1).

The pilot study

Dr Khan readily agreed to help and initially it was decided that Dr Bell would refer to him those men who he felt had significant psychiatric illness. Very soon, however, it became apparent to Dr Khan that the psychiatric morbidity

Figure 1 Sefton General Hospital, Liverpool

was frequent and severe, and he suggested that all Far East POW admitted to Sefton Hospital be seen by himself. This formed the basis of the Pilot FEPOW Psychiatric Study, comprising 65 consecutively admitted men seen in 1976 and 1977. These men all underwent a standard psychiatric history, and in particular enquiries were made into:

- Occupational history (before and after captivity)
- Armed services details
- Experiences and morale in captivity
- Medical illness in captivity
- Psychiatric illness in captivity
- Reaction to repatriation
- Psychiatric illness since release
- Physical illness since release

The assessments and interviews were held 31 to 32 years after repatriation. As well as standard psychiatric evaluation, a number of psychometric questionnaires were used to quantitatively examine mental state in general, as well as the degree of anxiety and depression.

Of the 65 Far East POW, the average age was 59 years and most were married. The majority had been captured at the fall of Singapore, and initially held in Changi POW Camp. Thereafter they were moved to many other camps, and a number worked on the notorious Thailand–Burma Railway. All had difficult experiences in captivity and in particular suffered from lack of food and physical beatings from the guards. They described an atmosphere of 'tension and edginess' in the camps, and also physical illnesses were common – especially malaria, dysentery and beriberi. Many men described difficulties following repatriation, though they had rarely discussed this with anyone. For example, 62 per cent recalled difficulties in re-establishing relationships with family and friends, and 74 per cent had experienced difficulties with social activities.

With regard to psychiatric illness since repatriation, 39 (60 per cent) reported that at some stage they had 'had some trouble with their nerves'. Details of full psychiatric evaluation are shown in Table 1. There were 29 per cent with a chronic anxiety neurosis, 34 per cent with a chronic depressive illness, and 37 per cent with a mixed picture of anxiety and depression. Though the onset of symptoms was often soon after repatriation, it was later than this in a significant number – thus in 49 per cent it was after 1955. Another frequent feature was that psychiatric symptoms varied with time, and there were remissions and exacerbations. This was true whether the psychiatric diagnosis was anxiety, depression or a mixed picture. Finally, the exacerbations could be quite brief – sometimes only a few hours or days.

Table 1 Details of psychiatric illness in 65 FEPOWs assessed in Liverpool 1976–77

1	Total with psychiatric illness	(60%)
2	Onset of psychiatric illness –	
	since repatriation	18%
	1945–1955	33%
	1955–1965	44%
	after 1965	5%
3	Psychiatric diagnosis –	
	Chronic anxiety neurosis	29%
	Chronic depression	33%
	Chronic anxiety and depression	37%

The psychological questionnaires used in this study included the Becks Depression Inventory (BDI), Hamilton Anxiety Rating Scale (HARS), and Present State Examination Schedule (PSES). The BDI showed high average scores consistent with frequent depression in the group. The HAR, however, did not correlate well with the common anxiety-related symptoms. In the discussion to this part of Dr Khan's PhD thesis of 1987, it is pointed out that the explanation may be the very intermittent nature of symptoms in the FEPOW anxiety/depression syndromes. The BDI explores symptoms in the last four weeks, whereas the HAR reflects symptoms at the time of completing the questionnaire. Thus if a former POW with a chronic relapsing anxiety state fills in the HAR at a time when their symptoms are in remission, then the result may be normal or near-normal, and not reflect their chronic psychiatric diagnosis. The BDI however, with its questions reflecting symptoms in the past 4 weeks, is more likely to 'capture' chronic though variable depressive symptoms.

Moving forward – the main psychiatric study

In 1977, Dr Khan was appointed Consultant Psychiatrist at Clatterbridge Hospital in Wirral, just across the River Mersey from his previous appointments in Liverpool. After discussions with Professor John Copeland of the Department of Psychiatry at the University of Liverpool, he registered for a part-time PhD degree, to undertake a more ambitious and detailed project on the mental health of Far East POWS.[1] The plan was to assess in a similar way to the Pilot Study, 100 ex Far East POWs from the north-west of England. There would also be a comparative (or 'control') group of 100 Burma Star Veterans (BSV), to be psychiatrically assessed in the same way. The BSV group had fought in the Burma Campaign of the Second World War. They were therefore all males and of similar age to the Far East POWs, and had also been posted to the same geographical location. The only difference was that the BSV group had not been imprisoned.

To obtain the patients to be studied, the help was enlisted of Mr Steve

Cairns, National Welfare Adviser for the National Federation of FEPOW Clubs and Associations (NFFCA). Steve lived in Manchester and was able to provide Dr Khan with a list of north-west Far East POW known to the Federation. Publicity for the project also provided a list of Far East POW volunteers, some not known to the FEPOW Federation. All were written to and asked to provide names of other POWs they may know locally. This 'cascade' system eventually resulted in a list of 653 Far East POWs in the study area. A similar search strategy was used for the Burma Star Veterans, and a total of 497 were found.

From these two lists of POWs and BSVs, 100 of each were randomly selected for study. Some did not respond to the invitation to participate, or declined to be interviewed; and the final samples for study were 80 POWs and 74 BSVs. All these men were assessed in a similar way as the POW participants in the Pilot Study, as previously described. At this point, it should be emphasised what a massive undertaking this project was. Each assessment lasted two to three hours and was carried out individually on all 154 subjects. The work was undertaken in addition to Dr Khan's busy full-time work as a Consultant Psychiatrist. The help of Steve Cairns was important in many ways. One example was that he organised the hire of a room in the YMCA at Manchester on Saturdays, so that Dr Khan could carry out the assessments there on POW or BSV participants who lived in the area.

Results of the comparative study (FEPOW v BSV)

The main results of the comparative study are shown in Table 2. These show details of the two groups with Far East POW in the left hand column and BSV in the centre column. The right hand column shows the statistical significance of the differences between the groups. This is a mathematical tool, using in this case what is known as the 'Chi-Square' test, which gives a 'p' value. The purpose of this is to detect whether the differences could have occurred by chance. A 'p' value of less than 0.05 means that there is a below 5 per cent chance of the differences occurring coincidentally. The numerical figures after the means ('±') are standard deviations, which give a measure of 'spread' or 'range' of the figures in each group.

It can be seen that the two groups were of similar age and gender, and that there was no difference in a family history of psychiatric illness. There were highly significant differences in the presence of severe anxiety and depression during wartime service, with a clear excess amongst the Far East POW. They also had greater difficulty repatriating than the BSV group, and suffered significantly more psychiatric disease since repatriation. Unlike the pilot study, the depression (BDI) and anxiety (HARS) questionnaires showed significantly higher scores amongst the Far East POW veterans. It was also once again noted that there was often a significant delay in the onset of psychiatric symptoms after repatriation, and that the anxiety and depression frequently occurred in exacerbations, with remissions between attacks.

Table 2 Details of the FEPOW and BSV groups in the main comparative study, including psychiatric morbidity

	POW	BSV	Significance
Age (mean)	61 ± 4 y	59 ± 4 y	NS
Gender	All male	All male	NS
Family history of psychiatric illness	17%	12%	NS
Severe anxiety during service	9%	0%	$p = 0.03$
Severe depression during service	8%	0%	$p = 0.001$
Difficulty on repatriation	32%	12%	$p = 0.001$
Psychiatric illness since 1945	52%	30%	$p < 0.01$
Beck's Depression Inventory (BDI)	10.9 ± 8.4	6.7 ± 5.9	$p = 0.001$
Hamilton Anxiety Rating Score (HARS)	5.4 ± 3.5	5.0 ± 4.0	$p = 0.05$

Case histories

As well as these hard figures, a number of specific case histories were recorded anonymously, and some of these are summarised below. They give an insight into their POW experiences and the aftermath. None of the individuals cited below were later interviewed for the oral history study.

Case 1 A 65-year-old man had suffered beatings, recurrent illness and weight loss during captivity. He had difficulty settling down after release, and often felt tense and edgy. About ten years after release his symptoms worsened, and he experienced intermittent bouts of depression, lasting for a few hours to several days. He felt very emotional and cried easily.

Case 2 A 64-year-old man suffered a lot of beatings and punishment, as well as several attacks of malaria and dysentery. He had never completely settled down after repatriation, feeling tense and anxious. He had frequent nightmares and would often wake up screaming. Once his wife awoke to find he had his hands round her throat. Subsequently, they slept in separate rooms. He had difficulty holding down a job and had been unemployed for four years.

Case 3 A 59-year-old labourer had suffered several episodes of systemic torture at the hands of the Japanese. He had great difficult integrating back into life in the UK and his marriage later broke down. He became withdrawn and did not speak to anyone for several days at a time. At the time of interview it was clear that he had a clinically severe chronic depressive illness.

Case 4 A 61-year-old builder had suffered severe illness in captivity. On return to the UK he found his father had died whilst he was imprisoned. He took to heavy drinking and later lost his job due to this. He later moderated

Figure 2 Meg Parkes with Dr Khan, August 2014

his drinking and married, but the relationship suffered from his moodiness and low libido. At interview he admitted to frequent suicidal thoughts.

Case 5 A 68-year-old retired process worker had suffered severe beatings and torture, and also lost many of his friends to illness and malnutrition during captivity. After release he suffered recurrent nightmares, and felt agitated, gloomy and despondent. He had become isolated, and was very bitter about the flourishing market of Japanese goods in the UK. Some years before interview, his son had bought a Japanese stereo sound system, and he had stopped speaking to him since then.

Case 6 A 59-year-old office worker had been captured at Singapore, and later moved to work on the Thailand–Burma Railway. He suffered many beatings, as well as several attacks of malaria and dysentery. At a remote up-country railway camp there was a cholera outbreak, and his job was to burn the bodies of cholera victims. On the fire, their bodies would often twist and writhe, as though they were still alive. He had relived these horrific scenes in nightmares ever since. At interview, he admitted that this was the first time he had spoken of this, and he burst into tears.

Conclusions

The brutal treatment, overwork, illness and malnutrition suffered by Far East prisoners of war is clearly documented. This is demonstrated by their overall 25 per cent mortality in captivity, compared with the 5 per cent mortality of allied servicemen in the German and Italian theatres of war. Considering the experiences of Far East POW it is perhaps not surprising that a number developed subsequent mental health problems. However, Dr Khan's study was unique in that it showed the extent and characteristics of the psychiatric after-effects. It also showed that these problems were clearly related specifically to the Far East POW experience, by comparing the Far East prisoners of war to the comparative control group of Burma Veterans.

The Far East POW psychiatric syndrome described by Dr Khan's studies affected nearly one-half of survivors, over 30 years after release. Some had pure anxiety neurosis, some pure depression, and a number had a mixture of the two conditions. It was notable that in many there was a delay in onset of their symptoms after release, sometimes for ten years or more. Also notable was the periodicity of symptoms, with severe bouts lasting hours or days, followed by a period of relative remission. Over twenty years after the completion of his work, in an interview Kamal Khan[2] commented that the illness he described was

> a very unique kind of depression ... they had a feeling of apprehension and anxiety ... basically suffering a low grade depression most of the time, but every now and then becoming more depressed. And it affected their quality of life, their relationship with their spouse, their work pattern and their ability to cope with life in general.

Dr Khan termed this a 'chronic intermittent depressive illness'. By modern terminology, the mental health effects of Far East captivity could be considered to be post-traumatic stress disorder (PTSD). This diagnosis was evolving during the 1980s, so during the early part of this study was not a known or accepted concept. There certainly are features of classical PTSD which are consistent with the Far East POW psychiatric syndrome – depression, agitation, and nightmares, for example. However, the marked periodicity of symptoms, and frequently delayed onset, are not entirely consistent with modern concepts of PTSD.[3]

Although essentially a research study, Kamal Khan additionally undertook the treatment and follow-up of many psychiatrically affected Far East POW veterans. Using a combination of drugs and supportive psychotherapy, he saw many regularly for several years at a 'Monday afternoon slot'. The gratitude of these men was enormous – they could for the first time speak of their experiences and the effect it had on them, and they realised that what they suffered from was an illness, not a weakness. In conversation, one commented that 'Dr Khan saved my life' (see Harry Hesp interview, page 200). In 1995, Kamal Khan retired, and the FEPOW clinic had to stop. He recalled that at their last visit, many left the clinic in tears.[4]

Kamal Khan's Far East POW psychiatric study is a remarkable project, in that it combined science with clinical experience and evaluation. This led to a clear definition of the features of the psychiatric sequelae of Far East captivity. Finally, and perhaps most importantly, from the study evolved Dr Khan's FEPOW Clinic, where countless numbers of these men found long-term support, sympathy, treatment and perhaps salvation.

FAR EAST POW WELFARE

THIS APPENDIX IS IN two parts: the first is an overview of the work of the National Federation of FEPOW Clubs and Associations (NFFCA) and its two welfare fund trusts. Much of the background information has been provided by former Far East prisoner of war, Bob Hucklesby. Bob was the last chairman of the Central Welfare trusts from 2007 until they were finally wound up and the funds gifted to the Royal British Legion in 2011. Bob began his association with FEPOW Clubs as the first secretary of the Lowestoft Association in 1950 and has had a long and distinguished record serving in various capacities in different FEPOW Clubs since that time.

In Chapter 4 brief reference is made to of the start of the FEPOW Club network around Great Britain and the establishing of the National Federation of FEPOW Clubs and Associations. The FEPOW Club movement was a remarkable example of self-help and social welfare in action. Clubs were starting up in 1946 by newly returned veterans of Far East captivity, the object being to assist and support each other initially. Very quickly the needs of fellow ex-POW and their families became a priority for club members and that has remained so ever since.

From the start the clubs were run entirely by the members. Although very few of the clubs are still in existence as membership naturally dwindled and clubs closed, there are still a few continuing, most notably Birmingham FEPOW Association, the Java FEPOW 1942 Club and the London FEPOW Remembrance Social Club.

The second part of this Appendix is a tribute to former Far East POW welfare adviser, Steve Cairns. It may seem to some to be invidious to single out one man from the many who similarly worked hard for many years for the clubs and their members, but Steve's contribution is by any standards quite remarkable. It was Steve who, from 1947 onwards, was inextricably involved in the development of, and continuing support for the FEPOW project at the Liverpool School of Tropical Medicine. Given that the unique collaboration between the School and these veterans is at the core of this book, it seems only right that his pivotal role in this regard should be acknowledged. To date no definitive history has been published about the FEPOW Club movement and this summary does not purport to be one. Here we provide a brief outline from the particular perspective of the FEPOW welfare links with the Tropical School.

Part I – Outline of the Clubs and the National Federation

In 1946 the first FEPOW Club was formed in Dereham in Norfolk. East Anglia was home to the largest single group of British Far East captives, the men of the 18th Division. Very soon afterwards, clubs had started up in the North West, notably in Merseyside, Manchester and Blackpool and then quickly across the country. In the large cities groups of clubs formed into Associations and eventually there were 72 clubs, large and small; members could belong to more than one club.

Each FEPOW Club or Association elected its own officers to undertake the day-to-day running, including a welfare officer who kept in close touch with the membership visiting families and the men when they were in hospital, offering assistance in all manner of practical ways.

In 1950 with each keeping its independence, the clubs decided to affiliate giving them one voice at a national level and in July 1952 formed the National Federation of FEPOW Clubs and Associations (NFFCA). It was agreed that the Federation should hold an annual conference where local representatives could meet to discuss issues like health and welfare. The National Federation eventually elected Steve Cairns to be the National Welfare Adviser, in large measure due to the vast knowledge he had accrued over many years and his understanding, from a layman's perspective, of tropical diseases. It was his job to liaise on a regular basis with all of the Welfare Officers in the local clubs (he still continued as the Manchester Association's Welfare Officer, a role he had had since 1947) disseminating pension and welfare legislation and also health-related information from the Tropical School and other organisations. He also prepared a detailed annual report for conference.

Following lobbying and representation to the Government, first by the clubs and later through the National Federation, from 1952 to the end of 1956 each former Far East prisoner of war received in three instalments a payout amounting

Figure 1 Blackpool 1984 National Federation Conference, Sir Weary and Lady Dunlop chatting with Steve Cairns (*courtesy Steve Cairns*)

to £76.50 each from monies handed to the International Committee of the Red Cross from the sale of Japanese assets in neutral countries or those that had been at war with the Allied powers. An interesting article entitled, 'Compensating the Railwaymen', charting the history of the Far East prisoner of war compensation claim and written by academic Dr Clare Makepeace, was published in *History Today* (April 2014, pp. 51–57).

The much respected Liverpool banker and businessman, and former Senior British Officer at Tamarkan camp in Thailand, Brigadier (later Sir) Philip Toosey, was one of the prime movers in the establishing of FEPOW Clubs across the North West of England in the early days. In addition, he was instrumental in establishing early links with the Liverpool School of Tropical Medicine. This was vital, as it secured the necessary specialist medical expertise needed then, and later, by sick Far East veterans (see Chapter 5), and was to have a profound effect on Far East POW health and welfare matters long into the future. This relationship formed the bedrock of a six decade long collaboration between the Tropical School and former Far East prisoner of war. Toosey used his considerable influence, diplomacy and powers of persuasion to great advantage to further the Far East POW cause, not least in encouraging the National Federation at its inception to invite General Percival to be their first President in 1951. Thereafter, Toosey and Percival worked closely together at the highest level, lobbying parliament regarding compensation and pension rights, work that was to continue long after both men had died.

The National Federation organised annual conferences and every two years or so the conference would be combined with a Reunion attended by hundreds more Far East POW. Bob Hucklesby helped to organise one in 1995 in Bournemouth to which 800 FEPOW, wives and relations came. These were large social gatherings, each year held in different towns and cities across the country and hosted by one of the local clubs, to which many VIP guests were entertained, including HRH Prince Phillip, Lord and Lady Mountbatten of Burma, and the Australian surgeon, Weary Dunlop, who is pictured on page 229, meeting Steve Cairns (right, with his back to the camera).

In the mid-1950s the National Federation elected to create an independent welfare fund to more effectively manage the monies raised specifically to relieve hardship. The first, the Central Welfare Fund (CWF), was set up in 1954 and this was followed by a second, the Far East (Prisoners of War and Internees) Fund (FEF) in 1959, each having a separate board of Trustees.

The Federation continued until 2005 when, due to naturally dwindling numbers forcing the closure of many clubs, the decision was made to wind it up and hand over the reins to the next generation in the form of a charity repre-senting the children and families of Far East prisoners of war (COFEPOW). This organisation had come into being to run a fundraising campaign to build the country's first, dedicated Far East POW Memorial Building and museum. The building is situated at the National Memorial Arboretum (NMA) at Alrewas in Staffordshire. On VJ Day (15 August) 2005 the country marked the 60th anniversary of the ending of the Second World War. At the NMA, following their successful fundraising appeal, COFEPOW officially opened the Far East prisoners of War Memorial Building in front of an audience of 3,500 guests, including over 300 veterans and internees, the families and friends of Far East POW, VIPs and dignitaries.

The welfare work, especially social welfare previously carried out by the Funds' Trustees and in association with the Royal British Legion, was taken on by a new organisation, the National FEPOW Fellowship Welfare Reunion Association (NFFWRA), formed in 2010 of which Bob is the President. It continues to work alongside the few remaining organisations, most notably the Java FEPOW Club, whose Welfare Officer, Margaret Martin supports Far East POW, internees, wives and widows, irrespective of whether or not they were ever a member of a FEPOW Club.

Central Welfare Trust (CWF)

This was established in November 1954 when the National Federation's Executive Committee acknowledged that welfare was an important factor which was beyond the resources of individual Clubs and Associations. At a meeting on 18 January 1955 it was resolved to set up the Far East pris-oners of war Central Welfare Fund with seven trustees, all appointed by the

National Federation, as well as an Honorary Treasurer and Secretary and with appropriate objects and conditions. This resolution became the Governing Instrument of the Fund and the basis of the Trust Deed and it was registered under the War Charities Act 1940.

Money for the fund was initiated by a large and generous donation from the 18th Division Officers' Association. There then followed donations from individual Far East POW as well as from clubs and associations. Subsequently, the CWF received grants from the Ministry of Pensions and National Insurance from the residual balances of Japanese assets after the per capita distributions, amounting to £56,166.55. The Trustees drew up a Welfare Guide setting out how welfare claims had to be made either through a club or association, or through recognised voluntary organisations such as the Royal British Legion, and which was regularly revised and updated over time. Day-to-day matters were dealt with by a Management Committee set up by the Fund, consisting from the 1970s of chairman of the Fund Reuben Kandler, vice chairman Harold Payne and the Honorary legal adviser Charles Elston.

The Far East (Prisoners of War and Internees) Fund (FEF)

This second Trust Fund was created in 1959 by the Trustees of the CWF when further assets from Japanese interests, amounting to £132,000.00, were donated by the International Committee of the Red Cross. They directed that the monies should be used for welfare, including now for the benefit of former civilian internees.

So now there were two Funds and they reported to the National Federation Conference each year. As the objects of FEF, set out in a Deed of Trust, were more precisely defined, from then on most of the funds forthcoming were channelled into that one. Monies could be and were transferred from one Fund to the other as necessary.

It is important to note that welfare funds are still available to all Far East POW, Internees and widows in need, whether or not they have been, or are, a member of a Club or Association, only now through the Royal British Legion. Also, both Trust Funds have always had contact with other similar charities such as the Royal British Legion and the Soldiers' and Sailors' Families Association (SSAFA) and on many occasions they shared in providing the welfare grants. Welfare claims could be for hospital treatment, a sack of coal, children's clothing or fees for specialist education, whatever was deemed necessary to those eligible and in greatest need by Club Welfare Officers. Welfare grants were never given directly to the individual but rather to the provider of the service or goods with two exceptions, one hospital payments and two grants for care home residents.

In about 1967 the Trustees of both Funds realised that its welfare money was running out and would not be able to meet the needs of the growing number of welfare cases. The Chairman (who chaired both funds) and the Vice Chairman of the CWF, one with connections in the City the other in military circles, set out to raise funds. In all, including donations from the Queen Mary's Roehampton Trust, the King's Fund and Regimental Associations plus a radio appeal by Dame Vera Lynn and donations from the POW veterans themselves well over £410,000 was raised. This money was used to top up the Fund and, through a wise and careful investment strategy managed by the Trustees, it continued increasing. It was used to top up funding up until the closure of Trust funds. The Welfare Fund Trusts were finally wound up in two stages between 2009 and 2011. First monies in the FEF was transferred to the CWF, prior to the drafting of a Deed of the Declaration of Trust to avoid complications caused by the restrictions set out in the forming of the FEF. The CWF ceased to attract any further funding from November 2009 when its assets were donated to the Royal British Legion coupled with a Declaration of Trust which safeguarded the Funds' policies and ensured that those monies were ring-fenced for use only for and by former Far East POW and their widows until there are no more claims and then any money left could be used for normal Royal British Legion welfare.[1]

Part II – Steve Cairns MBE OBE (1918–2012)

Steve Cairns forged and maintained links between Far East POW and the Liverpool School of Tropical Medicine, from the late 1940s until his death in 2012. In his welfare work he was largely self-taught, a driven, hardworking man, plain speaking and mischievous, always the joker. But this belies the capable and serious man beneath the public persona. Steve knew and understood suffering and he cared deeply about people, most especially his comrades and fellow survivors, and he fought tooth and nail to defend them. Both they, and the staff at the Tropical School, grew to admire and respect him and his tireless work. Much of what follows has been drawn from notes, extracts from his and other oral history interviews, as well as from his extensive archive of papers, lodged with the Tropical School between 2008 and 2012.

Percival Steven Cairns was born in Stretford in Manchester on 9 July 1918. His father died in 1920 as a result of mustard gas poisoning during the war and Steve was raised by his invalid mother, Cissie Cairns. He left school at fourteen and was apprenticed to Metropolitan Vickers. His interviews for the study (he gave three in all) are long and detailed and peppered with humorous anecdotes. One lovely example concerns Steve as a teenager, describing how he sought to enliven the Sunday School classes he took.

I had a popular class, all my class were seven- and eight-year-olds. I used to pick a story from the Bible and tell it in modern parlance. In the Bible stories I told, they all had cars and bicycles! [long pause while Steve gaffaws].

In July 1939, along with a thousand other 21-year-olds, he reported to the tented militia summer camp at Arrowe Park in Birkenhead, to join 'Hore-Belisha's Militia' (Leslie Hore Belisha being the Minister for War who had introduced the militia as a form of conscription). Steve recalled 'I'd just completed my apprenticeship as a gun fitter at Metropolitan Vickers. And when they found out … [they] immediately made me a Lance Bombadier, sent me to Southampton University College of Science where I passed out my exams and became … a gun artificer.' He spent the next two years with DEMS, Defence Equipment Merchant Shipping based in Hull, fitting guns to merchant ships and training crewmembers. Steve was sent to Durban in South Africa in September 1941, from where he was drafted to Singapore, landing in November 1941. In late January 1942 he sustained a gunshot injury which needed surgery, after which he was moved to a temporary hospital at Gilman Barracks near the docks just before Singapore fell.

I was the senior NCO in a party of 28 … in two wards, one doctor, a surgeon and a padre. Well the Japs started shelling the hospital … We were mustered out on to a lawn in front of the hospital … four machine guns trained on us … they brought the surgeon out with his hands tied behind his back, and the padre. I don't know what happened to the doctor … they just pulled a revolver out and shot 'em both.

After a few months in Changi POW camp, Steve was in one of the first parties to leave for Thailand where he built embankments and excavated cuttings until the railway was completed. In 1945 at Tamarkan camp, having been discovered smuggling batteries for the hidden camp radio, he was taken by the Kempetai (Japanese secret police) to Kaorin camp where he was tortured, his life saved only by the sudden ending of the war. Steve returned home via military hospitals in Rangoon, Calcutta, Poona and Bombay before boarding the French Hospital ship the SS *Louis Pasteur* to Southampton.

He made it home to his mother on Christmas Eve but was admitted to Manchester Royal Infirmary the day after Boxing Day. Soon after he was transferred to Smithdown Road Hospital in Liverpool (later renamed Sefton General), where he spent almost two years as an in-patient, under the care of doctors from the Tropical School. It was there that he learned that due to his injuries, he would never be able to father children. At his interview in 2008 Steve reflected on this.

I have no bitterness against the Japanese … we all do horrible things to each other in wartime, I think we're all guilty of that. If I was asked had I forgiven the Japanese … I'd quietly say, 'No', because they deprived me of the one thing I wanted and that was a family of my own. And I hate them for that … the fact they stopped me having children. I've never stopped hating them for that. I sometimes sit quietly in church, I have many friends in the church … and they've all tried to teach me the art of reconciliation. Dear old Ray [Rossiter], he's been at me for ages.

From late 1945, newly promoted Brigadier Toosey made regular welfare visits to fellow POW residing on the 'Tropical' wards at Smithdown Road, offering help and support. In a letter dated 27 September 2008, Steve recalled his ward there and meeting Brigadier Toosey.

In charge was Matron Wood, she was like a mother to us all … I was over-whelmed with the warmth, concern and hospitality of the Liverpool folk … I asked Matron Wood if I could help in any way and I virtually became her clerk. I learned how to use an old upright Remington typewriter … She asked me one day if I would like to take the specimen slides to Pembroke Place, the Tropical School, each day. I was delighted … stool and blood specimens on glass slides contained in a wooden box, six inches long with a leather strap carrying handle … Smithdown Road, that's where my education started … Toosey, who I knew by reputation although I'd never met him in the prison camps. And we became very close friends; he encouraged me in all sorts of things … I spent two years studying and I thought well, I'm damned lucky.

In early 1946 Toosey accompanied Steve to Chester Castle, where he was to give sworn evidence related to his torture for the War Crimes Trials in Tokyo. Toosey must have recognised in the pugnacious, young Mancunian, a tenacity and determination that could be put to good use. He

Figure 2 1949, Steve feeding the pigeons in Trafalgar Square on his way to the annual FEPOW conference.

urged Steve to enroll at night school to learn about welfare work and war pension rights, even helping out with train fares when necessary. In late 1947 Steve, now back home in Stretford, finally took up his old job at Metropolitan Vickers. He joined the Manchester FEPOW Association (a branch of which met at the Stretford Working Men's Club) and was soon appointed as Welfare Officer. He was also closely involved with the Returned Far East Prisoner of War Association whose President was the Countess Mountbatten of Burma. In a letter, dated May 1951, the organisation wrote asking him to distribute consignments of food and clothing sent from Australia to Far East POW families in the area. Over the years his employer was very supportive, allowing him time off for his welfare work. As the Manchester Association's FEPOW Welfare Officer from the late 1960s to mid-1990s, he encouraged and chivvied thousands of men to go for TDIs.

From 1962 to 1983 he was Chairman of the Department of Employment's Disabled Advisory Committee; from 1962 to 2000 he also chaired of the War Pensions Welfare Committee. In the late 1960s Steve and others met with Paul Dean of the Department of Health and Social Security when it was agreed that a special FEPOW Unit would be set up at the Ministry of Pensions at Norcross in Blackpool to process Far East POW referrals for TDI's to designated hospitals around the country. Steve made it his business to learn about the Law and he was not afraid to speak his mind even in a courtroom, if the case warranted it.

In 1972, when he extended his role from Manchester FEPOW club's Welfare Officer to working for the National Federation, he expected to continue using that title. At interview in 2009, FEPOW Padre Ray Rossiter recalled Steve's contribution with affection and great admiration while noting it wasn't always plain sailing. The Federation insisted that Steve would be known as an 'Adviser' and not an 'Officer'.

Figure 4 Steve (left) next to Professor Herbert Gillies and Revd Ray Rossiter, at the presentation of the optical scanning machine to Dr Wendi Bailey (2nd right) in 1983. Also present, 3rd right, Les Martin, Liverpool FEPOW Club secretary *(courtesy Steve Cairns)*

There's a distinction. You see, we are not like the usual run of ex-servicemen's associations, we haven't got a headquarters and branches. We've got 70-odd autonomous clubs and associations who are separate entities but banded together under the umbrella of a federation. And we have to make that [distinction]. Oh it annoyed Steve terrifically when he was told he couldn't be called a Welfare Officer. Welfare Adviser? Oh, he couldn't understand that at all. But of course, the Federation has no officers because the individual clubs have their welfare officers, and Steve over all, advising. We reconciled him to it, eventually.

Despite his teasing tone, Ray expressed sincere admiration for Steve's untiring work and his commitment to FEPOW welfare matters.

He was always willing to involve himself in somebody's troubles ... he's amassed this vast amount of knowledge, I don't suppose there's a person in the United Kingdom that knows more about [FEPOW] pensions than Steve Cairns. He's got it all at his fingertips. A remarkable man, remarkable man.

In the Queen's Silver Jubilee Honours in 1977 Steve was awarded the MBE for services to FEPOW welfare. In 1983, he spearheaded an appeal among

FEPOW clubs to raise £4,000 needed to buy an optical scanning machine to aid the diagnosis of *Strongyloides* infections (see Chapter 5).

It was presented later that year to Dr Wendi Bailey, head of the Tropical School's Diagnostic Laboratory (Figure 3). In his 1987 report to conference, Steve noted the long-awaited FEPOW psychiatric study, and thesis, by Dr Khan, consultant psychiatrist, was completed. He also commented that 'in 1979, an interim pilot report ... was published. The D.H.S.S. FEPOW Unit statistics showed a marked increase in War Pension Awards for psychiatric problems, indicating they ranked third amongst FEPOW disabilities, e.g. of 835 claims to date, 600 were successful, thanks to Dr Khan.'

Ten years later in 1997 a landmark legal ruling was made which was to have a beneficial effect on the success of Steve's Pension Appeals' work. A test case was brought to challenge stringent new rules introduced in 1995 that had made it much more difficult for disabled veterans to claim a war disablement pension later in life due to a deterioration in their health, caused or exacerbated by war service, if they could not produce documentary proof of what had happened. On Friday 17 October 1997, High Court Judge Mr Justice Alliott, sitting in Court No. 11 at the Royal Courts of Justice on the Strand in London, ruled in the case of a former serviceman (Cyril Bennett, a D-Day veteran and not a Far East POW) that his war service pension appeal should be allowed regardless of there being no evidence from the time of the incident to prove that it had happened.

Mr Justice Alliott's ruling was that a man or woman's word was to be accepted if he or she was deemed to be a 'credible' witness. The ruling led to thousands of veterans, including former Far East POW, who had been refused war pensions due to a lack of evidence, having their cases reviewed. Coupled with the continuing work of the Tropical School this ruling helped many

Figure 5
Steve Cairns (standing), NFFCA National Welfare adviser addressing a FEPOW conference in the 1970s

more Far East veterans to at last get the assistance they were entitled to.

Returning to Ray Rossiter's interview, as well as paying tribute to Steve's extensive knowledge and his commitment, he also made a point of acknowledging the role of Steve's wife, Gwen.

> Of course he was lucky in a way because Gwen, his wife ... did all the decorating, all the gardening ... and Steve was left to get on with his welfare work, no let or hindrance, she was a great help to him.

In Steve's case he was indeed blessed. At interview he pointed out, 'I had two wonderful women in my life. I'm very fortunate, very fortunate indeed.' He was referring to Gwen and to Peggy Cooke. Peggy's husband, Bill, had served in the Royal Navy and been a POW in Hong Kong for nearly four years. The two couples had known each other for years but when Gwen died Steve did not cope well. Peggy was also widowed and in time she invited Steve down from Manchester to just outside Bridgewater in Somerset for short holidays to try and help him. Eventually, in 1998, she offered him a home and much-needed companionship. Both were always at pains to tell people that their relationship was purely platonic. Peggy helped him regain his balance so he could carry on with his life's work but inevitably in time she became Steve's carer.

Steve recalled at interview how, early in 2000, he had been invited to have lunch with Her Majesty Queen Elizabeth the Queen Mother at Clarence House, when they discussed, among other things, how to make the best gin and tonic! Steve relished telling the story. What must it have meant to the lad from Manchester?

By February 2001 at the age of 83, Steve noted that he had referred 11,372 men for TDIs; undertaken 9,564 war pension claims for POW and widows and presented 653 appeals at Pension Appeal Tribunals, with a success rate of 48 per cent.[2] He was rightly proud of his record. Over the decades he relished nothing more than painstakingly preparing a case for an appeal tribunal.

Just three months earlier, in November 2000, after a 15-year campaign (following decades of appeals and refusals), Prime Minister Tony Blair announced that the Government was to make an ex-gratia award to each former Far East POW, FEPOW widow and Civilian Internee. In Steve's written report to the Federation's annual conference that year, he paid tribute to one of the many who had worked hard for this outcome. 'Again, we have to thank ... Major Philip Malins MBE, who instigated the special FEPOW Gratuity Claim ... [all] surviving FEPOW at November 2000, or their widows, would receive £10,000 each.'[3]

Steve was asked by the Department of Pensions to oversee the application screening process as he had the most accurate FEPOW records available.

Figure 6 Steve enjoying a joke (probably one of his own!), as many will remember him … at the Tropical School's FEPOW meeting, February 2010 *(author's photograph)*

Peggy readily agreed and so, from the dining room of her bungalow near Bridgewater, and with the help of a small volunteer army of her friends, Royal Mail delivered sacks full of applications daily, which were painstakingly processed. It went on for many, many months.

In February 2002, with the team processing on average 40 claims per week, Steve reported to the National Conference that to date they had received 27,944 claim forms in all (from Far East POW, widows and Internees), of which 22,945 had been paid out, 8,655 being to Far East POW veterans. Claims from widows and Internees amounted to 14,424, of which 12,400 had been paid out. There were 4,465 rejected claims and 469 still under investigation. Sadly, but inevitably, some claims were bogus. But there were also others made by widows believing they had a claim, only to find that their late husbands had never actually been in captivity in the Far East. By any standards the statistics were impressive, but given the voluntary effort involved, the mountains of biscuits and gallons of tea consumed, never mind the temporary loss of Peggy's dining room, they are exceptional.

In 2002, the Golden Jubilee year, aged 84, Steve was back at the Palace to receive the OBE in recognition of over 50 years' voluntary service to FEPOW welfare. For over 60 years Steve Cairns was a constant link for staff at the Tropical School, the personification of the FEPOW motto: To keep going the spirit that kept us going. When Reg Coite, Secretary to the Manchester FEPOW Association, addressed the 20th Annual National Federation Conference in Buxton, in 1971, he finished with this:

> In the camps we learned to look after ourselves and each other. We tried, as far as we were able, to look after the sick and the defenceless … and that, as an Association, is just what we are doing today. … Inevitably, as the years roll by, our ranks will thin out and I am sure that when the trumpets sound 'on the other side' for the last FEPOW, something quite unique will have vanished from this land.

Steve Cairns was one of those unique Far East prisoners of war.

APPENDIX III

LIST OF INTERVIEWEES

(Name, countries held captive in, year interviewed)

Alexander, Stephen, C., Singapore, Thailand (2007)
Anckorn, Fergus G., Singapore, Thailand (2007)
Arkush, David, Singapore, Thailand (2007)
Audus, Leslie J., Java, Spice Islands, Java (2009)
Bailey, Kenneth 'Ken' A. G., Singapore, Thailand (2007)
Baker, Alfred 'Alf' T. J., Singapore, Rabaul New Britain (2007)
Barton, Peter, Java, Japan (2007)
Baxter, F. John, Java, Japan (2008)
Berkeley, Sydney J., Sumatra (2007)
Boardman, Thomas 'Tom', Singapore, Thailand (2009)
Bolitho, William 'Bill' S., Sumatra (2007)
Brown, John 'Jack' R., Singapore, Thailand (2008)
Brown, William 'Bill', Singapore, Thailand (2007)
Cairns, P. Steven 'Steve', Singapore, Thailand (2008)
Chalker, Jack B., Singapore, Thailand (2007, 2008, 2010)
Cole, Victor A., Singapore, Thailand (2007)
Darch, Ernest 'Ernie' G., Java, Singapore, Borneo (2009)
Davis, Reginald 'Reg' G., Hong Kong, Japan (2007)
De Wardener, Hugh E., Singapore, Thailand (2007)
Drower, William 'Bill' M., Singapore, Thailand (2007)

Dunstan, Peter G., Singapore, Thailand (2008)
Edwards, J. Hugh, Java, Japan (2008)
Elston, Charles H., Singapore, Thailand (2013)
Eva, Owen V., Singapore, Thailand (2007)
Evans, Thomas 'Tom' H., Singapore, Thailand (2008)
Fogarty, Derek R., Java, Spice Islands, Sumatra (2008)
Frankland A. William 'Bill' Singapore (2012)
Hesp, Harry A., Singapore (2007, 2008)
Holland, George, Singapore, Thailand (2008)
Holland Kenneth 'Ken' A., Singapore (2011)
Hucklesby, F. Robert 'Bob', Singapore, Thailand (2014)
Jackson, W. Thomas 'Tom', Java, Japan (2008)
Jones, H. Cyril, Java, Japan (2007)
Kinmonth, Maurice H., Java (2007)
Knight, Edgar 'Ed' F., Java, Japan (2007)
Lock, Harold E., Java, Spice Islands, Java (2007) check
Manning, Leopold, Singapore, Thailand, Japan (2007)
McCreath, Henry G., Singapore, Thailand
Moon, Roger Singapore, Thailand (2009)
Morley, Denis J., Hong Kong, Japan (2008
Morrell, Robert 'Bob' E., Java, Spice Islands, Java (2007)
Naylor, W. Maurice, Singapore, Thailand (2009)
Peach, A. Nowell H., Java (2007, 2008)
Peall, Charles G., Singapore, Thailand (2008)
Pratt, John L., Singapore, Thailand, Saigon (2007)
Rossiter, Raymond 'Ray' S. D., Singapore, Thailand, Saigon (2009)
Ryall, Frederick 'Fred' T., Java (2008)
Scarr, Francis 'Frank', Singapore, Thailand (2008, 2009)
Seiker M Frederick 'Fred' C., Singapore, Thailand (2007)
Skippen Douglas 'Doug' O., Singapore, Burma (2008)
Smith Alexander 'Alex' F., Java, Japan (2008)
Smith, J. Gordon, Malaya, Thailand (2007)
Stobbart, W. Edward 'Eddie', Singapore, Thailand (2009)
Stott, Geoffrey H., Celebes, Japan (2007)
Surr, James 'Jim', Java, Singapore, Sumatra (2008)
Tidey, John T., Singapore, Thailand, Japan (2008)
Titherington, T. Arthur, Singapore, Taiwan (2008)
Turbutt, Arthur F., Java, Haruku, Java (2009)
Urquhart, Alistair K., Singapore, Thailand, Japan (2007)
Vickerstaff, N. Stanley 'Stan', Singapore, Taiwan (2014)
Voisey, Rouse O., Java, Spice Islands, Java, Sumatra (2008)

Wakefield, James 'Jim' T., Hong Kong (2007)
White, Arthur H., Hong Kong, Japan (2007)
Whitehead, Sydney, Java, Singapore (2007)
Wyatt, R. Franklin 'Frank', Singapore, Korea, Japan (2009)
Yerbury, Franklin 'Frank', Java, Singapore (2007)

OTHERS

Wool, Jane, daughter of Ken Bailey
Bailey, Pearl, wife of Ken
Buchanan, Stanley, crew member Orbita to Liverpool (2010)
Fogarty, Mary, wife of Derek Fogarty
Freeman, Marie, RAF Cosford, nee Goddard, widow Fred Freeman (2008)
Hannaford Rambonnet, Nini, widow (2008)
Neilson, Kathleen, ATS, Resettlement Unit (2011)
Smallridge, Emily, widow of Ken
Turbutt, Lola, wife of Arthur (2009)
Wearne, widow of Padre 'Tiny' Wearne (2008)
Yerbury, Olive, wife of Frank

National FEPOW Fellowship Welfare Reunion Association (NFFWRA) weekend in Llandudno, October 2014. Standing in front of the War Memorial on the Promenade are the following FEPOW veterans, from left to right: (front row) Vic Pugh, Arthur Howard, Jim Crossan, Arthur Bowen, George Housego, Stan Burridge, Ernie Boswell (second row) Eric Adie, Bill Macauley, **Tom Boardman**, **Maurice Naylor**, **Bob Hucklesby**, Jack Jennings (third row) Tom McKie, who is next to FEPOW chaplain Mrs Pauline Simpson and Nick Roberts (NFFWRA Standard bearer). Tom, Maurice and Bob were interviewees for the oral history study.

NOTES

Notes to Introduction

1   There are two excellent histories of LSTM – H. J. Power. *Tropical Medicine in the Twentieth Century. A history of the Liverpool School of Tropical Medicine 1898–1998.* (London, 1999); and P. J. Millar *Malaria, Liverpool – an illustrated history of the Liverpool School of Tropical Medicine, 1898–1998.* (Liverpool, 1998).

2   P. N. Davies. *The Man Behind the Bridge. Colonel Toosey and the River Kwai.* London 1991.

3   J. Summers. *Phillip Toosey The Colonel of Tamarkan and the Bridge on the River Kwai.* London, 2005.

4   This work is presented in more detail in Chapter 5 of this book. A summary article of the Liverpool FEPOW research was published in 2009 – D. Robson, E. Welch, N. J. Beeching, G. V. Gill. Consequences of captivity – health effects of Far East imprisonment in World War 2. *Quarterly Journal of Medicine* 2009; 102: 87–96.

5   G. V. Gill. Coping with Crisis. Medicine and disease on the Burma Railway 1942 – 1945. PhD thesis. University of Liverpool, 2009.

6   See bibliography.

7   Oral history interviewee and author of *My World War II Travels.* 1997 private publication.

8   See also John Coast *Railroad of Death*, July 1946 and Ronald Hastain's *White Coolie*, 1947.

9   Captain Andrew Atholl Duncan, Argyll and Sutherland Highland regiment.

10 Part I – *'Notify Alec Rattray...'* and Part II – *'...A.A.Duncan is OK'.*

11 Historian Jonathan Moffatt; biographer Julie Summers; Mike Parkes; www.research-ingfepowhistory.org.uk.

12 M. H. Parkes. 'Life, Health and Social Issues among ex-Far Eastern Prisoners of War' – an oral history enquiry. MPhil dissertation. University of Liverpool, 2012.

13 K. Khan. Psychiatric Morbidity amongst ex-Far Eastern prisoners of war more than thirty years after repatriation. PhD thesis. University of Liverpool. 1987.

Notes to Chapter 1

1 W. M. Drower. *Our Man on the Hill: A British Diplomat Remembers.* 1993, private publication.

2 Rod Beattie, *The Death Railway – A Brief History.* (Bangkok: 2005) NB figures given are revised as at 2014.

3 L. J. Audus. *Spice Island Slaves* see bibliography.

4 The term 'hellship' was coined by Far East POW at the time; see reverse of the Liberation Questionnaire of John Francis Clement, 5th Field Regiment, question 5, TNA WO344.

5 T. I. E. Moe. Starvation and mistreatment of British POWs aboard the *Singapore Maru* November 1942. 1945. TNA WO235/1043.

Notes to Chapter 2

1 C. W. Maisey. *Diary and report of work carried out from the time of the capitulation in Java – 9 March until 12 April 1942.* TNA. ref WO344/391/1. Typed from notes and memory on board the SS *Orantes* 24 November 1945 and submitted to MI9

2 Sergeant Harry Hall, 197 Field Ambulance RAMC (diary, courtesy Hall family).

3 Post-war, Wynd became a celebrated novelist, his 1977 book *The Ginger Tree* reflecting his deep knowledge and understanding of Japanese military history.

4 A. MacCarthy. *A Doctor's War.* p. 76.

5 F Samethini. *The Sky Looked Down. A Memoir of the Burma Railway.* Private publication. 1992; see http://theskylookeddown.blogspot.co.uk/; also http://hansamethini.blogspot.com/2009/04/10-prison-camp-musician-december-1944.html.

6 My thanks to Midge Gillies, author of *Barbed Wire University*, for sending me a copy of this article.

7 See https://www.bell-foundation.org.uk.

8 The original medical notes from his study into burning feet are with his family.

9 E. Welch, A. N. H. Peach, M. Parkes and G. V. Gill. 'Burning feet syndrome: an old tropical syndrome revisited.' *Annals of Tropical Medicine and Public Health.* 2013. 6. 65–70.

10 H. E. de Wardener. Cholera Epidemic among prisoners-of-war in Siam. *The Lancet.* 1946; 1: 636–640; and H. E. de Wardener & B. Lennox. Cerebral beriberi (Wernicke's Encephalopathy). *The Lancet* 1947; 1: 11–17.

11 Private papers of Captain Patrick MacArthur RAMC, held in the Documents and Sound Section of the Imperial War Museum. IWM ref Documents.18736.

12 *Scenes from Sumatra*, p. 50.

13 http://digitalcommons.macalester.edu/thdabooks/1/.

14 IWM. ref 67/330/1 this poster drawn by Geoffrey Barlow Gee was found among the papers of Major Claude Aylwin.

15 For more about Sid Scales see Java FEPOW 1942 Club. *Prisoners in Java* (2007).

16 *The Changi Murals.* (Changi Museum, 2002); http://www.petrowilliamus.co.uk/murals/painting/painting.htm.

17 M. Parkes. *'Notify Alec Rattray...'* (2002) pp. 66–74.

18 M. Parkes. Churchill in Captivity. *Memo Magazine.* Vol. 32. Churchill Museum, Missouri. Fall 2009 pp. 8–13.

19 Birkenhead Central Library Wilfred Owen memorial window; Birkenhead Priory HMS *Conway* memorial windows; St Hildeburgh's Church RNLI memorial window, Hoylake, Wirral.

20 Thanks to Richard Upton for his kind permission to quote from his father's post-war report.

Notes to Chapter 3

1   P. MacArthur. IWM Ref Documents.18736.

2   D. Skippen. *My World War II Travels.* (1997), p20.

3   T. H. Hewlett. Report on Fukuoka No. 17 Omuta, Japan. Presented to meeting of the American Defenders of Bataan and Corregidor, December 1978, see www.mansell.com.

4   H. P. Bryson. Eating rubber seeds and other internment memories. *Malaysia.* 1966: 24–25.

5   L. J. Audus. Archives of Hamilton Health Sciences and the Faculty of Health Sciences, McMaster University, Dr Charles Roland Oral History Collection 1994.44.16 HCM 17–86: 11–14; see Audus. 1946; 211–215.

6   E. E. Dunlop. Clinical lessons from prisoner of war hospitals in the Far East. *The Medical Journal of Australia.* (1946) 1: 22: 761.

7   J. Markowitz. I was a Knife, Fork and Spoon Surgeon. *Canadian Digest.* 1946; 87.

8   P. MacArthur. IWM Ref Documents.18736. p. 175.

9   Jack Spitttle's son Brian, not only made this fascinating collection available to the study but also published extracts on a blog which is highly recommended (see https://bspittle.wordpress.com/2014/08/).

10 Copy in LSTM collection; also published in H. Howarth's book *Where Fate Leads* (1983).

11 I. L. Duncan. (1983). p. 30.

12 Bryson. (1966). pp. 24–25.

13 B. Wheeler. The Man Sent from God. *Reader's Digest* (1983), pp. 159–191.

14 Coates. *Med J Aust.* (1946). p. 755.

15 See Dunlop. *BMJ.* (1946), p. 484; A. E. Coates. Surgery in Japanese Prison Camps. *The Australian and New Zealand Journal of Surgery.* 1946; XV : 3: 156.

16 Smith. (2008); also *Creativity Behind Barbed Wire*, Routledge 2012. Copyright (© 2015) From Chapter 4 Tins, Tubes and Tenacity, Inventive Medicine in Camps in the Far East in *Cultural Heritage and Prisoners of War, Creativity Behind Barbed Wire* by Meg Parkes/ eds Harold Mytum and Gilly Carr. Reproduced by permission of Taylor and Francis Group LLC, a division of Informa plc.

17 P. McArthur. IWM Ref Documents.18736

18 H. E. de Wardener. Cholera epidemic among prisoners of war in Siam. *Lancet.* May 1946; 1: 640.

19 E. E. Dunlop. Clinical Lessons from Prisoner of War Hospitals in the Far East. *Australian Journal of Medicine.* 1946; 1:22:763.

20 Hewlett (1978).

21 G. Bras. Dr Charles Roland Oral History Collection. Archives of Hamilton Health Sciences and the Faculty of Health Sciences. McMaster University. 1994.44. HCM 24 – 86: 16.

22 Dr Thomas Wilson MB, B.Ch, qualified in Belfast in the late 1920s. He joined the Malayan Medical Service as a Health Officer in Malacca, in 1931. While serving with the

Federated Malay States Volunteer Force (FMSVF) he transferred to the 6th Anti-Malaria Unit (RAMC). In February 1942 Captain Wilson was captured in Singapore along with an entomologist colleague, Major John Reid RAMC, who pre-war had worked at the Institute for Medical Research (IMR) in Kuala Lumpur.

In April 1943 both men left Changi POW camp attached as advisers on anti-malarial work and nutrition to "F" Force, a party of 7,000 Australians and British POW destined for Songkurai, a notorious work camp on the Thailand-Burma Railway. For the next eight months Wilson and Reid undertook extraordinarily detailed research studies into both nutrition and malaria among the party.

Returning to Changi at the end of 1943 with the remnants of "F" Force (over half had died up country) Wilson and Reid made lengthy secret reports to the POW HQ medical staff. Both survived captivity and eventually returned to the Malayan Medical Service. They published extracts from their reports in 1947 and again in 1949 (see Bibliography).

In 1949 Wilson joined the IMR becoming Director from 1956-1959. After returning to Britain, in 1962 he joined the staff of LSTM where he headed the Department of Tropical Hygiene, working on filariasis in Southeast Asia for which he and his team received international recognition. In 1971 he returned to the IMR as a consultant. Thomas Wilson died in 1988.

(Thanks to Jonathan Moffatt, historian to the Malayan Volunteers Group, for information for included here).

23 R. F. Braithwaite. *Medical report on conditions at No. 3 camp Pakenbaroe, Sumatra, July 1944– August 1945.* NA. ref WO344/366/1: 1–2.

24 J. Simpson. *Report on malnutrition at Chungkai April – May 1943.* Private papers.

25 Duncan. (1983). p. 30.

26 Braithwaite. p. 1.

27 H. P. Bryson. Nationalized Snails. *Malaysia.* Dec 1965.

28 Dunlop. *BMJ.* (1946). p. 484.

29 J. C. Collins. *Report on the Prisoner of War camps at Kuala Lumpur, Changi and Kranji Singapore – 1942 /1945.* Changi Report. Army Medical Services Museum (AMSM). ACQ3081. pp. 15–16.

30 Wheeler. (1983). p. 165.

31 M. E. Barrett. *Blood Transfusions by Amateurs.* Wellcome Library IOT.AA9 report written 24.9.45.

32 Wheeler. (1983). p. 172.

33 Coates. *ANZJS.* (1946). p. 150.

34 P. McArthur. IWM Ref Documents.18736.

35 Rawlings. (1972). p. 75.

36 I. Duncan. 1983. p. 30 account of Dr Bras' homemade microscope used for blood typing.

37 E. E. Dunlop. *BMJ.* (1946). p. 484.

38 M. E. Barrett (1945); also Wheeler. (1983). p. 182.

39 Markowitz. (1946). p. 83; Smith. (2008). p. 111; Wheeler. (1983). p. 182.

40 Coates. *Med J Aust.* (1946). p. 776; also A. E. Coates. *ANZJS.* (1946). p. 154.

41 Wheeler. (1983). pp. 172–173.

42 LSTM oral history interview with Frank Scarr (2009); J. Markowitz. *I Was a Knife, Fork and Spoon Surgeon.* Canadian Digest. (1946). p. 84.

43 F. K. Ellwell. IWM. ref LD7189.

44 Engineering. January 7, 1949. Vol.167 pp. 2–3.

45 Dunlop. *BMJ.* (1946). p. 485; see Coates. *ANZJS.* (1946). p. 153.

46 Gottrup and Leaper. Wound Healing: Historical Aspects. European Wound Management Association. (2004). Vol. 4. no. 2.

47 Taken from transcript of Captain Ennis's diary by kind permission of his daughter Mrs Jackie Sutherland; the post-mortem reports are lodged with the Liverpool School of Tropical Medicine.

Notes to Chapter 4

1   Fletcher Cooke. (1971; republished by Pen & Sword 2013). pp. 227–231.

2   Parkes. (2003). p. 120.

3   Fletcher Cooke. (1971). p. 216; Parkes. (2003) p. 121.

4   C. H. Bailey. *Life and Times of Admiral Sir Frank Twiss Social Change in the Royal Navy 1924–1970.* (Gloucester,1996). p. 95.

5   B. Hately-Broad, *War and Welfare.* (Manchester, 2009). pp. 142–145.

6   P. G. Cambray and G. G. B. Briggs. *Red Cross and St John: The official record of the humanitarian services of the War Organisation of the British Red Cross Society and Order of Saint John of Jerusalem 1939–1947.* (1949). p. 298.

7   B. Shephard. *A War of Nerves.* (London, 2000). p. 314.

8   A. L. Vischer. *Barbed Wire Disease: A Psychological Study of the Prisoner of War* (1919).

9   Far East. British Red Cross archives. September 1945 ref JWO/7/710 p. 3.

10 *The Naval Review.* Vol. XXXIV: 1: (1946); p. 36. see http://www.naval-review.org/about. asp.

11 W. L. Davis. IWM. ref 66/308/box 7.

12 P. G. Cambray and G. G. B. Briggs. Red Cross and St John War History 1939–1947. (1949). p. 312.

13 J. D. Harris. Report on work of recovery team 48, 22 September 1945. IWM. ref 95/5/1, 4.

14 G. V. Gill. University of Liverpool PhD thesis. *Coping with Crisis*: Medicine and disease on the Burma Railway 1942 – 45 THESIS 20951.GIL : 198.

15 Sitwell letter to wife 22 August 1945. Private papers Sitwell family.

16 H. D. W. Sitwell. IWM. ref 66/229/1.

17 P. Maltby. *The Diary of a Prisoner-of-War in the Far East 1942–1945.* (1997), p. 244. Private publication Maltby family.

18 Photograph by Cyril Restorick RN, crew member HMS *Implacable*; see online archive: www.maritimequest.com/warship_directory/great_britain/pages/aircraft_carriers/hms_ implacable_86_cyril_restorick_collection_page_2.htm.

19 W. M. Drower. Q Form. TNA ref WO235/867.

20 Japanese POW record cards.TNA. WO345/1–58.

21 *Welcome to Rangoon!!* Printed circulars produced by Indian Red Cross. Akhurst private collection; also see private papers of P. W. Stevens. IWM. Ref 95/9/1.

22 *No Welcome For Men From The Far East. Liverpool Evening Express*, September 19, 1945 p. 4.

23 A. Baker. *What Price Bushido.* (2001). pp. 103–104. Published memoir. For fate of 600 Gunners party see p. 19.

24 Daws. (1994). p. 345.

25 TNA WO 32/14550

26 L. J. Audus. *A Botanist's War.* pp. 181–182. Post-war private memoir, Audus family collection.

27 *Far East*, Vol. 1. No. 11, November 1945 p. 8; copy of *News from Britain*. IWM. Newspapers and journals ref E.J.5685.

28 Author's conversations with her mother Elizabeth Duncan and Iris McGowran, widow of Tom McGowran.

29 H. Churchill. *Prisoners on the Kwai.* (Dereham, 2005). p. 131.

30 www.britishpathe.com, film archive ID: 2058.10.

31 Steve Cairns' papers, LSTM collection.

Notes to Chapter 5

1 J. H. Walters, J. P. Caplan & E. W. Hayward. *A FEPOW Survey.* Report to the DHSS from Queen Mary's Hospital, Roehampton, 1971.

2 See: C. J. Smith, F. Patterson, K. J. Goulston et al. Evidence of hepatitis virus infection among Australian prisoners of war during World War II. *Medical Journal of Australia* 1987; 147: 220–30. Also: GV Gill, DR Bell & EM Vandervelde. Horizontal transmission of hepatitis B virus among British 2nd World War soldiers in south-east Asia. *Postgraduate Medical Journal* 1991; 67: 39–41.

3 A number of well-conducted US research projects explored FEPOW mortality patterns in the early post-war years. See, for example: R. J. Keehn. Follow-up studies of World War II and Korean conflict prisoners. III Mortality to January 1st 1976. *American Journal of Epidemiology* 1980; 111: 194–211.

4 The paper describing the 15 per cent prevalence of strongyloidiasis amongst FEPOWs seen in Liverpool was published in 1979 (G. V. Gill & D. R. Bell, *British Medical Journal* 1979; 2: 572–574). The overall results of the study appeared in: G. V. Gill & D. R. Bell, Persisting tropical diseases amongst former Far East prisoners of war of the Japanese. *Practitioner* 1981: 225: 531–538. The study was presented in more detail in: G. V. Gill. Long-term Health Effects of Former Prisoners of War of the Japanese. MD Thesis. University of Newcastle-upon-Tyne, 1980.

5 J. P. Caplan. Creeping eruption and intestinal strongyloidiasis. *British Medical Journal* 1949; 1: 396.

6 Gill & Bell, 1979.

7 G. V. Gill, E. Welch, J. W. Bailey, D. R. Bell & N. J. Beeching. Chronic *Strongyloides stercoralis* infection in former British Far East prisoners of war. *Quarterly Journal of Medicine* 2004; 97: 789–795.

8 W. A. Bailey. A serological test for the diagnosis of *Strongyloides* antibodies in ex-Far East prisoners of war. *Annals of Tropical Medicine and Parasitology* 1989; 83: 241–247.

9 L. K. Archibald, N. J. Beeching, G. V. Gill, J. W. Bailey & D. R. Bell. Albendazole is effective treatment for chronic strongyloidiasis. *Quarterly Journal of Medicine* 1993; 86: 191–195.

10 D. I. Grove. Strongyloidiasis in Allied ex-prisoners of war in South-East Asia. *British Medical Journal* 1980; 2: 598–601.

11 J. B. Stewart & B. J. Heaps. Fatal disseminated strongyloidiasis in an immunocompromised former prisoner of the Japanese. *Journal of the Royal Army Medical Corps.*1985; 131: 47–49.

12 There were a number of post-war descriptions in the medical literature of the FEPOW Burning Feet syndrome. See, for example: J. Simpson. Burning feet in British prisoners of war in the Far East. *Lancet* 1946: 2: 959–961.

13 H. E. de Wardener & B. Lennox. Cerebral beriberi (Wernicke's Encephalopathy). *Lancet* 1947; 1: 11–17.

14 G. V. Gill & D. R. Bell. Persisting nutritional neuropathy amongst former war prisoners. *Journal of Neurology, Neurosurgery and Psychiatry* 1982; 45: 861–865.

15 G. V. Gill, L. Henry & H. A. Reid. Chronic cardiac beriberi in a former prisoner-of-war. *British Journal of Nutrition* 1980; 44: 273–274.

16 K. Khan. *Psychiatric morbidity amongst ex-Far East Prisoners of War more than thirty years after repatriation.* PhD thesis, University of Liverpool, 1987.

17 C. Tennant, K. Goulston & O. Dent. Clinical psychiatric illness in prisoners of war of the Japanese: forty years after release. *Psychological Medicine* 1986; 16: 833–839.

18 H. J. Richardson. *Report of a study of Disabilities and Problems of Hong Kong Veterans.* Report to Canadian Pension Commission, 1964–65.

Notes to Postscript

1 While in Liverpool for the meeting, on a visit to the university's Victoria Gallery and Museum to view the dental exhibits, David mentioned a former colleague, Colin Cardwell, who had trained in dentistry with him in Liverpool during the early 1930s. Both men later joined the Royal Army Dental Corps and were posted to Singapore. Captain Cardwell was among the staff murdered by Japanese forces during the notorious Alexandra Hospital massacre on 13–14 February 1942. Noticing that Cardwell's name was not included on the University's war memorial board at the museum, David asked if it could be added. This has since been done.

2 Glasgow City Archives ref GB243 TD1764. Papers of John Francis Clement.

Notes to Appendix I

1 K. Khan. Psychiatric morbidity amongst ex-Far East Prisoners of War more than thirty years after repatriation. University of Liverpool PhD Thesis, 1987.

2 Interview with Dr Kamaluddin Khan by Meg Parkes, 15 June 2009. Liverpool School of Tropical Medicine archives.

3 J. I. Bisson. Post-traumatic stress disorder. *Brit Med J* 2007; 334: 789–793.

4 K. Khan, interview with M. Parkes; p. 6 of transcript.

Notes to Appendix II

1 I interviewed Bob Hucklesby in October 2014 and asked him about his experiences as a Far East prisoner of war. I also wanted to know more about his involvement with Far East POW welfare over the years. At the end of his interview I asked him if there was anything he would like to add to what he had told me. He said simply that, 'No organisation exists without there being a number of people prepared to take responsibility, and have the expertise to deal with that responsibility.

2 Steve Cairns' papers, File 1, item 3, LSTM

3 Steve Cairns' notes to the Java FEPOW 1942 Club

ACKNOWLEDGEMENTS

There are very many people who have contributed to the research which underpins this book.

Firstly, sincere thanks must go to all the former Far East prisoners of war and their families (listed on pages 240–242) who welcomed me and shared so openly for the oral history study, as did a number of wives and widows. They had known from my introductory letter that I was the daughter of a returned Far East prisoner of war, which may have helped me; but undoubtedly it was because I represented the Liverpool School of Tropical Medicine (LSTM) that each man so readily accepted the invitation to participate. Thanks too, to Stan Buchanan, former merchant seaman and crewmember of the repatriation ship *Orbita*, and to Edith Neilson who worked in the Civilian Resettlement Camps in 1945–46. Thank you all for sharing your memories in order that future generations could better understand the history of Far East captivity during the Second World War.

Next, grateful thanks to my mentor and *Captive Memories'* co-author, Geoff Gill, who gave me this extraordinary opportunity, and to his colleague and my other supervisor, Sally Sheard, Professor of the History of Medicine at the University of Liverpool, both of whom steered me through my MPhil. I would also like to thank physicians Dr Nick Beeching, Dr Andrew Larner, Dr Tim O'Dempsey, and historian Dr Kent Fedorowich from the University of West England, who all supported me in various ways through my academic work.

I would like to pay special tribute to the late Dr Dion Bell who cared for most of the Far East POWs seen at the Tropical School. His meticulous record keeping led the way for the research projects described in Chapter 5. Other tropical physicians involved in the care of these veterans were Dr Alistair

Reid, Dr David Smith and Dr George Wyatt. Dr Wendi Bailey led the Tropical School's Diagnostic Laboratory and developed the serological test which greatly aided *Strongyloides* worm infection diagnosis. Dr Nick Beeching was closely involved with various POW research projects, Dr Ellen Welch with strongyloidiasis and neuropathy research and Dr Debbie Robson worked on *Strongyloides* hyperinfection. My thanks also go to those at the Tropical School who accepted me as part of a very special team, especially Professor David Lalloo, Jenny Howley, Jean Taylor, Teresa Hewitt, Einion Holland, Billy Dean, Robbie Prendergast and librarian Sarah Lewis-Newton.

I am indebted to Dr Kamal Khan for allowing us to publish, for the first time, summary findings from his FEPOW Psychiatric Study and PhD thesis.

A special tribute must be paid to artist, the late Jack Chalker, for his help, guidance and kind permission to reproduce several of his drawings and paintings, both in the book and on the *Captive Memories* website.

Next, I must thank Keith Andrews whose father, like mine, survived Far East captivity. Keith's self-taught and extensive knowledge of the FEPOW holdings at The National Archives, and his diligence in seeking out and sharing countless useful documents and references, has been absolutely invaluable to my research and I am indebted to him for his support.

For permission to reproduce extracts, illustrations or quotes from private diaries and collections, sincere thanks go (in alphabetical order) to other children and grandchildren of Far East POW including: Clare Adams, David Akhurst, Selina Ballance, Keith Bettany, David Blythe, Maddie Brook, Richard Brown, Frank Clement, Peter Doyle, Carol Friend, Trish Groves, Monica Hall, Sarah Hunt, Robin Kalhorn, Ann-Louise Kinmonth, David and Mollie Lodder, Rod Margarson, Marcia McInerney, Sally McQuaid, Anne Oliver, John Pollock, Fiona Pushman, Helen Simpson, Carole Skippen, Brian Spittle, Ben Stallard, Jackie Sutherland, Andy and Ian Turbutt, Richard Upton, Martin Vaughan and Frank Williams. And thanks also to Paul and David Bartholomew for their generosity in sharing information about Far East POW artist Ashley George Old.

Museums and Archives

Thanks go to staff in the Imperial War Museum's departments of Documents, Sound Archives and Art, and the library. The oral history project was run in conjunction with the IWM's Sound Archive where copies of the recordings and transcripts are lodged. I am indebted to Jenny Wood, who recently retired from the IWM's Art Department, for her time, patience and expertise.

I wish to pay a special tribute to the former Keeper of the IWM's Department of Documents, the late Roderick Suddaby, to whom this book is in part dedicated. No question or enquiry was ever overlooked. He made his time and expertise available to me, always ready to help and, if possible, put me in touch with somebody who might know more; he never made me feel I might be wasting his time.

I owe grateful thanks to the Thackray Medical Research Trust and to Bill Mathie in particular, for support and encouragement during the inventive medicine research study.

To the many librarians and curators in archives and museums across the UK and abroad who have assisted me many thanks for your help, given willingly and often at short notice. In the UK they include Jane Davies, curator of the Queens Lancashire Regiment Archives in Preston; Pete Starling (retired curator) Army Medical Services Museum in Aldershot; staff at the University Library, Cambridge and at the City Library; archivists at the Regimental archives of the 9th Royal Northumberland Fusiliers at Alnwick Castle; the National Library of Scotland, Edinburgh; the staff at Glasgow City Archives and the Mitchell Library; Stewart Mitchell, curator at the Gordon Highlanders' Museum, Aberdeen. In London, staff at the Science Museum's store; National Army Museum's Art Collection; librarians at the Royal Artillery Museum Woolwich and the Wellcome Library; and the unknown librarian at the Inner Temple Library in London who recently, and at very short notice, dug out a reference for retired Appeal Court Judge Hedley on my behalf!

To institutions overseas, many thanks for invaluable help and guidance go to Jeya Jeyadurai, Director of Changi Museum in Singapore; Rob Beattie, Director of the Thailand-Burma Railway Centre, Kanchanaburi in Thailand; the Minister and parish office at All Saints Anglican Church in Jakarta; Wes Injerd (www.mansell.com) and the late Roger Mansell; and staff at the State Library of Victoria, Australia.

To fellow Far East prisoner of war history researchers and others who have helped, supported and shared their work with me over the years, thank you so very much. They include (in alphabetical order) Bernice Archer, Tony Banham, Lesley Clark, Jon Cooper, Sarah Edwards, Sears Eldredge, Rosemary Fell, Midge Gillies, Clare Makepeace, Margaret Martin, Brian McArthur, Tim Mercer, Jonathan Moffatt, Lizzie Oliver, Martin Percival, Phil Reed, Stephen Rockcliffe, Pauline Simpson, Nigel Stanley, Pam Stubbs and Julie Summers.

To Jill Thompson, Tracey Kellaway and David Ritchie at Pensby High School for Girls in Wirral and to Paul Cook, the former curator of Ness Botanical Gardens and his staff at the time, sincere thanks for their unstinting work on the Heritage Lottery-funded FEPOW Education Project and creation of the FEPOW Bamboo Garden.

To Anna and Lucy at Carnegie Publishing and Palatine Books, thank you so much for guiding me through this process.

Permissions

I am grateful to the Trustees of the Imperial War Museum for allowing access to their collections and to the copyright holders for their permission to quote extracts from the following papers:

Kareen Rogers for permission to use Geoffrey Barlow Gee's drawing (in Major C D L Aylwin's file, ref 67/330/1).

Sincere thanks to Taylor and Francis Group for their kind permission to quote from *Cultural Heritage and Prisoners of War, Creativity Behind Barbed Wire*, Routledge 2012; to Anne McKeage, Archivist/History of Health and Medicine Librarian, Health Sciences Library, McMaster University, Ontario Canada for permission to quote from Leslie Audus and Gerrit Bras' oral history interviews; Jeya Jeyadurai, Changi Museum, for permission to use Des Bettany's illustration on page 136; to Readers' Digest Association Inc, for permission to quote from Dr Jacob Markowitz's article, *I was a Knife, Fork and Spoon Surgeon*, in the *Canadian Readers' Digest* in 1946; to Grubb Street for permission to quote from *A Doctor's War*; Rod Beattie for permission to quote from *Death Railway. A Brief History* (2005); Gordon Smith for permission to use his sketch of the Tamarkan Still, previously published in *A Medical Student in Malaya* (2008); Robin Kalhorn for permission to quote from his father Frank Samethini's diary; to Ruth Alexander for permission to quote from her late husband Stephen's book *Sweet Kwai, Run Softly*; to Mrs Luba Estes for her kind permission to reproduce her father's, Lieutenant Alexander Skvorzov HKVDC drawing of the post-mortem.

Every effort has been made to trace copyright holders. The publishers will be glad to rectify in future editions any errors or omissions brought to their attention.

Finally, to good friends and family, including Sally, John and Jacqueline, Judith and Lawrence, Midge and Jim, Ann and George, Hannah, Luke, Denny, Pat and Kim, thank you all for offering sanctuary, good food and much-needed help on my numerous and often hectic research trips to London and elsewhere over recent years; to all my family, for understanding that this was something I had to do; and to Mike, who drove many thousands of miles around the UK, enabling me to read and make notes before every interview or archive visit, and who then listened patiently to the de-brief, always interested; thank you so much for knowing just what this has meant to me.

To anyone I have unintentionally omitted, who knows how much I have appreciated their help, apologies and sincere thanks.

Meg Parkes
March 2015

BIBLIOGRAPHY

Books:

Alexander, S. *Sweet Kwai Run Softly,* 3rd edition (Merriotts Press: Bristol 2006)

Archer, B. *The internment of Western Civilians under the Japanese 1941-1945, A Patchwork of Internment* (Hong Kong University Press: Hong Kong, 2008)

Audus, L.J. *Spice Island Slaves* (Alma: Surrey, 2001)

Baker, A.T.J. *What Price Bushido,* 2nd edition, private publication (2001)

Beattie, R. *The Death Railway,* (Bangkok: 2005)

Bell, F. *Undercover University* 2nd revised edition (Cambridge, 2001)

Coombes, J.H.H. *Banpong Express,* private publication (1948)

Campbell Hill, M.A. *Scenes from Sumatra* (Almondsbury, 2002)

Changi Museum *Don't ever again say It Can't Be Done!* (Changi University Press: Singapore, 2005)

Churchill, H. *Prisoners on the Kwai: Memoirs of Dr Harold Churchill,* edited by Dr Susan Palmer (Larks Press: Dereham, 2005)

Darch, E. *Survival in a Japanese POW camp with a Chungkol and Basket* (Minerva: London, 2000)

Daws, G. *Prisoners of the Japanese* (Robson: London, 1995)

Drower, W. M. *Our Man on the Hill* (IGS: Berkeley California, 1993)

Dunlop, E. E. *The War Diaries of Weary Dunlop* (Lennard: Hertfordshire, 1987)

Gibbs-Pancheri, P. *Volunteer!* private publication (1995)

Gillies, M. *Barbed Wire University* (Aurum: 2011)

Hardie, R. *The Burma-Siam Railway The Secret Diary of Dr Robert Hardie 1942–45* (Quadrant: London, 1984)

Hastain, R. *White Coolie* (Hodder & Stoughton: London, 1947)

Hately-Broad, B. *War and Welfare* (Manchester University Press, 2009)

Havers, R.P.W. *Reassessing the Japanese prisoner of war experience: the Changi POW Camp, Singapore, 1942-1945* (Routledge, 2012)

Howarth, H. *Where Fate Leads* (Ross Anderson: Bolton, 1983)

Kinvig, C. *River Kwai Railway The Story of the Burma-Siam Railroad* (Conway: London, 2005)

Kramer, R. *Lost Track* (Uitgever Neo Lux: Netherlands 2010)

Lewis Bryan, J.N. *The Churches of the Captivity in Malaya* (London, 1946)

MacCarthy, A. *A Doctor's War* 2ⁿᵈ edition (Grub Street: London, 2006)

Marshall, G.K. *The Changi Diaries* private publication (1988)

Martin, M. (ed) *Prisoners in Java: Accounts by Allied Prisoners of War in the Far East (1942-1945),* (Hamwic, 2007); extracts from the Java FEPOW 1942 Club's quarterly newsletters *Java Journals*

McQuaid, S.M. (ed) *Singapore Diaries: Hidden Journal of Captain R.M.Horner* (Spellmount: Stroud, 2006)

Mytum, H. and Carr, G. *Cultural Heritage of Prisoners of War Creativity Behind Barbed Wire* (Routledge: 2012)

Parkes, M. *'Notify Alec Rattray...'* (Kranji, 2002)

Parkes, M. *'...A.A.Duncan is OK'* (Kranji, 2003)

Philps, R. *Prisoner Doctor* (Book Guild: Lewes, 1996)

Power, H.J. *Tropical Medicine in the Twentieth century* (Kegan Paul: London, 1999)

Poiedevin, L. *Samurais and Circumcisions,* private publication (1985)

Rawlings, L. *And the dawn came up like thunder* (Rawlings Chapman Publications, 1972)

Richards, R. *A Doctor's War* (Harper Collins: Sydney, 2006)

Shephard, B. *War of Nerves* (Jonathan Cape: London, 2000)

Skippen, D.S. *My World War II Travels,* private publication (1997)

Smith, J.G. *War Memories: A Medical Student in Malaya and Thailand,* private publication (2008)

Summers, J. *The Colonel of Tamarkan* (Little Brown: London, 2005)

Urquhart, A.K. *The Forgotten Highlander* (Little Brown: London, 2010)

Theses:

G.V. Gill, 'Coping with Crisis. Medicine and disease on the Burma Railway 1942 – 1945', PhD thesis (University of Liverpool, 2009).

K. Khan, 'Psychiatric Morbidity amongst ex-Far Eastern prisoners of war more than thirty years after repatriation', PhD thesis (University of Liverpool, 1987)

E.V. Oliver, 'Interpreting Memories of a Foreign Army: Prisoner of War narratives from the Sumatra railway, May 1944 – August 1945', PhD thesis (University of Leeds, 2014)

M.H. Parkes, 'Life, Health and Social Issues Among Far East Prisoners of War – an Oral History Enquiry', M.Phil dissertation (University of Liverpool, 2012).

Journals/magazines:

L.J. Audus, 'Biology Behind Barbed Wire', *Discovery, Magazine of Scientific Progress,* 1946; VII: 211-215

R. Bradley, 'A Small Lathe Built in a Japanese Prison Camp', *Engineering.* January 7, 1949.167: 2-3

H.E. de Wardener & B. Lennox, 'Cerebral beriberi (Wernicke's Encephalopathy)', *The Lancet* 1947; 1:11-17

H.E. de Wardener, 'Cholera Epidemic among prisoners-of-war in Siam', *The Lancet.* 1946; 1. 636-640

J. Markowitz, 'I was a Knife, Fork and Spoon Surgeon', *Canadian Digest* (adapted in part from an address given over the Canadian Broadcasting Corporation). 1946; 6:81-87

J.A. Reid, and T. Wilson, 'Report on nutrition and discussion of the main causes of death, "F" Force, Thailand'. *Journal of the Royal Army Medical Corps.* 1947, 89: 149–165

D. Robson, E. Welch, N.J. Beeching and G.V. Gill, 'Consequences of captivity: health effects of 'Far East imprisonment in World War II', *Quarterly Journal of Medicine.* 2009; 102: 94

E. Welch, A.N.H. Peach, M.H. Parkes and G.V. Gill, 'Burning feet syndrome: An old tropical syndrome revisited', *Annals of Tropical Medicine Public Health.* 2013; 6: 65-70

B. Wheeler, A Man Sent from God. *Reader's Digest.* (December 1983)

T. Wilson and J.A. Reid, 'Malaria among prisoners of war in Siam ("F" Force)'. *Transactions of the Royal Society of Tropical Medicine and Hygiene.* 1949, 43: 257–272

Private Papers:

C.D.L. Aylwin, private papers. Imperial War Museum (IWM) ref. Documents. 67/330/1

P. MacArthur, private papers. IWM ref. Documents.18736

Unpublished diaries and memoirs:

Kenneth Bailey, *The Face of Adversity* (undated)
Owen V. Eva, *A Captivity Remembered* (1992)
Harry Hall, pharmacist Changi POW camp
Harry Hesp, *All for the Love on an Empress* (1992)
Harold Lock, *The Forgotten Men* (1995)
Diaries of Air Vice Marshall Sir Paul Maltby
Sir Roger Moon Bt, *An Autobiography* (1988)
R.F. Spittle, *Changi notebook 1942–44*
R.F. Spittle, (1945) Book C

ebooks and websites:

Frank Bell https://www.bell-foundation.org.uk/ (2014)
Sears Eldredge http://digitalcommons.macalester.edu/thdabooks/1/ (2014)

INDEX